Beliefs and Values in
Science Education

DEVELOPING SCIENCE AND TECHNOLOGY EDUCATION

Series Editor: Brian Woolnough,
Department of Educational Studies, University of Oxford

Current titles:

John Eggleston: *Teaching Design and Technology*
Richard Gott and Sandra Duggan: *Investigative Work in the Science Curriculum*
David Layton: *Technology's Challenge to Science Education*
Keith Postlewaite: *Differentiated Science Teaching*
Michael J. Reiss: *Science Education for a Pluralist Society*
Jon Scaife and Jerry Wellington: *Information Technology in Science and Technology Education*
Joan Solomon: *Teaching Science, Technology and Society*
Clive Sutton: *Words, Science and Learning*
Brian Woolnough: *Effective Science Teaching*

Beliefs and Values in Science Education

MICHAEL POOLE

Open University Press
Buckingham · Philadelphia

Open University Press
Celtic Court
22 Ballmoor
Buckingham
MK18 1XW

and
1900 Frost Road, Suite 101
Bristol, PA 19007, USA

First published 1995

A catalogue record of this book is available from the British Library

Library of Congress Cataloging-in-Publication Data
Poole, Michael (Michael W.)
    Beliefs and values in science education / Michael Poole.
        p.   cm.   (Developing science and technology education)
    Includes bibliographical references and index.
    ISBN 0-335-15646-0. — ISBN 0-335-15645-2 (pbk.)
    1. Science—Study and teaching. I. Title. II. Series.
    Q126.9.P66   1995
507′.1—dc20   94-41387

Typeset by Type Study, Scarborough
Printed in Great Britain by St Edmundsbury Press, Bury St Edmunds, Suffolk

An Educational Model

'the sensible educator . . . will not expect or intend to produce an educated adult who has no beliefs, values, or attitudes, which he cannot rationally defend against all comers and who is incapable of settled convictions, deep-seated virtues, or profound loyalties. But neither will he treat his pupils in such a way as to leave them with closed minds and restricted sympathies. The process of being educated is like learning to build a house by actually building one and then having to live in the house one has built. It is a process in which the individual inevitably requires help. The extreme authoritarian helps by building the house himself according to what he believes to be the best plan and making the novice live in it. He designs it in such a way as to make it as difficult as possible for the novice to alter it. The extreme liberal leaves the novice to find his own materials and devise his own plan, for fear of exercising improper influence. The most he will do is to provide strictly technical information if asked. The sensible educator helps the novice to build the best house he can (in the light of accumulated experience). He strikes a balance between the need to produce a good house and the desirability of letting the novice make his own choices; but he is careful that the house is designed in such a way that it can subsequently be altered and improved as the owner, no longer a novice, sees fit.'

Professor Basil Mitchell
The Durham Report

Contents

Series editor's preface

It may seem surprising that after three decades of curriculum innovation, and with the increasing provision of a centralised National Curriculum, that it is felt necessary to produce a series of books which encourage teachers and curriculum developers to continue to rethink how science and technology should be taught in schools. But teaching can never be merely the 'delivery' of someone else's 'given' curriculum. It is essentially a personal and professional business in which lively, thinking, enthusiastic teachers continue to analyse their own activities and mediate the curriculum framework to their students. If teachers ever cease to be critical of what they are doing, then their teaching, and their students' learning, will become sterile.

There are still important questions which need to be addressed, questions which remain fundamental but the answers to which may vary according to the social conditions and educational priorities at a particular time.

What is the justification for teaching science and technology in our schools? For educational or vocational reasons? Providing science and technology for all, for future educated citizens, or to provide adequately prepared and motivated students to fulfil the industrial needs of the country? Will the same type of curriculum satisfactorily meet both needs or do we need a differentiated curriculum? In the past it has too readily been assumed that one type of science will meet all needs.

What should be the nature of science and technology in schools? it will need to develop both the methods and the content of the subject, the way a scientist or engineer works and the appropriate knowledge and understanding, but what is the relationship between the two? How does the student's explicit knowledge relate to investigational skill, how important is the student's tacit knowledge? In the past the holistic nature of scientific activity and the importance of affective factors such as commitment and enjoyment have been seriously undervalued in relation to the student's success.

And, of particular concern to this series, what is the relationship between science and technology? In some countries the scientific nature of technology and the technological aspects of science make the subjects a natural continuum. In others the curriculum structures have separated the two, leaving the teachers to develop appropriate links. Underlying this series is the belief that science and technology have an important interdependence and thus many of the books will be appropriate to teachers of both science and technology.

Increasingly, teachers have become aware that science and technology are not objective, impersonal, amoral activities but that they have, underlying them, fundamental issues relating to the very nature of the subjects and the purposes for which they are to be used in society. Teachers and curriculum developers have increasingly sought to see science in this wider, cultural context, to see how scientific ideas have developed and how they have been influenced by the world-view held by society at that time. Alongside such a broadening has been the influence of constructivism as the theory underlying the way that students learn science, the belief that students need to construct for themselves their own meaning for science. Both of these trends add important perspectives to science teaching but together they raise the possibility of suggesting a relativistic view of science. The suggestion that because scientific theories have been influenced by social conditioning that they are *only* social constructs. The suggestion that because students need to make sense of science for themselves that there is nothing absolute 'out there' for students to seek to understand. Michael Poole challenges us to resist such a relativist position, which undermines not only the teaching of science but the very worth of scientific endeavour itself. He points out the logical inconsistencies of scientific relativism, and argues for a clear,

unambiguous world-view that gives science a purpose to seek understanding of our world as it exists. Furthermore, he clarifies the out-dated myth of an inherent conflict between science and religion by considering four central concepts in science which have often been misused to illustrate such a simplistic view point. This is a fundamentally important book which demands that we take seriously the very nature of science and how our own beliefs and values affect the way we teach it.

We hope that this book, and the series as a whole, will help many teachers to develop their science and technological education in ways that are both satisfying to themselves and stimulating to their students.

Brian E. Woolnough

Preface

When a former President of the University of Chicago defined a university as a collection of departments held together by a heating system, he was rather cynically drawing attention to the fragmentation of knowledge. In recent years, considerable educational efforts have been made to stress the integrated nature of knowledge and explore cross-curricular themes. Traditionally, science has not been seen as concerning itself with beliefs or values, but recent studies in the history and philosophy of science have indicated how thoroughly they permeate the scientific enterprise.

This book itself starts from a set of beliefs – that beliefs and values are integral to the scientific enterprise, the theory and practice of education and hence science education, and that it is educationally desirable to explore such matters in class. Other beliefs I hold will quickly become evident and, where appropriate, I have attempted some justification.

In science education, beliefs and values appear in such diverse matters as the nature and status of science, gender issues, and the place of history of science in teaching science. They impinge upon the origins of the universe in general and humankind in particular. They inform judgements about appropriate attitudes to the environment, whether science is a worthwhile activity, what counts as good science education and whether beliefs and values should be taught, or simply taught about.

With such a range of topics to choose from – and the list is by no means exhaustive – any single book must necessarily be highly selective. A whole range of books is necessary, many already written, including a number in this present series. I have selected the following subjects for my seven chapters; my aim in so doing is to indicate how deeply beliefs and values are embedded in science and to provide resource material which can be adapted for classroom use. I hope it may help science teachers to show how spiritual, moral, social and cultural factors affect science and assist them to promote pupils' development in these areas.

Chapter 1 starts by looking at ways in which beliefs and values are located within science and within education and quickly moves on to fundamental matters about the bases of belief systems. Ultimately, the beliefs and values which people hold about a whole variety of issues stem from their *world-views* – their foundational beliefs about the world, human nature and destiny. This is a recurring theme of the book. The difficulties presented socially and pedagogically by the plurality of beliefs and values are then explored and some popular positions examined.

Chapter 2 considers how beliefs about the nature of the scientific enterprise have affected popular views about the status of science, and the particular educational task this presents. The first two chapters are the most theoretical ones, but unless these matters of principle are addressed at the outset, what follows for science education is seriously compromised. The breadth of ideas involved means in some cases one section, or even a single paragraph, touches on a subject which elsewhere has a book devoted to it! To enable such subjects to be followed up, I have provided an extensive list of references.

The ways in which beliefs and values affect the language of science, its models and metaphors, is the theme of Chapter 3. For example, the metaphors of the earth as a *machine* or as a living *organism* shape views about the environment, a topic addressed in Chapter 4. This chapter, along with the remaining three chapters, is concerned with particular areas of science teaching in which beliefs and values play a significant part.

Chapter 5 is about teaching the Earth in space and traces out current interest in metaphysical as well as physical questions about origins. The topic lends itself to promoting the 'awe-and-wonder' aspect of pupils' spiritual development. It also offers opportunities for teaching about the limitations of science through a discussion of the nature of *explanation*. Chapter 5 paves the way for looking, in Chapter 6, at one historical episode in cosmology – the Galileo affair. The final chapter also focuses on the beliefs and values involved in particular historical events – the Darwinian controversies. The materials can help in teaching pupils about the nature and history of scientific ideas, essential for science education. They also provide opportunities for examining the nature of scientific evidence, proof and change, as well as distinguishing between claims and arguments based on scientific factors and those which are not.

The subject matter of this book also offers resources for fulfilling, in science teaching, some key aims set out on page 6 of the National Curriculum Council (1993) discussion paper, *Spiritual and Moral Development*:[1]*

> The knowledge and understanding essential to both spiritual and moral development, and the ability to make responsible and reasoned judgements should be developed through all subjects of the curriculum. In most aspects of the curriculum pupils should encounter questions about the origins of the universe, the purpose of life, the nature of proof, the uniqueness of humanity and the meaning of truth. They should be encouraged to reflect on the possibility of certainty, and to question the often exaggerated view of the infallibility of science as the only means of understanding the world, and the equally exaggerated view of the inadequacy of religion and philosophy.

This passage encapsulates much of what this book is about – science, philosophy and religion. Any examination of beliefs and values about the nature of science must address some basic issues in philosophy. Also, much of the historical development of science over the last few hundred years can only be understood against the background of the religious (specifically Christian) beliefs and values held at the time. In the words of an Open University Course on Science and Belief, covering a similar period:

> This is not a matter of partisan selection; it is simply a fact of historical reality that, during this crucial and formative period for Western science, it was Christian belief that it chiefly encountered at every stage of its development and with which it reacted in a great variety of significant ways.[2]

A growing recognition within education of the importance of the interplay between science, philosophy and religion is reflected in the emphasis currently being placed on promoting pupils' spiritual, moral, social and cultural development *across* the curriculum, an undertaking in which science education has its part to play.

M. W. Poole
King's College London

* Superscript numerals refer to numbered notes at the end of the book.

Acknowledgements

I should like to acknowlege my debt to a number of colleagues in the preparation of this book. I am grateful to Professor Roger Trigg, Head of the Philosophy Department in the University of Warwick, for reading and commenting on Chapters 1 and 2. My debt to his own writings will be evident. I should also like to thank John Brooke, Professor of History of Science in the University of Lancaster, for reading and commenting on drafts of Chapters 3, 6 and 7. Again I should like to record the particular benefits I have received from his writings.

I have singled out these two colleagues for special mention, although my indebtedness to a vast number of other people will be evident from the extensive lists of references. Chapter 6 is developed from my article of the same title which appeared in the *School Science Review* in September 1990 and I am grateful to Andrew Bishop for his permission to do this. My appreciation goes to Dr John Martin, Reader in Physics at King's College London, for his comments on Chapter 5. My thanks also go to John Bausor, formerly Staff Inspector for Science with the Inner London Education Authority, for reading and commenting on the whole manuscript. Needless to say, the errors that remain are my full responsibility!

It is quite a long time ago that Brian Woolnough first slipped half a sheet of exercise paper (I still have it!) across the table during a meeting, asking, 'Would you be interested in writing a book . . . ?' My thanks go to Brian for his encouragement and valuable suggestions as the book has developed.

So, too, my thanks go to John Skelton, Managing Director of the Open University Press, to Shona Mullen and Sue Hadden and to Pat Lee, Editorial Assistant, whose cheerfulness and helpfulness have been a constant inspiration.

Copyright acknowledgements

Verse extract on p. 20 is from Edel, A. (1955) *Ethical Judgement: The Use of Science in Ethics*, p. 16, Glencoe, IL, The Free Press. Copyright © 1955 by The Free Press; copyright renewed 1983 by Abraham Edel. Reprinted with permission of the publisher.

Extract on p. 5 is from 'Indoctrination', in *The Durham Report*, p. 358, London, National Society/SPCK. Reprinted with permission of Professor Basil Mitchell.

Photographic acknowledgements

To Cavendish Laboratory, Cambridge for Figures 2.2 and 3.7; to National Aeronautics and Space Administration (NASA) for Figures 4.4, 5.1 and 5.5; to Dr G.B.R. Feilden CBE FEng FRS for Figure 5.3; to Royal College of Physicians for Figure 6.7; to The Royal College of Surgeons of England for Figure 7.1 and Lady Lyell and the former Department of Geology, King's College London for Figure 7.4.

CHAPTER 1

'Everybody needs Standards'
– bases of decision-making

The double meaning of this advertisement for a London evening paper is a reminder that we constantly appeal to norms which are taken for granted. 'That's not fair!', 'You shouldn't have lied!' or 'That's *my* pen you've taken!' is typical classroom talk. It arises from beliefs like, 'people from different social backgrounds should have equal educational opportunities', 'truth-telling is a good thing', or 'stealing is wrong'. Such beliefs result in valuing *justice*, *truthfulness* and *honesty*.

Values typically involve *thinking*, *feeling* and *willing*. Valued beliefs are sometimes referred to as 'dispositions' or 'commitments'. The element of commitment is not bypassed by choosing not to make decisions. It is possible to be committed to 'fence-sitting', a commitment which is reflected by a disposition to avoid making decisions!

Evidence for the beliefs and values which people hold comes from what they *do*, for 'preparedness to act upon what we affirm is admitted on all hands to be the sole, the genuine, the unmistakeable criterion of belief'.[1]

Fig. 1.1 Attitudes to nuclear power reflect underlying beliefs and values

Beliefs and values in science and education

Beliefs and values are integral to science, to education and, consequently, to science education. They appear at different logical levels:

- *Level 1*: beliefs *about* science and *about* education, e.g. science is a worthwhile activity, education is a good thing.

- *Level 2*: beliefs (i) *within* science – the *orderliness* and *intelligibility* of the world; (ii) *within* education – the choice of subjects taught and the resources allocated indicates society's preferred beliefs and values.
- *Level 3*: within the subjects taught, the choice of topics to be included reflects a further set of values.
- *Level 4*: the *ways* in which individual topics are taught reflects the beliefs and values of society and the individual teacher. In science education, beliefs and values are likely to be in evidence in dealing with nuclear power and reproduction.

Furthermore, the educational process itself is based upon beliefs about human nature. Stevenson[2] surveys seven such views, sharing one point of agreement – that there is something wrong with the human race. Ideas about human nature underlie such educational concepts as critical rational autonomy; they also shape views about matters like class control.

Education is permeated with beliefs about what *ought* or *ought not* to happen in the classroom: pupils *ought* to be encouraged to make informed choices for themselves; 'indoctrination' *ought* to be avoided. The very idea that there are things which ought and ought not to take place introduces a whole new area of discourse – the moral *universe of discourse*, constituted by the concept of obligation. Within it, words like 'ought', 'duty', 'right', 'wrong' and also 'responsibility' – which currently has a high public profile – acquire currency.

It would be nice . . .

Among the many sayings attributed to Einstein is 'Everything should be made as simple as possible, but not simpler'.[3] It would be nice if the treatment of beliefs and values were simple, but it is not. The consensus which exists within science, even after allowing for disagreements among scientists, is enormous by comparison with agreement about beliefs and values.

There are various possible responses to the educational difficulties posed by the plurality of beliefs and values: (1) pretend that beliefs and values are not there; (2) say 'it's not our job as science teachers'.

1 'No beliefs or values lurking around here!'

Trying to avoid the difficulties by pretending they are not there replaces one problem by another. Facility is gained at the loss of authenticity. Underlying beliefs and values about science, education and their social interactions remain unexamined, accepted uncritically as what 'everybody believes'. The values of a dominant ideology may appear neutral and get glossed over.

Their widespread acceptance makes them less vulnerable to having their underlying assumptions scrutinised. Pupils need to reflect critically on the foundations as well as the superstructure of the educational endeavour.

2 'It's not our job!'

This alternative was advocated in a letter in *School Science Review*, addressed partly to 'teachers of religion . . . teachers of history, or any other subject that feels it has overlaps with science':

> Science teachers have more than enough to do, especially in these days of trying to fit three subjects into two, in teaching science properly. They should not allow themselves to be seduced into taking heed of the desires of non-scientists to adulterate science syllabuses with non-science.[4]

This position is likely to elicit considerable sympathy. The workload has been enormous, the resources inadequate, the goalposts keep moving and behind everything lies a deep-rooted conviction that 'constant change is here to stay' – and now they are asking us to *do* beliefs and values as well!

Another lure of the 'it's-not-our-job' stance is that it is easier to teach 'science' if beliefs and values are not explicitly raised. But the quotes around 'science' are to indicate that this is an expurgated version. The relative simplicity with which conclusions about the content of school science can be justified, compared with conclusions about beliefs and values, tends to vest science with a certain prestige, sometimes verging on imperialism. But some of the most important facets of life are not amenable to scientific testing. Furthermore, what are sometimes seen as 'soft' considerations of less easily treated beliefs and values may be neglected for amassing 'hard facts' and getting university places.

Educationally, the question is not 'should we bring beliefs and values in to science teaching?', but 'how do we best teach a subject which already has beliefs and values embedded in it?' An exploration of the role of beliefs and values in science classes need not be a last straw upon a groaning camel. Some of the case studies, like those of

Galileo and Darwin, cited later, can prove intensely interesting in showing how prevailing beliefs and values affect the development of science and shape its public image. It can also prove intriguing to see how beliefs and values lie behind the continuing folklore portrayals of episodes like these, despite the different perspectives painted by recent studies in history of science.

A few more problems

The teaching difficulties presented by the lack of consensus about beliefs and values are compounded by a divergence of views about what procedures to adopt in order to steer towards consensus – or, even more radically, whether consensus is possible or desirable. A further dilemma arises through trying to avoid the spectre of 'indoctrination' when making beliefs and values explicit. Then there are complications arising from the powerful *emotional* and *volitional* factors existing alongside the *cognitive* ones. When people's *feeling* and *willing* are motivated by powerful drives like survival, sex, politics and religion, the cognitive and moral factors may get overridden in acts of rationalisation.[5] The power of the 'survival' drive can be illustrated by the rationalisation of moral compromises made by teachers under pressure to teach Nazi ideology in German schools in the 1930s. The power of the sexual and political drives are evidenced by a frank admission Aldous Huxley once made about the role of rationalisation in human affairs:

> For myself, as, no doubt, for most of my contemporaries, the philosophy of meaninglessness was essentially an instrument of liberation. The liberation we desired was simultaneously liberation from a certain political and economic system and liberation from a certain system of morality. We objected to the morality because it interfered with our sexual freedom; we objected to the political and economic system because it was unjust . . . There was one admirably simple way of confuting these people and at the same time justifying ourselves in our political and erotic revolt: we could deny that the world had any meaning whatsoever.[6]

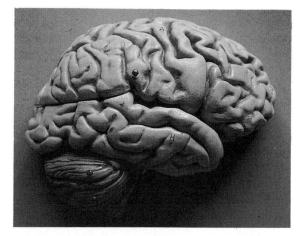

Fig. 1.2 Model of a human brain

All beliefs and values are subject to scrutiny, but even to examine them invokes a foundational belief – that of human rationality. J.B.S. Haldane wrestled with the question of why we hold this belief, saying:

> If my mental processes are determined wholly by the motion of the atoms in my brain, I have no reason to suppose that my beliefs are true . . . and hence I have no reason for supposing my brain to be composed of atoms.[7]

Darwin's puzzlement over the same matter crops up in Chapter 3. But even to discuss whether or not we are rational creatures involves the assumption that we are, otherwise our utterances are just noises. That may appear to be trivially true and not something which need detain us. But such is not the case. The matter of human rationality is part of a complex of issues which has featured prominently in recent debates about education, science and hence science education. So these matters must be examined in detail before proceeding to more specific aspects of science teaching. The complex of issues includes the bases of belief systems, as well as pluralism, relativism and rationality. It encompasses associated topics like choosing between beliefs and values, 'indoctrination' and teaching controversial issues. To these matters we now turn.

Bases of belief systems

Answers to questions about human nature and significance stem from beliefs expressed in *world-views*, *value systems* or *stances for living*. A world-*view* is an *evaluation* of the world, not to be confused with a world-*picture*, such as the Ptolemaic or Copernican ones. A world-view is concerned about such questions as, 'is the universe a cosmic accident?' or 'is there a purpose behind it?'

Such questions broaden the enquiry from *scientific* considerations about nature (Gk. *phusis*, hence physics), to further questions which arise *after* (Gk. *meta*), questions about 'the interpretation of ultimate reality'. These belong to the realm of *meta*physics, which is 'an attempt to discover the most general and pervasive facts about the world'.

Although metaphysics has at times been treated like a philosophical outcast, as under logical positivism, it draws attention to the existence of assumptions beyond the competence of science to justify. It includes three dominant concepts:

1 *Ontology* – about 'being' or 'what exists'.
2 *Epistemology* – about 'how' and 'whether' what exists can be known.
3 *Axiology* – about 'values' and their relation to ultimate reality.

Science itself has a metaphysical basis,[8] encountered in the next chapter; and these three dominant concepts of metaphysics permeate science.[9] Speculations in modern cosmology about Theories of Everything (TOEs) show that metaphysical questions are increasingly being asked.

Making moral decisions

Each of the three elements in values, *thinking*, *feeling* and *willing* (or *cognitive*, *affective* and *volitional*), have been appealed to as bases for making moral decisions within what is often termed the 'moral maze'.[10]

1 *Appeals based on the thinking, or cognitive, element:*
   - *Naturalism* claims that by looking at the nature of the world and the nature of human-kind, certain moral truths can be discerned. Goodness and badness are seen as natural features of the world and of people.
   - *Intuitionism* holds that every reasonable person knows by intuition what he or she ought and ought not to do.

2 *Appeals based on the feeling, or affective, element:*
One group claims that morality is about feelings in general and it divides into two:
   - *Subjectivism* holds that morality is just a matter of taste, of personal preference.
   - *Emotivism* holds that it is expressing our emotions on a subject and persuading others to feel the same way.

These positions tend towards *relativism*.

A second group holds that morality is specifically about feelings of pleasure and it splits three ways:
   - *Egoism* sees self-interest/selfishness as the basis of moral judgements.
   - *Hedonism* is that particular form of egoism based on pursuing pleasure and avoiding pain.
   - *Utilitarianism* is based on hedonism and is the social theory developed by Jeremy Bentham and John Stuart Mill. It is summarised in Bentham's words, 'The greatest happiness of the greatest number is the foundation of morals and legislation'.[11] He even devised a calculus for quantifying the Greatest Happiness Principle.

3 *Appeals based on the willing, or volitional, element:*
   - *Existentialism* starts from the belief that the world is meaningless and seeks to create meaning by exercising the will. Choice is unavoidable and makes us what we are. By choosing, we create our own morality.
   - *Prescriptivism* goes further than existentialism by saying that individual moral choices do not make for a common life and that the corporate nature of morality should be seen as prescribing, not simply what the individual should be doing, but what everybody else should do in the same situation.

To these moral stances can be added those so-called 'scientific' approaches which claim that morality can be reduced to one basic factor such as animal behaviour, psychology or economics. Finally, there are the religious approaches which see morality as relating to the divine will.

Pluralism and choice between beliefs and values

An enormous range of beliefs and values are represented in society,[12] schools and even a single science department. Some beliefs – about styles of music, fashions in dress, or holidays abroad being better than holidays in Britain – do not appear of great moment. Similarly, valuing hand-made goods more than machine-made ones, or perennials more than annuals, seem little more than matters of taste. But some beliefs and values reflect people's deepest convictions about right, wrong and the purpose of life. These generate strong feelings which make for confrontation and conflict.

Pluralism, as pupils are well aware, raises the matter of choice. People's upbringings affect their beliefs and values, although humans are able to transcend their cultural backgrounds – otherwise there would be no reformers. Pupils may make the beliefs and values of their upbringing their own, or they may choose new ones. So does it matter what they choose, as long as they make their own rational autonomous choice and their beliefs are sincerely held?

Sincerity, surely, is a good thing, but as a criterion for choice it is inadequate. A sincere belief, that the contents of a bottle on the medicine shelf will heal, is of no avail if a bottle of poison is taken by mistake. Beliefs need to reflect the way things are.

Some people, however, argue that all beliefs and values, including moral ones, are simply matters of taste and personal choice, and that no one set of beliefs and values takes precedence. Such a claim requires careful scrutiny. Despite divergence of practice, some common ground is found across societies over matters like property rights, care of the elderly, sexual practices and murder. Two issues, one theoretical and one practical, arising from the plurality of beliefs and values, will occupy the rest of this chapter. They are (1) accounting for variety and (2) the treatment of controversial issues.

Accounting for variety

Possible responses to the plurality of beliefs among pupils, science teachers and society in general, depend in turn on *other* sets of beliefs. If, for instance, it is believed that there are (1) objective truths about the physical world, (2) universal moral truths like 'stealing is wrong' and (3) metaphysical truths like 'there is a God', then the task would appear to be to try to discover these truths, 'truth' being taken as some kind of correspondence to what is the case.

1 Reflects a *realist* view of the scientific enterprise as attempting to discover the nature of a physical world which exists independently of observers.
2 Might result in investigating the commonality of moral values within different cultures.
3 Might be pursued by considering *The Justification of Religious Belief*,[13] as does Mitchell in a book of that title.

The brevity of these comments belies the magnitude of the tasks! Responses (1)–(3) interpret variety partly as the outcome of incomplete knowledge – knowledge being taken as what corresponds to the facts.

Alternatively, if variety is interpreted as a consequence of there *being* no absolute truths, then no one set of beliefs takes precedence over any other. However, as a matter of logic, there is no way of arriving, from the *fact* of plurality, at the conclusion that all beliefs and values *are* of equal worth. Such a belief might be imported into a pluralism discussion, but it cannot be derived from it.

Relativism

The package of beliefs which claims 'there are no absolute truths, all is relative', is one variety of *relativism* which, in its ethical form, can be summed up in a verse by Abraham Edel:

It all depends on where you are,
It all depends on when you are,
It all depends on what you feel,
It all depends on how you feel.
It all depends on how you're raised,
It all depends on what is praised,
What's right today is wrong tomorrow,
Joy in France, in England sorrow,
It all depends on point of view, Australia or Timbuctoo,
In Rome do as the Romans do.
If tastes just happen to agree
Then you have morality.
But where there are conflicting trends,
It all depends, it all depends . . .[14]

If all beliefs and values are of equal worth, or so the argument proceeds, we *ought* to be tolerant of other people's beliefs and values and *ought not* to try to persuade them to adopt our own. The form of the 'argument' is:

1 A *description* – there *is* plurality.
2 Importing an inconsequent *belief*, that all beliefs and values are of equal worth.
3 A *prescription*, not justifiable from (1) and (2), that everyone *ought* to be tolerant of other people's beliefs and values and *ought not* to try to persuade them to adopt their own.

Relativism and a demand for universal tolerance go hand in hand.

Is relativism a good solution to the problems presented by pluralism? Everyone is free to choose their own sets of beliefs and values from the supermarket shelf. Any feelings of guilt about choosing those easiest to keep can quickly be allayed. After all, if no one set of beliefs is more worthy than any other, it seems eminently sensible to opt for the set which is least demanding and easiest to keep, in order to stand the best chance of living up to one's ideals. Furthermore, if nobody ought to try to persuade us to adopt their beliefs and values, and we ought not to try to persuade anybody to adopt ours, there, surely, lies the recipe for living harmoniously together in a pluralist society.

The note of irony will not have gone undetected. Is it really as simple as this? A central difficulty concerns the claim, on which all else depends, that 'there are no absolute truths, all is relative'. Is it true? Oddly enough, if it is true, then it is *not* true! For then there would be at least one absolute truth, namely 'there are no absolute truths, all is relative'! If on the other hand it is *not* true, why take the claim seriously? Worse still, the claim *itself* is incompatible with the demand for universal tolerance; for if relativism is true, tolerance is only *relative to particular contexts*. The central claim of simple relativism is technically incoherent; it paints itself into a corner.

In practice, a relativist position tends not to be held consistently; indeed, it is arguable that its self-refuting nature ensures that it never could. A perceptive PGCE student at a Midlands university protested to one lecturer who taught two courses, 'On one of your courses you tell us that there are no absolute rights and wrongs, only what a particular society holds to be right or wrong. Yet on the other course you tell us that racism is always wrong. You can't have it both ways!'

Relativism is essentially conservative, with a small 'c'. It tends to preserve the *status quo*. Since, however, it is often those who would call themselves 'radicals' who are effectively saying 'people ought to believe in relativism', an odd paradox ensues.

According to the precepts of relativism, reformers like William Wilberforce were intolerant, because they said that slavery and racism were at all times and in all societies wrong, and they also tried to change the beliefs of those who thought differently.

Fig. 1.3a,b The old tree where Wilberforce spoke with Mr Pitt and the seat with an inscription from his diary, which says: 'I well remember after a conversation with Mr Pitt in the open air at the root of an old tree at Holwood just above the steep descent into the vale of Keston I resolved to give notice on a fit occasion in the House of Commons of my intention to bring forward the abolition of the slave trade.'

Tolerance

Even if the claim 'there are no absolute truths' cannot logically be sustained, might not universal tolerance still be claimed to be a good thing? But here again, there are difficulties. If we *ought* to be tolerant of everyone else's beliefs and values, ought we for instance – and this is not playing with words – be tolerant of a person who is intolerant of tolerant people? Or might it be better to be *intolerant* of intolerance? On a more sombre note, should we be tolerant of the beliefs of someone who wishes to promote a society based on apartheid or the principles of the Third Reich? Ought we not to try to persuade them otherwise?

A final difficulty for those who insist nobody ought (i) to try to persuade other people to change their beliefs and (ii) adopt the ones which *they* hold, is that they are being inconsistent. For this is precisely what *they* are trying to do; for they are saying (unless both parties already count universal tolerance as a virtue) (i) 'you *ought* to change your beliefs' and (ii) adopt my belief that 'you *ought* to be tolerant'.

> Relativism is only tolerant of relativists. *It does not matter what you believe, except that you must believe that it does not matter.*

The purpose of spelling this out in detail is not to score debating points, but to indicate the inescapable self-contradictions involved once the concept of objective truth – so important to science and science teaching – is denied. A person who claims there are no absolute truths, nevertheless wishes his or her claim to be believed as absolutely true!

The inadequacies inherent in any doctrine of universal tolerance should not be taken as a recommendation of the opposite – suppression, or universal intolerance! Part of the difficulty in discussing tolerance concerns the meanings of the word and the different reasons which are offered in its defence. Toleration is not indifference.

Toleration is a policy of patient forbearance in the presence of something which is disliked or disapproved of. Toleration . . . has an element of condemnation built into its meaning. We do not tolerate what we enjoy or what is generally liked or approved of . . . To tolerate is first to condemn and then to put up with or, more simply, to put up with is itself to condemn . . . toleration is far from an ideal policy; it is contaminated, so to speak, by that very implication of evil which its meaning contains.[15]

Toleration has sometimes in the past been defended on the grounds that, eventually, 'truth will out'. Nowadays it is frequently based upon belief in an unresolvable agnosticism about any beliefs and values underpinning the world or, more cosily, on the belief that 'everybody's right'. The cosy position falls foul of a fundamental principle of logic, the *law of non-contradiction* – two contradictory statements cannot both be simultaneously true – once mutually conflicting claims are made by different belief systems.

On an objectivist view of right and wrong, the best practice would seem to be to try to discern between right and wrong, realising that one may oneself be mistaken, and then (1) actively encourage what is right, (2) try to change what is wrong and (3) tolerate distinctions which are of little consequence. Considerable practical difficulties, of course, lie in knowing the difference in the first case and then in deciding how to treat controversial issues in the classroom.

In attempting to escape the fatal weakness of simple relativism, *it has been claimed that the deficiencies only arise if one accepts the laws of logic which are themselves culturally determined.* If the idea of truth, human rationality, the concepts and the reasoning processes of logic vary from culture to culture, then, it is argued, standards of rationality which are currency in one society cannot be used to judge the beliefs and values of a different one. This is a claim of *conceptual relativism.*

Conceptual relativism

Conceptual relativism also claims that concepts are social constructs which *determine* the world, rather than the world determining our concepts.

Fig. 1.4 'The concept of a unicorn is fairly well defined'

Certainly, concepts *are* formed through social negotiation, but that does not mean the world is the way it is *because of* our socially negotiated concepts. Possessing a *concept* of something does not mean that the 'something' exists. For example, a unicorn is depicted in heraldry as having the body and head of a horse, the hind legs of a stag, the tail of a lion, and in the middle of the forehead a single, long straight horn. The concept of a unicorn is fairly well-defined, even though we do not believe such creatures exist. But if we questioned whether they did, the matter could not be decided by appealing to the existence of the socially negotiated concept of a unicorn; only by searching for a unicorn in a world in which unicorns either did, or did not exist, independently of unicorn-concept-possessing hunters.

The consequences of beliefs about conceptual relativism, if they could be sustained, would be far-reaching for education in general and science education in particular. Science is a social activity and if its contents are regarded as arising *solely* out of social conditioning, rather than out of objective truths about the natural world, then the value of the entire scientific enterprise is thrown into question. This is why conceptual relativism and its allied claims need to be scrutinised in some depth, before considering the nature of science in the next chapter.

However, while an examination of conceptual relativism is a necessary component of the theoretical underpinning of what follows, some readers may prefer to pass over the detailed arguments at a first reading and return to them later. If so they can turn now to the treatment of controversial issues on page 27.

As with simple relativism, conceptual relativism interprets the variety of beliefs and values as a consequence of there *being* no absolute truths, 'truth' being only what a particular society counts as truth. Typically, the argument goes, if individuals or societies interpret the same data in different ways, it seems likely the reasons should be sought in the effects of social conditioning rather than in the things themselves. If so, an entirely different programme is presented. Attention is diverted away from the truth or falsity of the beliefs to *why* they come to be held. But once what people believe is taken as *just* a result of social conditioning, then no set of beliefs takes precedence, with serious consequences for science – but also for conceptual relativists!

Cultural anthropologists have provided fascinating insights into how the beliefs and values of different cultures came about. Decisions to 'bracket-out' questions about the truth or falsity of the beliefs *can* simply be a convention adopted within anthropology – a methodological principle – *provided* it is not claimed that truth and falsity are unimportant issues. But frequently such studies have not stopped at phenomenology – *describing* the phenomena observed. They have offered *explanations* of the beliefs – an ambiguous phrase which hides two quite distinct ideas: (1) why the belief came to be held, i.e. its *genesis*; (2) the belief itself, i.e. its *content*.

The distinction can be illustrated by considering the belief that performing a particular dance makes it rain. An explanation of (1), the *genesis* of the belief, might be that sooner or later, after the dance, it always rains. Then it is incorrectly assumed that if 'b' follows 'a', then 'b' must have been caused by 'a', overlooking the essential distinction between *correlation* and *causation*. Thus (on the assumption that dancing does not cause rain) a plausible explanation has been given of why this false belief came to be held.

But conceptual relativists go much further than this by claiming, not only that the *genesis* of the belief has been explained, which is unexceptionable, but the *content* of the belief also, simply by explaining the social factors producing it. This collapses the distinction between (1) the belief itself and (2) the reasons for believing. It also collapses the traditional distinction between (1) the *context of justification* of what is believed and (2) the *context of discovery*. These well-tested differentiations mark out the traditional distinction between the history and the philosophy of science.

What is believed may be true or false, but this stems from the way the world *is*, not from whether people believe it or not. The *genetic fallacy*[16] is the mistake of supposing that the source of a belief affects its validity, or that, because the origins of a belief can be explained, the belief itself is somehow explained *away*. Someone *might* have first heard that the earth was spherical from a madman, but that is quite irrelevant as to whether it is spherical or not. An illustration of the genetic fallacy in science comes from Stephen Jay Gould:

> The theory of natural selection is a creative transfer to biology of Adam Smith's basic argument for a rational economy . . .
>
> Many people are distressed to hear such an argument. Does it not compromise the integrity of science if some of its primary conclusions originate by analogy with contemporary politics and culture rather than from data of the discipline itself?[17]

Whether or not Gould's view is true, the point is that the answer to his question is 'No'.

> . . . the *source* of an idea is one thing; its *truth* or *fruitfulness* is another. The psychology and utility of discovery are very different subjects indeed.

Darwin may have cribbed the idea of natural selection from economics, but it may still be right. As the German socialist Karl Kautsky wrote in 1902: 'The fact that an idea emanates from a particular class, or accords with their interests, of course proves nothing as to its truth or falsity'.[18]

Dr Frederick Temple's contribution to practical work in science education while Head of Rugby School has been referred to in this series.[19] When he later became Archbishop of Canterbury, a student said to him, 'Archbishop, . . . you believe what you believe because of the way you were brought up'. Temple is reported as replying, 'That is as it may be. But the fact remains that you believe that I believe what I believe because of the way I was brought up, because of the way you were brought up'.[20]

Apart from the futility of the ensuing stalemate of the infinite logical regress, such rhetoric fails to distinguish between *causes for belief* (social and psychological factors) and *grounds for belief* (evidential factors). To attempt to argue as the student did is to wield a double-edged sword for, as the story shows, if it *were* a valid argument it would be as damaging to the sceptic as to the believer. But apart from illustrating the *genetic fallacy*, the story makes a number of other relevant points. What we believe *is*, of course, powerfully affected by the way we were brought up; but that says nothing about the truth or falsity of what we believe – we can be disposed towards true beliefs just as we can be disposed towards false beliefs. The fact of our particular upbringing does not distinguish between the two. So whereas social explanations of the *origins* of knowledge are logically possible, social explanations of the *contents* of knowledge are not.

The implication of the student's accusation was that Temple *only* believed what he believed because of the way he was brought up and that evidence for the truth or falsity of what he believed were irrelevant. For this fallacy, a variant of the genetic fallacy, Flew introduces 'the appropriately shaming nickname "The Debunker's Fallacy"'.[21]

Conceptual relativists are saying something similar to the student. They are claiming that each society sets its own standard of truth and that there is no common basis for adjudicating between them, that is they are *incommensurate*. Customs, moral beliefs and even the concepts of science are said to be valid only within the context of a particular society and they have no validity outside.

Redefining words

By taking the consensus of social groups as baselines, rather than how things are in themselves, words like truth, fact, knowledge, rationality, reality and evidence get redefined to mean *what a particular social group counts as* truth, fact, knowledge, rationality, reality or evidence, a meaning which I shall henceforth indicate by referring to 'truth', 'fact', 'knowledge', etc. (in quotes), to distinguish them from what is more generally understood by these words.

Traditionally, *truth* has been taken to mean correspondence to the facts. The statement *Andrew is seven years old* is true *iff* (a term meaning if, and only if) Andrew *is* seven years old. If someone believes Andrew is seven and, having seen his birth certificate has good grounds for the truth of that belief, they can correctly say that they *know* that Andrew is seven. If their belief is true

Fig. 1.5 *'Iff* Andrew *is* seven years old'

and they are justified in believing it (for a justified belief can be false and an unjustified one can be accidentally true), the word *know* is appropriate. Someone who believed that Andrew was eight, but later discovered he was only seven, could correctly say 'I believed Andrew was eight, but I was wrong' but could not correctly say – indeed it would sound very odd – 'I *knew* that Andrew was eight, but I was wrong'. Whereas one can *believe* something which is not true, one cannot *know* something which is not true.

This would hardly need saying except that this is precisely what some students of society have denied. Instead of taking *truth* as some kind of *correspondence* with the way things objectively are, independently of knowing subjects, they have taken it as the *consensus* of believing people. Thus the phrase, 'pupils construct their own reality', encountered in science education in *constructivism*, sounds linguistically odd because it seems to be saying that an objectively existing world exists because somebody thinks it up. On a realist view it can only mean that 'pupils construct their own "reality" (i.e. what counts to them as reality).' Similar odd-sounding expressions like *true for you* or *not true for me* mean 'true' for you or not 'true' for me. Confusion arises when words like *truth* and *reality*, already common currency, are given *stipulative definitions*, without an appropriate warning (such as those provided by quotes) that they have different meanings from usual. But even more radical among the ideas under review are claims made about human rationality.

Rationality

The claim has been made that standards of rationality are not universal but particular to a culture. So no other culture can judge another culture's beliefs and values to be 'right' or 'wrong' – they are incommensurate – since there are no culturally independent criteria for doing so. 'Truth' and 'knowledge' on this view is treated, not as some kind of correspondence with the way the world is, but as an expression of what people in societies believe. 'Truth', 'knowledge' and 'reality' can be negotiated and constructed, whereas truth, knowledge and reality cannot, they simply have to be reckoned with:

> 'I accept the universe' is reported to have been a favourite utterance of the New England transcendentalist, Margaret Fuller; and when some one repeated this phrase to Thomas Carlyle, his sardonic comment is said to have been: 'Gad! she'd better!'[22]

If these claims about human rationality could be justified, they would have enormous implications for science and science teaching, which depend on constructing *valid arguments* and *inferring* conclusions from evidence. So the question of whether there are alternative standards of rationality is foundational and must be examined carefully.

What it is reasonable to believe depends on what is already known, so rationality is a relative concept. It might appear *irrational* to us for the ancient Greeks to have believed in a geocentric system, but to them it was eminently *rational*. The earth *felt* stationary, the sun *appeared* small and moving, and there was no detectable stellar parallax, as would be expected with a heliocentric system.

Culture *does* play a significant role in standards of rationality and this aspect of rationality has been termed *context-dependent* rationality.[23] But cultural relativism claims more than this – that *the very processes of reasoning and the logical rules are not universal but culture-specific*. But *do* these processes vary in their entirety from society to society or is there a common core?

In defence of the idea of a common core it can be pointed out that if the *law of non-contradiction* were rejected, so that 'the sky is clear' and 'the sky is not clear' could both simultaneously be 'true' – whatever that might mean – then the basis for valid arguments would disappear, *whatever* the specific content involved. It is difficult to see that, without operable logical rules like *identity*, *negation* and the *law of non-contradiction*, any society at all could be credited with the possibility of (1) *arguing* or (2) *inferring*.

Logical rules

Identity: a mathematical and logical relation expressed by the '=' sign. So $4 + 3 = 7$ means that the number obtained by adding 4 and 3 is *identical with* $(=) 7$.

Negation: to assert the negation of a statement *p* is to deny *p*.

Law of non-contradiction: a statement *p* and a statement *not-p* cannot both simultaneously be true.

The *law of non-contradiction* is the basis on which other logical laws receive their justification. For instance, consider a valid, deductive argument:

Premiss 1	If the sky is clear, stars can be seen at night.
Premiss 2	The sky *is* clear.
Conclusion	Stars can be seen at night.

Arguments can be *valid* or *invalid*.
Premisses on which arguments are based can be *true* or *false*.

The truth or falsity of premisses does not of itself affect whether the argument is valid or invalid.

An argument is said to be valid in virtue of the fact that it is not possible to assert the premisses and to deny the conclusion without thereby contradicting oneself.

A valid deductive argument depends on the *form* of the argument, not on its *content*. It can include premisses which are false, in which case the conclusion may be false, for example:

Premiss 1	If the moon is made of cream cheese, the moon is edible.
Premiss 2	The moon is made of cream cheese.
Conclusion	The moon is edible.

To ensure the conclusion of a valid deductive argument is true, the premisses must be true.

1 *Arguing*: Without the *law of non-contradiction*, how could one *argue* for taking appropriate safety measures in *any* society where 'the man-eating tiger is alive' and 'the man-eating tiger is dead' could both be simultaneously 'true'?

2 *Inferring*: Or, how could one *infer* the state of one's pea-breeding experiment, anywhere in the world, while denying the validity of the following deduction:

Premiss 1	If a hippopotamus walks over my peas, my peas will be squashed.
Premiss 2	A hippopotamus has walked over my peas.
Conclusion	My peas will be squashed.

Some criteria of rationality are universal, while others depend on context.[24] The claim that totally distinct standards of rationality apply to different societies, with consequent incommensurability of their beliefs, appears unjustified.

The extreme claims of cultural relativism affect every discipline, not just science. An even more devastating consequence of such beliefs would be that, if there is no reality common to different societies, but only 'realities', then one society could not even understand the language of another. This would for ever preclude the possibility of having English/Chinese or French/Russian dictionaries for one thing. The implications for international science and science education would be catastrophic. If a society 'has a language, it must, minimally, possess criteria of truth (as correspondence to reality) and logic, which we share with it and which simply *are* criteria of rationality'.[25]

Furthermore, on moral issues, which are currently receiving emphasis in science education, it is not clear that one culture could have nothing to say about practices being right or wrong in another culture: 'even those who seem to be genuine outsiders – even people who are hearing about us for the first time – can make moral comments about us which we recognise as valid . . . there is such continuous and all-pervading cultural interchange that the idea of separateness holds no water at all'.[26] In similar vein, take the educational aspects of the apartheid issue, over which there has recently been real progress:

People speak of the evil of apartheid, for example, in a manner which suggests a judgement rooted in considerations more fundamental and universal than one expressed in terms of what is right or wrong *for me or for our society*. At the same time, however, the allegiance of World Studies teachers to the idea of a multicultural society and their endorsement of cultural pluralism often lead them into a kind of social relativism. I am not sure that such a position can be consistently maintained. Certainly its implications would come uneasily from the lips of most World Studies teachers – 'racial apartheid is wrong unless you happen to live, for example, in South Africa where it is right'? The morality of seeking change in society becomes difficult to explain in a context in which we are supposed to derive our moral precepts from those which already pervade that society.[27]

Sociology of 'knowledge'?

The relativistic ideas which we have examined come from cultural anthropology and a discipline which has taken upon itself the title of the *sociology of knowledge*. Its central thesis is that 'knowledge' is to be explained with reference to the conditions of the society of the knower, rather than the evidence offered for it. It rejects appeals to the objective existence of a world as the final arbiter of truth; and the significance for science teaching is obvious.

Thus the word *knowledge* in the phrase *sociology of knowledge* does not mean 'possession of the truth', because it is taken to depend on social conditioning and consequently to vary from society to society. However, if it is possible to have *A is B* in one society and *A is not-B* in another, both claiming simultaneously to be true, the concept of truth collapses – and so does the concept of knowledge as possession of the truth. So the label *sociology of 'knowledge'* is more appropriate where, on my notation, 'knowledge' signifies 'what counts as knowledge'. But since what people count as knowledge is what they *believe* to be knowledge, the sociology of *belief* would be an even better descriptor.

The sociology of 'knowledge' attempts to avoid the idea of objective knowledge by concentrating on the *beliefs* which people hold, which are affected by social factors. But the concept of objective knowledge is not avoided by shifting attention on to belief, for

> Belief requires the concept of truth just as does knowledge. Beliefs are propositions accepted as true, so 'belief' cannot be characterised without the concept of truth . . . The justification for holding a belief, then, will be the same as the evidence for its truth . . . A belief is justified, then, in the same way as knowledge is established.[28]

To believe, say, that cold fusion can occur is to believe that evidence can be produced to show that *it is true* that cold fusion can occur. The example is an appropriate one since the point is unaffected by the fact that beliefs can turn out to be false. The reason for holding beliefs is still that they are thought to be true.

I have felt it necessary to examine the foregoing views in detail since they have had wide publicity in some educational establishments during the last few decades and many teachers will have encountered them. In addition, the next section on controversial issues, as well as the following chapter on the nature of science, are significantly linked with the views which I have discussed.

The treatment of controversial issues

In recent years, science teachers have been dealing increasingly with controversial issues like nuclear energy, organ transplants, origins, fluoride in drinking water and the use of the Earth's resources. Three distinct matters are involved:

1 The *definition* of a controversial issue.
2 The *justification* for including or omitting such issues in school science teaching.
3 The *approach* to be employed if they are included.[29]

1 Definition

What it is that makes a matter 'controversial' is also a matter of controversy! This can be seen by looking at some of the problems encountered by those attempting to find an all-encompassing definition of a controversial issue.

L8	LI	B3 ↑⚡	LI	B3 ↑⚡	LI	B3 ↑⚡	LI	B3 ↑	LI	B3 ↑⚡	LI	B3 ↑⚡
....	....	1830	....	1918	....	1930	....	2018	....	2030	....	2118
..	....	1908	..	1946	..	2008	..	2046	..	2108	..	2145
....	....	1932	....	2002	....	2032	..	2102	..	2132	....	2202
1828	....	..	1858	..	1928	..	1958	..	2028	..	2058	..
1901	....	..	1931	....	2001	....	2031	....	2101	....	2131	....
1908	....	..	1938	....	2008	....	2038	....	2108	..	2138	....
....	1840	....	..	..	..	..	..	..	..	..	..	..
..	..	....	..	..	..	..	..	..	..	..	..	..
..	1911	....	..	..	..	..	..	..	..	..	..	..
1933	1936	....	2003	....	2033	....	2102	....	2132	....	2202	....
....	....	1945	....	2015	....	2045	2115	....	2145	....	2211	2215
1937	1941	1951	2007	2021	2037	2051	2121	2107	2151	2121	2207	2221
1939	1943	1953	2009	2023	2039	2053	....	....	....	....	....	....
1941	1946	1956	2011	2026	2041	2056	2111	2126	2141	2156	2211	2226
1945	1950	2000	2015	2030	2045	2100	2115	2130	2145	2200	2215	2230
....	1954	....	2020	....	2050	....	2120	....	2150	....	2220	....
..	1958	....	2024	....	2056	....	2124	....	2156	....	2224	....
..	2000	....	2026	....	2058	....	2126	....	2158	....	2226	....
..	2003	....	2029	....	2101	....	2129	....	2201	....	2229	....
1958	2007	....	2033	....	2105	....	2133	....	2205	....	2233	....
2002	2011	....	2037	....	2109	....	2137	....	2209	....	2237	....
2005	2014	....	2040	....	2112	....	2140	....	2212	....	2240	....
2011	2020	2024	2046	2052	2118	2124	2146	2152	2218	2224	2246	2252
2017	2026	2030	2052	2058	2124	2130	2152	2158	2224	2230	2252	2258
2026	2035	2036	2100	2106	2132	2138	2200	2206	2232	2238	2300	2306
..	....	2040	....	2109	....	2141	....	2209	....	2241	....	2309
..	..	2045	....	2114	..	2146	..	2214	....	2246	....	2314
..	..	2048	....	2118	..	2150	..	2218	..	2250	..	2318
..	..	2059	..	2130	..	2202	..	2230	..	2302	..	2330

Fig. 1.6 Disagreements about the scheduled time of the next train can be settled

Just because people disagree about something does not make it controversial. People may disagree about the scheduled time of the next train, who won a horse race, such as the Derby, in a certain year, or which is the shortest route into town. But that does not make these matters controversial. There are recognised procedures for settling such disputes, the answers to which are matters of fact. So there are difficulties about taking a behavioural criterion and saying 'an issue is controversial if numbers of people are observed to disagree about statements and assertions made in connection with the issue',[30] for

> If all that is needed is for a number of people to assert a counter-opinion for the matter to become controversial, regardless of that counter-assertion's ungroundedness, inconsistency, invalidity or mere expressiveness of a vested interest, then even the shape of the earth becomes at once controversial. Some say, and many more in the past have said, that its shape is flat. That is a matter of social fact. But what have such social facts got to do with the shape of the earth? This planet goes imperturbably on its way regardless of

our utterances, and its shape can be known by anyone concerned seriously to find out. The behavioural criterion of the controversial therefore encourages the thought that what is true should be collapsed into what some group regards as true, with epidemic relativism and a sociological carnival as the result.[31]

An alternative definition of *controversial* might be to say that 'a matter is controversial if contrary views can be held on it without those views being contrary to reason'.[32] However, that definition, too, has been regarded as inadequate, on two counts:

1 According to this criterion, a 'person would have to accept that some view contrary to his own could be equally sound and reasonable'.[33] The difficulty here, as Mary Warnock points out, is that:

> It is strictly impossible at one and the same time to say 'this is wrong' and 'but you need not think so' . . . if we have come to our moral judgement by the route of serious thought and a consideration of the evidence as fair as we can make it, then we cannot think that an opposite judgement follows equally 'validly' from this same evidence. If we have concluded that something is wrong, we *must* think that everyone ought to hold it wrong, even though we know that they do not and that we must put up with this . . . If we really believed that any moral view was as good and worthy to be adopted as any other, then we would of course make no moral judgements at all. And the same is true of all other, non-moral evaluations. We cannot evaluate, and accept another evaluation at the same time as equally sound.[34]

2 A second inadequacy is that the definition would prevent people from making a stand on a controversial issue, whereas

> . . . pupils need to realize that people take stands and commit themselves for grounds and reasons and because they believe that they have the best case; they need to realize that to take a stand and commit oneself is to believe one's opponents are wrong, and that such stands and commitments are often to be found at the cutting-edge of disciplines . . . the fact of disagreement is no reason for

lapsing into some form of relativism, such as subjectivism. Indeed, we may argue that it is only by rejecting relativism that the logic of disagreements can be explained.[35]

An early educational project which had to grapple with values and controversial issues was the Humanities Project. Stenhouse, introducing the project in 1970 – and Ruddock, more recently in 1983 – defined a controversial issue as 'one which divides students, parents and teachers because it involves an element of value judgement which prevents the issue's being settled by evidence and experiment'.[36] Stenhouse also said:

> In the consideration of value issues no evidence can carry authority, since all evidence implies a value position and needs to be critically examined. The word evidence, therefore, in this context does not carry implications for the status of the materials, only for their use.[37]

The latter statement moves into relativism, as it effectively redefines the word *evidence* as *what counts as evidence*. Once this is done, discussions on controversial issues can easily become rearrangements of individual prejudices where opinion is treated as having objective value. But it is important for pupils to recognise that, because there are differences of value judgements, it does not follow that there are never ways to resolve these differences. For

> . . .where value-judgements are concerned . . . to regard them as being controversial at least assumes a cognitive theory of ethics. What is controversial is precisely the truth, correctness or rightness of some view, which presumes that at least it makes sense to search for these things even if we do not attain them. Without that presupposition, there is nothing controversial but just different personal preferences, susceptible of explanation perhaps, but not appropriately open to calls for further justification or the citing of evidence.[38]

Furthermore, controversial issues do *not* always involve value-judgements. There are plenty of such issues to be found in science education, concerning the *content* of science, issues such as the development of the early universe and the nature of evolutionary change.

2 Justification

So, then, should controversial issues be taught in science classes? It is difficult to see how they could be totally avoided, even if desirable. They are often 'matters of widespread and enduring significance',[39] which, if neglected, would be likely to leave gaps in children's education, so 'the controversial is not simply an epistemological disaster area into which the responsible curriculum constructor should not care to go'.[40] Controversy is part of life. It arises because people hold different values and have different priorities and interpretations for the same values. So the questions again arise, 'Are such values simply socially relative? Purely subjective? God-given? Intuitively knowable? Rationally defensible?'[41]

A knowledge of the *content* of individual contentious issues and the *skills and processes* involved in analysing them are both educationally desirable. *Product-based* and *process-based* approaches each have points in their favour.[42]

3 Approach

It is a problem to decide how best to treat controversial issues in the classroom, for the very acts of discussion involve the valuing of (1) evidence, (2) the opinions of others and (3) one's own judgements. Various strategies have been suggested, based on the key concepts *balance*, *neutrality* and *commitment*, along with the avoidance of 'indoctrination'.

Attempting to present a balanced view raises the question: 'Should the sought-for balance be in each lesson or over a series of lessons?' Furthermore:

> . . . when considering a balanced approach it is also necessary to consider carefully whether we are talking about a genuine spectrum of alternative viewpoints or are limiting ourselves to those viewpoints which are generally accepted within, say, the broad consensus of liberal-democratic values or even the liberal-humanist ideology that pervades so much educational theory in Britain.[43]

'Procedural neutrality' in the classroom has been

advocated by Stenhouse to counter what he claims to be the following state of affairs:

> . . . the inescapable authority position of the teacher in the classroom is such that his view will be given an undue emphasis and regard which will seriously limit the readiness of the students to consider other views.[44]

This view has itself been questioned,[45] but the strategy of the 'neutral chairman' has its own difficulties: What does the impartial chairperson do if a range of views is absent from class discussions? Should teachers then argue for alternative viewpoints with which they may disagree?

World-views to which teachers are committed shape their teaching, something which has received particular attention in religious education:

> . . . all teachers, whatever their starting point may be, have a commitment for which to account.
>
> During the course of a discussion of this point by the writer and a teacher in an in-service training group, the latter maintained that, unlike the writer, she was *uncommitted* and so in a better position to be neutral. In other words she had no *religious* convictions. It was soon clear, however, that she had commitment of a secular kind in articulate abundance.[46]

Such 'uncommitted commitments' are evident in science education as well. However, commitments to 'procedural neutrality' present their own problems, not least the possibility of conveying the impression that making commitments (other than to being uncommitted) is undesirable. Additionally, it can leave the impression – a point made earlier – that all options are of equal worth as long as they are the person's autonomous choice.

Various texts explore the pedagogy of controversial issues.[47] Bridges, for example, identifies four different strategies which might be, and have been, adopted when teaching controversial issues: 'proselytisation and indoctrination; neutrality; reason and impartiality; and "oppressive tolerance" and counter-indoctrination'.[48] Reiss examines the application of the last three of these approaches to teaching the controversial topic of the interplay between science and religion,[49] but

leaves aside the first one, the matter of 'indoctrination', to which we now turn.

'Indoctrination'

There is a considerable literature on indoctrination, arising out of teaching controversial issues. What it is, whether it occurs and whether there is a distinction between education and indoctrination, have all been explored in detail. The word is almost always used perjoratively. 'In England . . . The term "indoctrination" has tended to preserve its connection with the teaching of Christian doctrine, at least in the minds of those who are opposed to such teaching'.[50]

What characterises indoctrination? Is it a way (*method*) of teaching? Is it possible to indoctrinate without realising it, or is the term only used when the aim (*intention*) is to bring about a certain result? Then, again, if that aim is not realised (*consequences*), would the teaching be termed indoctrination? Finally, does what is taught (*content*) have something to do with it?

It will not be surprising to know, from the above, that there is no single 'concept of indoctrination', but many. They may be broadly classified as those which are based on one or more of the following criteria: (1) teaching *method*, (2) lesson *content*, (3) *consequences* of the teaching and (4) *intentions* of the teacher. Of each of these it needs to be asked whether they are *necessary* and *sufficient* conditions of indoctrination.

The arguments are extensive and can be followed up in a number of the standard texts referenced. Some problems occur because 'indoctrination' can be used in both 'task' and 'achievement' terms. It can be argued that *method*, *content* and *consequences* are neither *necessary* nor *sufficient* criteria and that the *intention* criterion seems best to stand up to scrutiny. Snook offers the following as a necessary and sufficient condition of indoctrination: 'A person indoctrinates p (a proposition or set of propositions) if he teaches with the intention that the pupil or pupils believe p regardless of the evidence'.[51]

The charge of indoctrination is used imprecisely in popular speech to mean little more than 'I don't like what you're teaching', particularly where political or religious education is concerned – education is what *we* do; indoctrination is what *others* do! Yet it should not be overlooked that, if indoctrination occurs, it can be just as much towards the political right as the political left, into a secular humanist world-view as much as into a religious one:

> . . . the protest on behalf of the defenceless child who is subjected to a dominating adult commitment he would otherwise resist can be less a defence of the child than a plea to influence him from *another type* of committed position, a commitment based upon a different set of assumptions about the nature of human existence and destiny.[52]

Mitchell, in his paper 'Indoctrination', points out that 'the entire *liberal approach to education* (let alone the particular methods its protagonists choose to employ) depends on a "controversial" or "debatable" position. So equally does the authoritarian approach'.[53] Problems arise with a liberal approach, as Mitchell points out, from the claim that 'Most liberals feel, moreover, that man is innately biased in favour of the good and the right or, at worst, neutral with respect to them'.[54] He then raises the difficulty of trying to convince the victim of a school bully about this claim.

The problems of an authoritarian approach are perhaps the more obvious. That they can arise in science education is evident from the sixth-former who complained that, 'Our biology teacher was an atheist and often implied that science has once for all disproved religion'. But the issues which that complaint raises about the scope and limitations of science takes us into the next chapter.

CHAPTER 2

'What science cannot discover, mankind cannot know'? – beliefs and values about science

The most fundamental of all the *beliefs* of science is that a world exists to be observed, one which appears self-evident, but whose denial by some students of society is one concern of this chapter. There are also beliefs about the *intelligibility*, *orderliness* and *uniformity of nature*, presuppositions which underpin the scientific enterprise, but which cannot be established from within science itself.

The scientific endeavour, in addition to involving beliefs, also involves *values*; values such as *integrity* – in abstaining from scientific fraud, telling the truth and not plagiarising. In addition, it values *elegance*, *symmetry*, *unification* and *simplicity* in the construction of theories, appealing to such aesthetic criteria for theory selection as Ockham's razor – 'it is vain to do with more what can be done with fewer'.

Intelligibility

The most incomprehensible thing about the universe is that it is comprehensible.

Albert Einstein[1]

What attracts young men and women to the study of the physical world, and holds them to it despite the weariness and frustration inherent in research, is the marvellous way in which that world is open to our understanding.

John Polkinghorne[2]

Orderliness

the . . . belief that every detailed occurrence can be correlated with its antecedents in a perfectly definite manner, exemplifying general principles. Without this belief the incredible labours of scientists would be without hope. It is this instinctive conviction, vividly poised before the imagination, which is the motive power of research: that there is a secret, a secret which can be unveiled . . . there seems but one source for its origin. It must come from the medieval insistence on the rationality of God . . . Every detail was supervised and ordered.

Alfred North Whitehead[3]

The first part of this chapter sets out to examine one belief about science which has been deeply etched into the public consciousness since early in this century. It is summarised by the claim made in the chapter title. This leads on to a consideration of the limitations of science and of some reactions there have been to the claim within philosophy, sociology and science education.

The *content of science,* as well as the *nature of science*, is permeated by beliefs and values, as will be evident later in the Galileo affair and the Darwinian controversies. The degree to which beliefs and values are involved varies with the science concerned.[4]

Beliefs and values in science curricula

An extensive list of phrases can be collected to indicate how widely distributed beliefs and values are within science education. They include 'fair test', 'well-being', 'responsibility for the care of living things', 'genetic engineering', 'social and ethical issues', 'quality of life', 'healthy functioning of the human body', 'responsible attitude to sexual behaviour' and many more.

Currently, there is concern that pupils should recognise the limitations of scientific evidence and realise that science is not the only way of thinking about experience. This concern functions something like a gravestone. It indicates a body buried beneath which was very much alive early this century; one which lies in a shallow grave and is from time to time disinterred and resuscitated. Even where resuscitation has proved impossible and the body lies a-mouldering in the grave, its soul *still* appears to go marching on in popular thought and in many pupils' perceptions of science. The body is a body of ideas which sprang out of an imperialistic view of the scope and status of science. In their developed form, these ideas came to be known as *logical positivism*; their cradle was in that view of science called *positivism*.

Fig. 2.1 Logical positivism – the 'body' beneath

Positivism

Positivism is particularly associated with the influential nineteenth-century French philosopher *Auguste Comte* (1798–1857) and *Saint-Simon* (1760–1825) his patron, but its ancestry goes back much further. Saint-Simon set out 'the law of the three stages', according to which the history of the sciences passes through the *theological*, the *metaphysical* and the *positivist* stages, the progression being seen as inevitable and irreversible. Comte sought to apply the scientific attitude not only to the sciences but to human affairs as well, coining the term *sociologie*. His emphasis was on physical observables. It was a philosophy which was essentially optimistic of the benefits which science would bring as it was applied to every walk of life. Comte also made himself 'high priest' of a new, non-theistic, rationalistic religion of humanity, whose 'saints' included Dante, Adam Smith and Shakespeare. But Comte did not address himself to fundamental issues about the nature of science and its possible limitations; this was left to Mach.

Ernst Mach (1838–1916) was a physicist and philosopher who taught that science had its origin and its base in sense experience. He stressed the need of verification based on sensation. Theories were seen as mental devices to aid classification, as temporary summaries of data awaiting direct sensory descriptions of physical phenomena. Hidden entities and causes were not postulated. Unobservables like atoms were seen simply as means of achieving economy of thought and not as having existential status.

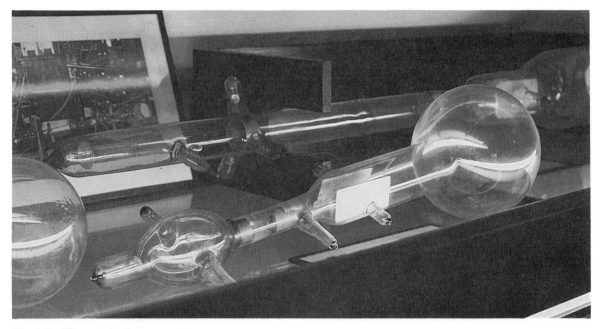

Fig. 2.2   Thomson's e/m apparatus

One of the ways in which this view of science had negative effects can be seen in what is generally regarded as the discovery of the electron by J.J. Thomson in 1897:

> Yet the same experiment was done in Berlin at just about the same time by Walter Kaufmann. The main difference was that Kaufmann's was better. It yielded a result for the ratio of the electron's charge and mass that today we know was more accurate than Thomson's. Yet Kaufmann is never listed as a discoverer of the electron, because he did not think that he had discovered a new particle. Thomson was working in an English tradition going back to Newton, Dalton and Prout – a tradition of speculation about atoms and their constituents. But Kaufmann was a positivist; he did not believe that it was the business of physicists to speculate about things that they could not observe.[5]

There were variants of positivism, but it was essentially anti-metaphysical. It took its name from the assumption that sensation gives direct experience of the physical world and we can be *positive* about it because it is 'given'. Positivism

can best be summed up by some words of Bertrand Russell, used in the title of this chapter: 'Whatever knowledge is attainable, must be attained by scientific methods; and what science cannot discover, mankind cannot know'.[6]

Sixty years on, Russell's antipathy towards religion, and the view that science is the only source of knowledge, still has its followers. At the time of the announcement of the setting up of the *Starbridge Lectureship in Theology and Natural Science* in the University of Cambridge in 1993, Richard Dawkins, an Oxford zoologist, wrote a letter to the editor of the *Independent*, which started:

> Sir: In your dismally unctuous leading article (18 March) asking for a reconciliation between science and 'theology', you remark that 'people want to know as much as possible about their origins'. I certainly hope they do, but what on earth makes you think that 'theology' has anything useful to say on the subject? Science is responsible for the following knowledge about our origins.

He then very properly listed the many things which science has told us, but appeared to regard the questions that science can answer about our origins as the only ones worth asking – 'What has "theology" ever said that is of the slightest use to anybody?' – and concluded his letter, 'What makes you think that "theology" is a subject at all?'

Logical positivism

In the 1920s and 1930s, a group of philosophers, known as the Vienna Circle and including Mach, applied the principles of positivism to a wholesale theory of language, calling it *logical* positivism because (1) it was a theory of the *meaning* of language and (2) its conclusions were considered to follow from positivism as a matter of logic. The philosophers Wittgenstein and Popper were on the periphery of the group, and its cause was championed in Britain by A.J. Ayer.

The basis of *logical positivism* was the famous Principle of Verification. Following criticism of its earlier formulations, the second (1946) edition of Ayer's *Language, Truth and Logic* declared 'a statement is held to be literally meaningful if and only if it is either analytic or empirically verifiable'.[7] So the logical positivists allowed only two classes of meaningful statements:

1 *Analytic* – true by definition (tautologies).
2 *Synthetic* – could be empirically verified.

Analytic statements contain the propositions of mathematics and formal logic as well as agreements about the meanings of words (definitions), such as 'a bachelor is an unmarried man'. Such analytic statements say nothing about any matter of fact – though they give new knowledge about the use of language – so they cannot be verified by empirical tests. It is no use collecting a sample of bachelors and doing an empirical test by examining public records to see whether they are unmarried, because the only means of knowing that everyone in the sample is a bachelor is to know that they are unmarried.

Synthetic statements synthesise two or more different aspects of reality to impart new knowledge. 'Roses are red' is a synthetic statement,

bringing together the concepts of 'roses' and 'redness'. It is open to empirical test and, in this instance, results in the need of the qualifier, 'some'. But statements like 'stealing is wrong' or 'there is no God', on the logical positivists' criterion of meaning, were relegated to the status of meaningless utterances. They granted 'stealing is wrong' represented an emotive expression of disapproval, equivalent to 'Stealing – ugh!', but that was all. Such statements were not declared untrue, but cognitively meaningless. If a statement is meaningless, its truth or falsity does not arise, since questions of *meaning* are logically prior to questions of *truth*. So in the couplet from Lewis Carroll's rhyme, *Jabberwocky* . . .

> All mimsy were the borogoves,
> And the mome raths outgrabe.

. . . before one can decide whether it is true that the borogoves were mimsy, one has to know whether the terms 'mimsy' and 'borogoves' have meaning.

The deification of science

Thus, with a sweep of the arm, the logical positivists dismissed as meaningless all moral, theological and metaphysical statements, supposedly in the name of science! Science was deified with a vengeance, exalted as final arbiter of what could rationally be believed. The legacy of this view survives among those who hold that science is devoid of beliefs and values and is anti-religious. So the logical positivists elevated the 'language of science' to the status of a *meta*-language against which all other utterances had to be judged. Here indeed was a golden image, but closer inspection showed it had feet of clay.

The ideas caught on like wildfire and the story of their growth forms an interesting study in the history of ideas. For two years earlier, Popper had already exposed fatal weaknesses in the position in his *Logik der Forschung* (1934–5), later translated, with additions, as *The Logic of Scientific Discovery* (1959). He pointed out that 'positivists, in their

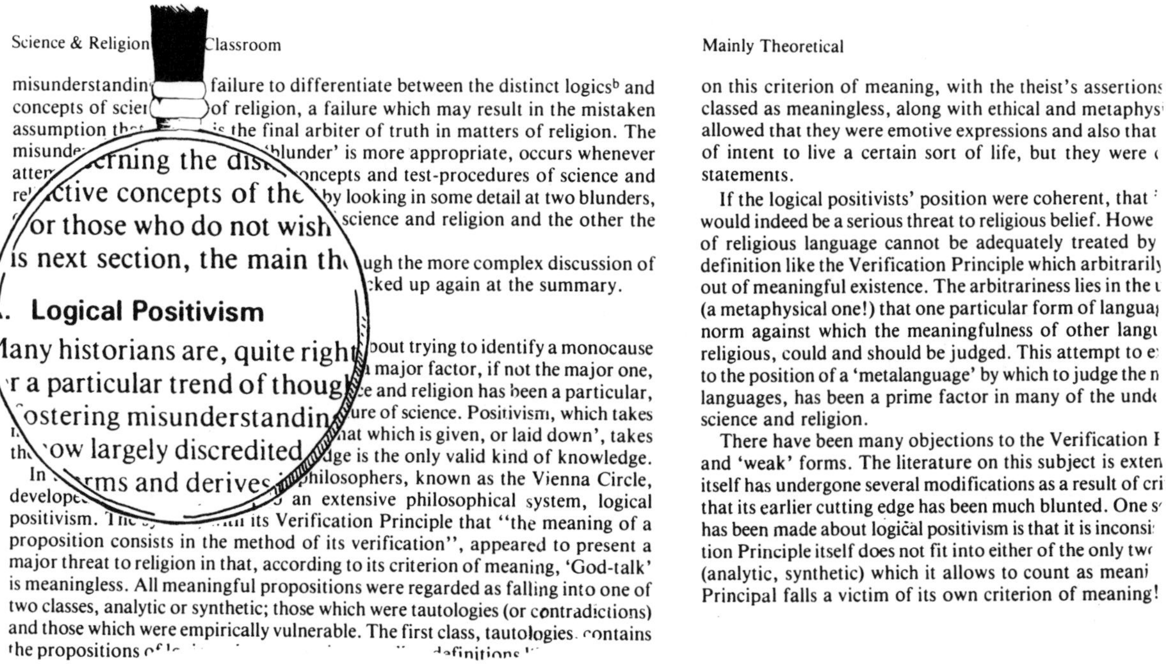

Science & Religion   Classroom

Mainly Theoretical

misunderstanding failure to differentiate between the distinct logics[b] and concepts of science of religion, a failure which may result in the mistaken assumption that science is the final arbiter of truth in matters of religion. The misunderstanding blunder' is more appropriate, occurs whenever attempts concerning the distinct concepts of science and respective concepts of the by looking in some detail at two blunders, for those who do not wish science and religion and the other the is next section, the main through the more complex discussion of picked up again at the summary.

Logical Positivism

Many historians are, quite right about trying to identify a monocause for a particular trend of thought major factor, if not the major one, fostering misunderstanding ence and religion has been a particular, the now largely discredited that which is given, or laid down', takes In terms and derives philosophers, known as the Vienna Circle, develops an extensive philosophical system, logical positivism. The Verification Principle that "the meaning of a proposition consists in the method of its verification", appeared to present a major threat to religion in that, according to its criterion of meaning, 'God-talk' is meaningless. All meaningful propositions were regarded as falling into one of two classes, analytic or synthetic; those which were tautologies (or contradictions) and those which were empirically vulnerable. The first class, tautologies, contains the propositions of logic definitions

on this criterion of meaning, with the theist's assertions classed as meaningless, along with ethical and metaphysical allowed that they were emotive expressions and also that of intent to live a certain sort of life, but they were statements.

If the logical positivists' position were coherent, that would indeed be a serious threat to religious belief. However of religious language cannot be adequately treated by definition like the Verification Principle which arbitrarily out of meaningful existence. The arbitrariness lies in the u (a metaphysical one!) that one particular form of languag norm against which the meaningfulness of other langu religious, could and should be judged. This attempt to e to the position of a 'metalanguage' by which to judge the n languages, has been a prime factor in many of the und science and religion.

There have been many objections to the Verification P and 'weak' forms. The literature on this subject is exten itself has undergone several modifications as a result of cri that its earlier cutting edge has been much blunted. One s has been made about logical positivism is that it is inconsi tion Principle itself does not fit into either of the only two (analytic, synthetic) which it allows to count as meani Principal falls a victim of its own criterion of meaning!

Fig. 2.3 Logical positivism: 'Here indeed was a golden image, but closer inspection showed it had feet of clay.'

anxiety to annihilate metaphysics, annihilate natural science along with it'.[8] For if, as the logical positivists insisted, 'a statement is held to be literally meaningful if and only if it is either analytic or empirically verifiable', then science itself falls victim to the Verification Principle, since it relies upon assumptions like the *uniformity of nature*, which are not themselves empirically verifiable.

Uniformity of nature

Since for most of Earth's history nobody has been around to observe nature, how can we be certain that it behaves uniformly? Only by assuming it functions, when unobserved, in the same way as when observed. But this is to assume the uniformity of nature, not to prove it. The argument is circular.

So science, upon which the whole superstructure of logical positivism claimed to have been erected, fell an early victim of its own criterion of meaning. It shot itself in the foot, and because the foot was made of clay, it shattered!

Worse still, awkward questions were asked about the Verification Principle itself. To which of the only two classes of statements it counted as meaningful did it *itself* belong? Was it an analytic statement? But it did not seem to be merely an agreement about the use of words. So if it was not to be relegated to the class of meaningless utterances, it would have to be synthetic. But in what way *could* it be 'empirically verified'? Disastrously, it appeared that the Verification Principle *itself* failed to match up to the very criterion for meaning it had erected. The Verification Principle was meaningless in its own terms! It was self-destructing. It was in fact a *stipulative definition*; worse than that, it was itself one of those *metaphysical* statements which the logical positivists themselves so abhorred!

Space forbids a resumé of the subsequent history and modifications of the Verification Principle. That can be followed up elsewhere.[9] Suffice to say its cutting edge was severely blunted and the philosophical inadequacies of making science the ultimate test of meaning have been widely acknowledged by subsequent philosophers. What the Verification Principle *did* help to do was to specify what counts as a *scientific* statement, rather than define what is a meaningful one. Wittgenstein departed from his earlier position and adopted a functionalist criterion of meaning – the meaning is the use. In his own words, there is a need to view language 'when it is doing work' and not when it 'goes on holiday'.[10]

Currently, although the debate about logical positivism is not dead, it is very subdued. But what is of present concern is the legacy which those lively debates have left to posterity and in particular to science education. A recognition of the inadequacy of this imperialistic view of science as the only way of knowing has resulted in:

1 The educational need to help pupils recognise the limitations as well as the strengths of science as one important way of thinking about experience, but not the only one.
2 The reinstatement of moral, theological and metaphysical questions as meaningful ones. These areas of concern are currently receiving considerable attention across the curriculum in general and in science teaching in particular, in consequence of the requirement to promote the spiritual and moral development of pupils across the curriculum.

1 The limitations of science

Although logical positivism now occupies a distant chapter in the history of recent philosophy, the view that science is omnicompetent still has its prophets and disciples. Peter Atkins, an Oxford physical chemist, wrote in the *New Scientist*:

Historically, the unstopped flow of science gives us reason to believe that it is omnicompetent . . . That science limits its domain of discourse is a

manifestation of its honesty and the springboard of its success. It does not mean that science has rejected any domains of enquiry from its method: their time will come. Science's cautious, publicly monitored gnawing at the cosmic bun is a far more honest approach to universal competence than religion's universal but empty gulping and the verbal flatulence that passes for theistic exposition.[11]

In similar vein, but without the purple prose, Richard Dawkins in his 1991 Royal Institution Christmas Lectures replied to his own question, 'What is the meaning of life?', with the declaration, 'if *science* has nothing to say, it's certain that no other discipline can say anything at all'.[12]

With a backward glance at the demise of logical positivism, such statements seem curiously anachronistic. Science is the study of events in the natural world, of nature. But there are other questions to be asked, metaphysical ones such as 'is there anything *other* than nature – God, for instance – to which nature owes its existence?' And it is no use going to science, which is the study *of nature*, to try to find out whether there is anything *other than nature* to which nature owes its existence.

The limits of science

The existence of a limit to science is, however, made clear by its inability to answer childlike elementary questions having to do with first and last things – questions such as 'How did everything begin?' 'What are we all here for?' 'What is the point of living?'

. . . It is not to science, therefore, but to metaphysics, imaginative literature or religion that we must turn for answers to questions having to do with first and last things.

Sir Peter Medawar[13]

The doctrine of the omnicompetence of science belongs to *scientism*, not to science:

In the fairy tale, the peasant induced the king to marry his daughter by boasting she could spin straw into gold. Having married her, the king promptly locked her up with a pile of straw and told her to get started. Science ought not to be put in this position.[14]

2 Spiritual and moral development through science education

The Office for Standards in Education (OFSTED) *Framework for Inspection* stresses that 'The promotion of pupils' spiritual, moral, social and cultural development is a "whole school" issue . . . other subjects [than religious education] can play no less significant a part in inviting pupils to reflect on the purpose and meaning of life'.[15] It defines spiritual and moral development:

Spiritual development relates to that aspect of inner life through which pupils acquire insights into their personal existence which are of enduring worth. It is characterised by reflection, the attribution of meaning to experience, valuing a non-material dimension to life and intimations of an enduring reality. 'Spiritual' is not synonymous with 'religious'; all areas of the curriculum may contribute to pupils' spiritual development.

Moral development is concerned with pupils' ability to make judgements about how to behave and act and the reasons for such behaviour. It requires knowledge and understanding and includes questions of intention, motive and attitude. Pupils should be able to distinguish 'right' and 'wrong' as matters of morality from the use of the words right and wrong in other contexts.[16]

It gives as evaluation criteria:

Spiritual development is to be judged by how well the school promotes opportunities for pupils to reflect on aspects of their lives and the human condition through, for example, literature, music, art, science, religious education and collective worship, and how well the pupils respond . . .

Moral development is to be judged by how well the school promotes an understanding of the moral principles which allow pupils to tell right from wrong, and to respect other people, truth, justice and property; and how well they respond, through their behaviour and the views they express.[17]

Science education has its part to play in promoting the spiritual and moral development of pupils, following the recognition of the inadequacies of imperialist views of science.[18]

A pot pourri of views about science

The legacy of logical positivism is an entrenched part of popular folklore and not easily dislodged. Science still gets deified. But this view now competes with components from the New Age movement, examined in more detail in Chapter 4. The New Age components are inhomogeneous and sometimes mutually contradictory. One component consists of a *denigration of science*. A second component, often accompanying the first, involves a rejection of rationality in preference for *subjectivism*, which locates truth in the mind of the thinker, or *relativism*, which locates it in the collective decisions of a society. A third component attempts to enlist certain aspects of science, such as quantum mechanics, to support mystical ideas of 'wholeness'. While the third view is arguably suspect,[19] the second would, if widely adopted, herald the *demise of science* – a possibility we shall examine after looking at the first component.

The denigration of science

Where there has been a repudiation of science, it has reflected a measure of public disenchantment on two counts:

1 *Science failed to come up to expectations.* The successful struggle for the professionalisation of science in the latter half of the nineteenth century, and the undoubted success of science, raised public hopes of it being the recipe for progress, peace and plenty. This hope was fuelled by the logical positivists' attempts to get science accepted as the ultimate judge of what could rationally be believed. When science failed to come up to the (unreal) expectations made of it, it came to be seen by some as a god that failed.

But it is not the fault of science that it cannot answer every type of question about life – and the questions do not go away. Indeed, schools are expected to have among their aims 'the integration in the pupil's personality of some overall view of knowledge and of the world'.[20] But it is not a good reason for deriding science that it failed to deliver what was never in its gift. It is foolish to kick the cat for failing to bark at intruders.

2 *Science had exceeded its bounds*. The First World War illustrated only too vividly that science and technology could be directed towards other ends than peace and plenty. A never-ending series of conflicts since that time has reinforced the point. More recently, concerns about the environment have given science and technology a bad press as being responsible for pollution. All this calls for a sober appraisal of the strengths and the limitations of science within science education – always assuming that science and science education continue to be practised at all.

The demise of science and science education?

There have been various reactions against the grandiose claim that science is the paradigm of rationality and truth. Where such reactions have resulted in a more sober appraisal of the scope of science, and a recognition that there are other standards of rationality and other kinds of truth than scientific ones, that seems entirely to the good. But in some quarters the pendulum has swung to the opposite extreme, with the dissemination of a particular view of science which, if it could be sustained, would put in jeopardy the whole of the scientific enterprise. The view arises from within the sociology of science and it is based on a relativist view of the nature of knowledge.

The sociology of science

The view referred to makes claims along the lines spelt out in Chapter 1. It denies an objective world existing independently of observers. 'Reality' is taken as what is agreed by the knowers – in this case, practitioners of science. Taken to its logical conclusion, this position leads to (1) some odd ideas about the nature of the scientific enterprise and (2) an awkward dilemma for some sociologists of science.

1 *Odd ideas about the nature of the scientific enterprise*. Science is usually taken to be a study of phenomena in the natural world. But on a particular view of science emerging from the sociology of 'knowledge', the factors which decide what shall count as science have nothing to do with the way the physical world *is*, but only with the effects of society determining the beliefs of its practitioners. So science is taken to be, not about an objectively existing world, but about social influences on scientists – the subject matter of sociology of science.

If this position could be defended, then sociologists of 'knowledge' would indeed reign supreme. For they alone would seem to be the unmaskers of ideologies in every discipline; they alone would possess *hegemony*, or *cultural supremacy*. Such a claim amounts to a struggle for cultural supremacy which outstrips even that which the newly emerging scientific professionals were conducting against ecclesiastical authority in the late nineteenth century. For if all knowledge is socially *determined* rather than simply socially *influenced*, then sociology must reign supreme. But the grand claim also entails its own undoing. It leads to . . .

2 . . . *an awkward dilemma for some sociologists of science*. It self-destructs, for since students of society have taken to their discipline the prestige title of *science* and called themselves social *scientists*, their principles can be legitimately applied to themselves – the problem of *reflexivity*.

Reflexivity . . .

The problem for the sociological view outlined is that the sociology of science cannot *itself* make any claims to *truth* about the practice of science, only to 'truth' – that is, what those sociologists count as truth about the practice of science. This raises the awkward question about why anyone should take their claims seriously.

Their position leads to an infinite regress, for it would then be up to another group of social scientists, if they wished, to study the practices of the first group of social scientists, who are themselves studying the practice of science. Their discipline would then be the sociology of the sociology of science. A further group of social scientists . . . and so forth! None of these groups would be saying anything about the way the world *is*; nor would their research papers be saying anything objectively true about the way that scientists view science, nor about the way that social scientists view the work of other social scientists. They would simply be describing the social conditioning that, say, sociologists of sociologists of sociologists of knowledge – and so on *ad infinitum* – have experienced, in a non-objective way. Flew incisively points out

> . . . the obvious and devastating objection . . . that this is to make the whole enterprise self-refuting. For it is to say, on the basis of supposed findings of social scientific investigations, that no such findings are to be relied on as real knowledge.[21]

Trigg, who spells out the arguments and the dilemmas at length, concludes that the demise of science is no empty threat, for

> The snag is that if they are right about the character of science as merely a social institution, the scientists who accept what they say may well find their own activities very pointless. It is not wholly fanciful to suggest that the sociology of science could so undermine the practice of science that ultimately there would be no scientists left for sociologists to investigate.[22]

The only way of avoiding the impasse of reflexivity in which the sociology of knowledge finds itself, is to abandon the grand claim of the social determinism of 'knowledge', whose consequence is to cast doubt on the value – and indeed the meaning – of sociology itself. Instead, a more moderate view can be adopted, that the locus of concern of the sociology of science is the social origins of scientific knowledge.

If the sociology of science aims to say what is objectively true about the social origins of science and the influences on what societies come to count as knowledge, then its contribution is both meaningful and extremely valuable. But the price of being meaningful and valuable is to relinquish sociological aspirations to occupy the supreme position as the exposer of ideologies – a position which confidently takes for granted the ability to spot ideologies lurking within its own camp.

. . . and other problems

The grand claim of social determinism suffers from a number of other fatal problems:

1 The belief in social determinism must *itself* be socially determined. What then if a sociologist has a colleague who lives in the same society, and one of them believes in social determinism and the other disbelieves? The same society appears to have resulted in opposite beliefs, but there is no possibility of saying that one is right and the other is wrong. But sociologists *do* argue their point as if they believe themselves to be right and those who disagree with them to be wrong.

2 If the reasons for a person's belief are wholly determined by social influences and not by the way things actually are, then the distinction between *rationality* and *rationalisation* collapses. If rationally held beliefs are determined by social conditioning – for the 'strong programme' of the sociology of 'knowledge' treats true beliefs and false beliefs symmetrically – then so too are the processes of rationalisation determined by social conditioning. Aldous Huxley's decision, referred to in the last chapter, to 'deny that the world had any meaning', in 'justifying ourselves in our political and erotic revolt', is not distinguishable from that of the person who does not engage in what appears to be verbal subterfuge but says openly, 'I engage in political and erotic revolt because I like it'.

'Indoctrination' revisited

A consequence for science education of a collapse of the distinction between rationality and rationalisation is that there would appear to be no good reason for using one means rather than another for achieving the required beliefs. A science teacher could not give *grounds* for saying to a class of pupils that they should believe what the teacher is saying, rather than what they already believed, for the possibility of *grounds for belief* has been denied. The teacher's beliefs, no less than the pupils' beliefs, would be the result of social conditioning and not of how things actually are, something which would prejudice the whole educational endeavour. A charismatic teacher could presumably use his or her powers of persuasion to inculcate the required beliefs. From there it seems to be but a short step to using less savoury forms of persuasion. The concept(s) of indoctrination, referred to in Chapter 1, collapse along with the collapse of a distinction between rationality and rationalisation.

A recurring theme of these first two chapters, crucial to the entire enterprise of science education, is that once the idea of objective knowledge is abandoned, one enters a morass of self-contradictions and pointless academic endeavour which actually saws off the branch it tries to sit on. Followed to its logical conclusion, the rejection of objectivity would spell the demise of science and consequently of science education.

Objectivity

Although objectivity has its own problems, it is coherent, which relativism is not. Furthermore, while not wishing to try to argue *ad numeram*, the fact that most practising scientists hold some kind of a realist view about what they are doing should not be dismissed lightly. One does not have to be a *naïve realist,* maintaining a one-for-one reading off of the world as it is. Some form of *critical realism* is a defensible position, for

> The critical realist thus tries to acknowledge both the creativity of man's mind and the existence of patterns in events not created by man's mind. Descriptions of nature are human constructions but nature is such as to bear description in some ways and not others. No theory is an exact account of the world, but some theories agree with observations better than others because the world has an objective form of its own.[23]

There are two types of objectivity:

1 Objectivity as *a reality which exists independently of any human observer*. This form of objectivity is sometimes referred to as *ontological objectivity*, since ontology is the study of what *is*, of existence, or being.
2 Objectivity as *impartial procedures of enquiry*. This is referred to as *epistemic objectivity*, since epistemology is about *what* we can know and *how* we can know it (grounds).[24] Both types of objectivity have been targetted for attack.

Objectivity as *a reality which exists independently of any human observer* has been dismissed for well-known reasons like 'all facts are theory-laden', 'all seeing is seeing-as' and that 'there is more to seeing than meets the eyeball'. These much-quoted phrases of Hanson and others rightly draw attention to the fact that the stimuli received by our senses from the outside world are processed by a brain which interprets them in the light of similar data which are already stored, so that we have *mediated*, rather than *direct*, contact with the world.

But that does not in itself give grounds for denying a world which exists, whether or not there are observers to view it, only for realising that there is a measure of uncertainty about what we can claim to know. It is not irrational to believe in the objective existence even of something which we cannot access. Astronomers, gazing through giant telescopes like that at Mount Palomar, do not regard it as irrational to believe that the galaxy of Andromeda presently exists, even though, at a distance of two million light years, there is no means of knowing it. Cosmologists do not regard it as irrational to speculate about what takes place beyond the event-horizon of a black hole, even though light can never escape to signal the state of

Fig. 2.4 Evening at Mount Palomar Observatory

affairs. Truth which is inaccessible is not a contradiction in terms. It can be rationally held that the task of science is to search for truth about a world which exists independently of observers.

Objectivity as *impartial procedures of enquiry* has been declared impossible due to bias, prejudice and the points of view of interested parties. The methods of arriving at knowledge and the uses to which knowledge is put are affected by partisan interests; facts are selected and, since knowledge is only partial, it is claimed that the pursuit of objectivity as a method is doomed.

Whereas the criticisms of both these types of objectivity are grossly overstated, the difficulties of trying to achieve objectivity are obvious. But that is not an adequate reason for denying it as an appropriate *goal*. It is no more justified than it would be for a judge to argue that, because complete justice is an unattainable goal, it should not be striven for, or for a doctor to say that, because perfect health cannot be achieved, medical practice should not aspire to it!

Of course facts are selected – they have to be out of the infinite number of possibilities – and knowledge *is* only partial. But although we do not possess the whole truth about anything, that does not mean that selection makes matters totally arbitrary.

> When, for instance, you are as a witness sworn to tell 'the truth, the whole truth, and nothing but the truth' you have not undertaken the impossible task of uttering an infinite collection of truths. What the court wants, and what in this and in other cases is meant by 'telling the whole truth', is that you should reveal everything which you know, *which is relevant to the business in hand*.[25]

> The fact that knowledge is incomplete would cast doubt on the existence of objective facts only if someone were prepared to argue that unless we have knowledge of everything, we have no knowledge of anything . . . The fact that selection has taken place does not make objectivity impossible. What is at issue is whether what is selected can be objectively described and explained.[26]

Selection and incompleteness are not of themselves grounds for denying objectivity as a goal. Nor are the factors of bias, prejudice and points of view. Everyone pursues an enquiry from some point of view, but that does not make the enquiry irredeemably subjective. Bias is something which, to a greater or lesser extent, we all have, but compensation can be attempted. Prejudice, too, can be recognised and allowances made for it; although in view of the frequent misuse of the word to dismiss the considered views of others with which one happens to disapprove, a reminder is appropriate that prejudice simply means 'judgements made prior to examining the evidence'.

Nothing that has been said implies the world is unaffected by observers. Interactions between observer and observed certainly needs to be taken into account in both natural science and social science. At the micro-physical level, the positions and velocities of electrons are certainly affected by observation (Heisenberg indeterminacy). In relativity, the observer's position and velocity are important with respect to the concepts of *simultaneity* and the measurement of mass, length and time. In society, an observer might be said to 'create reality' in the highly restricted sense that some aspects of the world would be different if they were not there. In the social sciences, where the objects of study and the observers have the same nature and interact, the problems are heightened. Everyone is aware of the 'announcement effects' of Gallup Polls and press leaks.

Kuhn and objectivity

The idea of objectivity in science has been challenged by Kuhn in *The Structure of Scientific Revolutions*[27] and in his subsequent writings. Kuhn's contributions to understanding the ways in which scientific ideas change, written from the perspective of an historian of science, have been valuable, and his views about scientific revolutions are well known. They involve a *pre-scientific phase* followed by the emergence of a *paradigm* within which the *normal science* of *puzzle-solving* is carried out. A period of *crisis and extraordinary science* leads to a *scientific revolution* and the *emergence of a new paradigm*, the process repeating itself.

The word *paradigm* has caused difficulties on account of the many different ways in which Kuhn has used the word. 'On my counting', says Masterman,[28] 'he uses "paradigm" in not less than twenty-one different senses'! One definition is that paradigms are 'standard examples of scientific work that embody a set of conceptual, methodological and metaphysical assumptions'. More recently, Kuhn has preferred terms like *disciplinary matrix*. The idea of a paradigm is more readily understood by seeing how the word is used. Biologists work within an evolutionary *paradigm*; physicists in the nineteenth century worked within the Newtonian *paradigm* – and for many purposes still do. But Newton's ideas of absolute space and time, and mass invariance, failed to account for phenomena like the precession of the perihelion[29] of the planet Mercury. This led to a crisis in normal Newtonian science and the emergence of the Einsteinian paradigm in which Special and General Relativity play key roles. In view of my earlier comments about relativism as a world-view, it may be worth pointing out that relativism has no logical connection with relativity in physics. It certainly does not follow from it. Relativity actually encompasses a prime absolute, the invariance of the velocity of light.

One aspect of Kuhn's thinking which has been a particular bone of contention, and is of importance here, is the challenge to objectivity through the notion that rival paradigms are *incommensurable*, a concept encountered in Chapter 1. The essence of the problem can be summarised thus:

> Incommensurability – the inability of competing paradigms to be directly compared, or judged according to a neutral standard – stems from Kuhn's contention that a paradigm contains its own criteria of evaluation, as well as laws and methods of application . . . Since there are no paradigm-neutral criteria of evaluation, paradigm debate can rely on no objective criteria of evaluation of paradigms; hence paradigm debate is irrational. The irrationality thesis thus rests on incommensurability, which in turn rests on the paradigm-bound nature of criteria of evaluation of paradigms.[30]

Thus Kuhn uses words like 'conversion' and 'gestalt switch' to describe the shift from one paradigm to another, saying: 'The conversion experience that I have likened to a gestalt switch remains, therefore, at the heart of the revolutionary process. Good reasons for choice provide motives for conversion . . .'.[31]

Kuhn has been repeatedly criticised over incommensurability. He complains, 'My critics respond to my views . . . with charges of irrationality, relativism, and the defence of mob rule. These are all labels which I categorically reject . . .'.[32] However, the difficulty which has been highlighted in many journal articles since 1962 is that on the one hand Kuhn *denies the irrationality charge*, and that on the other he *maintains his incommensurability thesis* – and the two positions are mutually incompatible.[33] Kuhn's very claim that 'Good reasons for choice provide motives for conversion' seems to undermine his incommensurability thesis, that different paradigms cannot be directly compared. Furthermore, the anomalies which precipitate the period of crisis and extraordinary science, and lead to the search for a new paradigm, strongly suggest these anomalies *do provide* a bridge between the old and the new paradigms. The anomalies must make sense in the old paradigm, otherwise they could not be judged to be anomalous. But they must also make sense in the new paradigm, otherwise it could not be considered to sort out problems raised by the anomalies in the old paradigm.

So if the anomalies must make sense in *both* paradigms, they cannot be totally incommensurable.

Kuhn's numerous attempts to resolve the dilemma of holding two mutually incompatible positions have not satisfied his critics and he has been charged with failing to differentiate between criteria for paradigm-choice which are *internal* to a paradigm and those which are *external*. A further objection is that if different theories are completely incommensurable, it becomes utterly baffling how one could ever determine whether two theories *were* in competition. Kuhn does not appear to have mounted a convincing case for denying objectivity as a goal in science.[34]

Some challenges to ideas of objectivity are reactions to the extreme empiricist claims of positivism. *Empiricism* may be defined as the belief that all knowledge of matters of fact, as distinct from logical relations between concepts, is based on experience. Empiricism tends to look upon experimental science as the paradigm case of knowledge. The mind at birth is taken to be a *tabula rasa*, in contrast to *idealism* which holds that human minds, encountering the world for the first time, already possess concepts and ideas. A reaction within science education to extreme empiricism has been that some of the philosophical ideas of *idealism* have been introduced.

Idealism

Idealism, in its various forms, shares the common belief that the so-called 'external world' is somehow created by the mind. Physical objects are viewed as existing only in relation to an experiencing subject, so that reality is conceived of in terms of mind or experience. Idealism, in its full-blooded form, holds that reality is mental and that matter does not exist except as ideas in the mind – the individual mind, minds in general, or the mind of God. It holds that our senses inform us about ideas, but not about material substances to which those ideas belong.

One of the challenges to objectivity, which has achieved great prominence in science education, uses some of the language of idealism and goes under the umbrella term of *constructivism*.

A comment on idealism

There once was a man who said 'God
Must find it exceedingly odd
If he finds that this tree
Continues to be
When there's no one about in the Quad.'

Ronald Knox (1888–1957)

A comment on the comment on idealism

Dear Sir, Your astonishment's odd:
I am always about in the Quad.
And that's why the tree
Will continue to be,
Since observed by Yours faithfully, God.

Anon.

Constructivism

Constructivism has been defined by Driver as 'The perspective . . . whereby individuals through their own mental activity, experience with the environment and social interactions progressively build up and restructure their schemes of the world around them'.[35] 'It has at its centre the importance of meaning as constructed by individuals in their attempt to make sense of the world'.[36]

There is much about the *practice* of contructivism in science education which is commendable, such as:

- its accent on starting where pupils are and understanding their current conceptual schemes;
- stressing active, rather than rote learning, using dialogue and argument;
- emphasising the importance of the social milieu within which learning takes place.

However, as Matthews has pointed out, constructivism is more than a psychological theory, it has a significant philosophical component, for 'The one-step argument from the psychological premiss "the mind is active in knowledge acquisition" to the epistemological conclusion "we cannot know reality" is endemic in constructivist writing'.[37]

Fig. 2.5   Objects to be reckoned with as we wend our way through a wood

It is the philosophical component which is my present concern. It appears in the literature in approaches to the teaching of science which 'view knowledge as personally and socially constructed, rather than "objective"'.[38] Russell and Munby say, 'The idea that we construct our worlds is central to our current research on the nature and development of teachers' professional or practical knowledge'.[39]

Phrases like 'constructing meaning', 'constructing knowledge', 'constructing our worlds', 'constructing reality' and 'making sense of the world' are endemic to constructivism,[40] hence its name. Such language is *idealist* – it makes 'reality' a construction of the human mind rather than of how things are. But many exponents of constructivism, while using the language of *idealism*, nevertheless assume there is a world which exists apart from our thinking about it, which is a *realist* view. For example,

> . . . although we may assume the existence of an external world we do not have direct access to it; science as public knowledge is not so much a discovery as a carefully checked construction.[41]

The mixture of terms appropriate to two distinct philosophical positions within individual writings is confusing. It highlights the need to preserve the distinction between (i) the world as it is and (ii) the world as we conceive of it. This distinction marks the difference between *realism* and *idealism*.

Realism, of which there are several varieties,[42] accepts that there is an objectively existing world, whether there are thinking subjects or not. It can accept all the well-rehearsed arguments about having mediated, rather than direct, access to the world on account of 'seeing-as' and the effects of prior theoretical commitments shaping what we 'see'. It recognises that what we claim to know about the world is partial, provisional and corrigible.

It is worth emphasising that these points apply equally well to everyday living. The realisation that our knowledge of trees and cars is mediated knowledge does not seem to hinder a view of their objectivity (i.e. as things to be reckoned with) as we wend our way through a wood or across a car park.

As we engage in the scientific enterprise, we do

not know whether we have 'got it right', but we can still have objectivity as a goal, making the metaphysical presupposition that certain criteria of scientific theories can be taken as pointers towards *verisimilitude*, criteria such as:

- *comprehensiveness* – taking into account all known data deemed relevant;
- *consistency* – free of internal contradictions;
- *coherence* – holding together as a whole;
- *congruence* – corresponding, coinciding with experience.

From a stance of realism, some of the language of constructivism, with its perplexing mix of realist and idealist terminology, is linguistically odd. This is the main thrust of what I am saying and it may well be that if some of the inconsistencies of language were ironed out, my objections would be largely resolved. However, as matters stand at present, it needs to be said that although you can construct a theory, or a model, or a *view* of reality or an *interpretation* of the world, you cannot construct *reality* and you cannot construct *the world*! Also, any interpretation of the world had better have as its goal the way the world is. Otherwise it invites the charge of 'living in a world of one's own', with all its implications! Furthermore, the aim of pupils 'constructing their own meaning' of the world will have little to commend it unless it has as its touchstone the world itself. At a trivial level, to say that someone's observations of the appearance of the moon means, to them, that it is made of cream cheese, appears to have little going for it. At a non-trivial level, this constructivist statement raises a number of questions:

> . . . students in science classes construct their own meanings for events and phenomena through personal reflection and social encounter. The science teacher (and the textbook) have access to one preferred set of meanings which have been constructed by scientists and have been accepted as particularly powerful and useful. These necessarily carry greater weight than students' personal meanings and there may be a need to introduce them into the discussion at some point (Driver and

Oldham, 1986: 119). But this does not negate the need to *discuss* and *negotiate* the meaning of observation and experiment in the classroom. The teacher cannot ever be sure that the student's own construction of meaning during a teaching episode matches the accepted view.[43]

The questions it raises are these: Why are the views of scientists so muted? – 'there may be a need to introduce them into the discussion at some point' – leaving the impression that it is a matter of little consequence whether one does or not, and that one could equally well concentrate exclusively on the students' meanings. Does this mean there are no criteria for preferring the consensus meanings of scientists to those of students?[44] Furthermore, why are the meanings of scientists 'preferred' and 'powerful' if not because they are more congruent with the way the world is? Is it their status, weight of numbers, the need for students to pass examinations, or what? Lastly, why should it matter whether 'the student's own construction of meaning during a teaching episode matches the accepted view', unless the 'accepted view' better fits the way the world is – a *realist* position?

In considering the nature of science, it is important to distinguish between the real objects of science and the theoretical structures and constructs of science. Otherwise, the scientific enterprise is reduced to a study of what socially conditioned believers believe. As such, it only tells us about our experience and says nothing about the way the world actually is. This is the path of *idealism* and leads to the slippery slope of relativism, discussed in Chapter 1.

Finally, the constructivist claim that 'knowledge is something which is constructed, not discovered', suffers from the same ubiquitous problem of reflexivity, encountered earlier. For presumably those who assert that 'knowledge is something which is constructed, not discovered' wish us to believe that the assertion is true, and that its truth was *discovered* and not simply constructed!

'Making sense of our world' is a common phrase used in constructivist writings about science. But is that an adequate goal for science education? The history of science is littered with ideas about our world which, at some time or other, have 'made sense'– a flat Earth, solid matter, the inability of humans to survive speeds of 60 mph, the impossibility of people living in the tropics and the need of an 'aether' for the propagation of light, to cite a few examples. But so much of science is counterintuitive. Hawking confesses about his postgraduate research:

> I was sure there was some other reason for the red shift. Maybe light got tired, and more red, on its way to us. An essentially unchanging and everlasting universe seemed so much more natural. It was only after about two years of Ph.D. research that I realised I had been wrong.[45]

In view of the increasing awareness of the counterintuitive aspect of science, 'making sense' seems a precarious goal for science education. 'Making sense of our world' is a worthwhile undertaking if there is an objectively existing world to investigate and make sense of. But if not, the undertaking reduces to 'making sense of our sense impressions'.

> 'Making sense' of our sensory inputs hardly seems sufficient warrant to maintain the scientific enterprise; and in a science classroom it hardly seems sufficient warrant for the teacher to disturb deeply ingrained and important beliefs of children. Finding out the truth might provide such warrant.[46]

CHAPTER 3

'Every comparison has a limp'
– language, concepts and models

'You should have heard their language!'

The idiot sat right on my tail for mile after mile. When he ran into me, after I had to stop suddenly, I was so steamed up I was nearly bursting. And when he had the nerve to blame me for stopping without warning, I just blew up and hit him! You know how it is, Your Honour, if you build up too much pressure in a boiler it explodes – and that's what happened to me.

The defendant's analogy illustrates:

1 The power of a comparison to evoke a more vivid mental picture than plain descriptive prose, like 'I lost control of my actions'.
2 The use of analogies as instruments of persuasion. The motorist wanted his actions excused as an inevitable consequence of his circumstances. So he picked an analogy which favoured his case and tried to exonerate himself on the grounds that you can't blame a boiler for bursting if the pressure exceeds a certain value. Of course, if there are independent grounds for claiming that a person who has had his car damaged is bound to exhibit catastrophically uncontrollable behaviour, then the analogy is splendidly illuminating. But there are plenty of people who, in similar circumstances, have not so lashed out. You cannot justifiably argue from analogies.
3 The way an analogy provokes further thought about a situation. For instance, the judge might have turned the tables, using the same analogy,

by pointing out that the defendant could have counted up to ten as a 'safety-valve'. This would have enabled him to 'let off steam' and 'taken the pressure off' in a tense situation.

So not only is language a vehicle for expressing beliefs and values, they in turn affect the choice of language. 'A resolute approach' could be declined as: *I am firm; you are unbending; he is pig-headed*! These expressions are not simply descriptions, they are evaluative metaphors, disclosing different beliefs about the propriety of a resolute approach when adopted by different people.

Evaluations and beliefs also lurk within the similes, metaphors and models used in education and science, for example the 'house-building' model for the 'sensible educator' in the frontispiece. This chapter is concerned with ways in which they affect the choices of analogies and models used in science and in science education.

Giant redwood trees

The first example comes from James Lovelock, author of the 'Gaia hypothesis', which we shall encounter in the next chapter. He wishes to persuade us that the Earth is alive. He defends this counterintuitive idea by appealing to a carefully chosen metaphor:

You may find it hard to swallow the notion that anything as large and apparently inanimate as the

Earth is alive. Surely, you may say, the Earth is almost wholly rock and nearly all incandescent with heat . . . the difficulty can be lessened if you let the image of a giant redwood tree enter your mind. The tree undoubtedly is alive, yet 99 percent is dead. The great tree is an ancient spire of dead wood, made of lignin and cellulose by the ancestors of the thin layer of living cells that go to constitute its bark. How like the Earth, and more so when we realize that many of the atoms of the rocks far down into the magma were once part of the ancestral life from which we all have come.[1]

Mechanism, organism or . . .

To take another example, a dominant view of the world used in science is that of the world as a *machine*. But other views have been taken, such as the world as an *organism*, favoured during the Greek period of science (*c.* 600 B.C. to A.D. 200). During the same period, *pantheistic* views were prominent, which saw the world as semi-divine; so to experiment on it was rather like committing sacrilege. Such a world-view had negative effects on experimental science.

The mechanistic view was promoted by Robert Boyle, a founder-member of the Royal Society, in the seventeenth century. He approved of the universal explanatory principle of 'matter and motion', for its clarity and comprehensiveness, but he also wished to de-deify nature. He objected to the Greek notion of the world as semi-divine, not only because he considered it idolatrous, but because the 'veneration wherewith men are imbued for what they call nature' was 'a discouraging impediment' to experimental philosophy.

One of the books he wrote was *The Christian Virtuoso*,[2] subtitled *shewing that, by being addicted to Experimental Philosophy [science], a man is rather assisted than indisposed to be a good Christian*. Boyle saw from his reading of the Bible that *pantheism*, which identified God *with* nature, was not taught there; indeed, there was no word for 'nature'. God was portrayed as distinct from, although involved with, the world. So Boyle thought the world should be conceived as a

mechanism like 'a rare clock, such as may be seen at Strasbourg, where all things are so skilfully contrived, that the engine being once set a-moving, all things proceed, according to the artificer's first design'.

This *mechanistic* world-view preserved the distinction between creator and creation by the analogy of the clockmaker and clock. Clearly, there were several other theological points it suggested – creation for a purpose, design, dependence of everything on God for its being, and so forth. But Boyle's comparison was later to backfire for reasons best given after looking generally at figurative language. The *organismic* world-view will be examined more closely when considering the environment in the next chapter.

Purity of language?

This preliminary encounter with figures of speech raises a number of questions. Should we try to 'purify' science and science education from them and deal only in the so-called 'plain, straightforward language of science'? Was the French physicist Pierre Duhem right when he called models 'disreputable understudies for mathematical formulas' and 'props for feeble minds'? But it is not clear, even if we were able to do so, how we could be articulate. We use figures of speech when other words fail us. The fact that science curricula make numerous references to pupils being able to generate and test theoretical models indicates the importance currently attached to understanding figurative language.[3] But if figures of speech are important, what is their status? How do they arise? What are their benefits and are there any pitfalls in their use? How do beliefs and values affect their choice and, conversely, how do they play back on beliefs and values?

We shall shortly explore some answers to questions like these with reference to some models and metaphors inherent in the subject matter of Chapters 4–7 inclusive. But first it will be useful to reflect upon the fact that models and analogies are only part of the much wider study of how language is used in science, something to which an entire book in this series has been devoted.[4]

Lost for words!

Ordinarily, language serves us well. Where fresh needs arise, as in a new branch (another metaphor!) of science, a fresh vocabulary has to be developed within a community of user-interpreters. This is evident from a university notice offering research training in 'Periodicity in the microstructure of invertebrate shells and its paleo-environmental significance'.

Cracks in language show up when asking questions like, 'what was it like before the universe began?', since spacetime is believed to come into being with the universe and 'before' is a time-dependent word.

The way the meanings of words depend on context can be seen by considering the word 'draw': We *draw* pictures, cheques, conclusions, lots, curtains and crowds. We *draw* out a story, *draw* in our horns, *draw* up regulations, *draw* down blinds, *draw* threads together and *draw* apart in relationships. Moreover, to illustrate the dynamic, changing nature of language, people used to speak about *drawing* water and, with decreasing frequency, talk about leaving the tea to *draw*.

In science, everyday words are often adopted and given a technical meaning. 'Work' then becomes 'the product of force and distance moved in the direction of the force' as well as that by which someone earns a living. 'Fields' may be grazing places for cows or regions of electric, gravitational or magnetic influence. One physicist declared in Heisenberg's presence that 'space was simply the field of linear operations'. 'Nonsense', said Heisenberg, 'space is blue and birds fly through it'.[5] But some words which have dual employment are much more slippery to handle. 'Force' and 'energy' have clear connotations in science, but when used in phrases like 'the *Force* be with you' or about 'psychic' *energy*, they carry with them metaphysical beliefs and values which are not derivable from science. Even more tricky is the distinction between the popular and technical uses of the word *chance*. The *technical* meaning of chance is metaphysically neutral, indicating 'unpredictable from prior data'. But it is sometimes surreptitiously replaced in cosmological and biological literature by the *popular* meaning of 'unplanned' or 'purposeless', something which will be referred to in Chapter 7. Examples like these start to raise a host of questions about appropriate and inappropriate uses of similes, metaphors, analogies and models in science and in teaching science.

'It is as if . . .'

When we try to describe something inaccessible, or conceptually demanding, we make comparisons with the familiar, on the assumption that both share a similar structure (*isomorphism*), showing resemblances between corresponding parts. Sometimes comparisons are made in the form of a *simile*, which uses *like* or *as* to make *explicit* comparisons between two essentially unlike things – light is *like* water waves; electricity behaves *as* water flowing through a pipe.

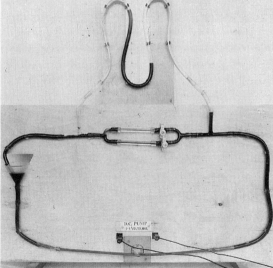

Fig. 3.1   Water circuit board

Omitting the word 'like' results in *metaphors*, in which *implicit* comparisons are made, e.g. light *waves*, electric *currents* which *flow* in wires. Such expressions are so familiar that their metaphorical nature is often forgotten. '"Computer virus" is particularly interesting in this respect because "virus" is currently well on the way to being literalised in the computer setting, the meaning of the word having changed in such a way that for some people the phrase is no longer a metaphor at all!'[6]

Metaphors are concise ways of expressing a great deal. Take, for example, the mass of theoretical ideas underlying light *waves*, or the image conjured up by saying the Earth is a *space-ship*. The latter metaphor illustrates their changing nature. Lovelock proposes a replacement metaphor: 'I see the world as a living organism of which we are a part; not the owner, nor the tenant, not even a passenger on that obsolete metaphor "spaceship Earth"'.[7]

Models

Some metaphors such as electric *current* and the *billiard-ball* metaphor of gas-molecules have been systematically developed under the label of *models*. They are called *models* and not simply *analogies* as an indication that the analogy is intended to suggest, not simply a correspondence between one thing and another, but a correspondence between one set of circumstances and another. Although a model will have a *key concept*, there will be an additional cluster of ideas, for the scope of a model is wider than a plain metaphor. Metaphors are used momentarily, models are systematically developed:

> . . . a model is a symbolic representation of selected aspects of the behaviour of a complex system for particular purposes. It is an imaginative tool for ordering experience, rather than a description of the world.[8]

Types of models

The word 'model' is used in a variety of ways, a common one being the small-scale models which pupils play with and may encounter in energy-transfer experiments. But the word may also be applied to *fashion models, model pupils* (!), *atomic models* and *mathematical models*, indicating that a central feature is the *representation* of something. Such a breadth of usage is an indication of the many different forms and functions of models, which vary across the sciences.[9]

The study of models has been extensively developed by Barbour,[10] Black,[11] Harré,[12] Hesse,[13] Ramsey[14] and a host of others. Hutten[15] differentiates between a *model of* something and a *model for* something, identifying five functions of models:

1 *Psychological function*: in the case of a building which, because of its size, is not easily visualised, a scaled-down *model of* the building gives a visual representation. There is also a sense, albeit a very different one, in which a *model for*, say, an atom – such as a miniature solar system – could be said to give a visual representation. But a major difference would be that the atom is not thought to have the appearance of a scaled-down version of the solar system.

Lord Kelvin once said, 'I never satisfy myself until I can make a mechanical model of a thing. If I can make a mechanical model I can understand it'.[16] But in science the scope for being able to make mechanical models – and indeed for *picturability* in models at all – is now seen to be severely limited.

A further psychological function of a model would be as a persuasive device, as already illustrated by the motorist and steam-boiler.

2 *Logical function*: the use of a computer as a working model for certain brain processes illustrates the logical function of a model.

3 *Explanatory function*: a model functions as an explanatory device. An ethological (animal behaviour) model can, for example, be used to explain human behaviour – a point to which we shall return later – and a flow of water can be used to explain electric current.

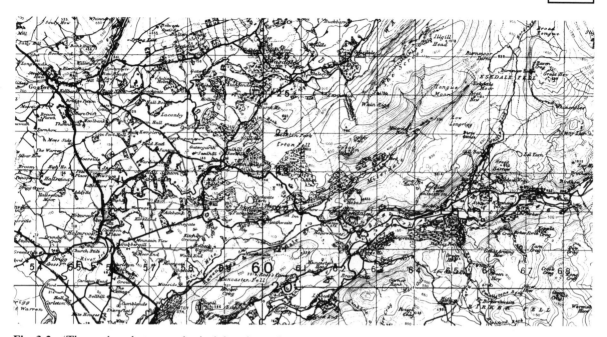

Fig. 3.2 'The analogy between physical theories and maps extends for quite a long way'

4 *Normative function*: a model can function normatively when it represents an ideal, as in the earlier examples of a model pupil (diligent, hardworking), a fashion model ('right' physical statistics) or a model husband/wife (loving, faithful).

5 *Interpretive function*: a model is an interpretation, an evaluation of a phenomenon. It acts like a filter, selecting, highlighting and suppressing features of the principal subjects. Evolutionary ideas, so successful in biology, have come to be taken as a model in many other areas of thought where they are unsuitable. In extreme cases, this has led to the undervaluing of data which do not fit the model, which then takes on the status of a *control* model, moulding, *a priori*, the interpretation of data. Two such *non-sequiturs* from different disciplines are that moral betterment must result from organic evolution as humans 'at last throw off their animal origins', and that monotheism must have evolved out of polytheism.

Models are used *within* science, but there are also models *for* the activities of science itself; and both are important in teaching science. We are mainly concerned in this chapter with the former, but here are two examples of the latter, provided by Toulmin and Popper, respectively:

> . . . the analogy between physical theories and maps extends for quite a long way . . . since the problems of method facing the physicist and the cartographer are logically similar in important respects, and so are the techniques of representation they employ to deal with them.[17]

Science does not rest upon solid bedrock. The bold structure of its theories rises, as it were, above a swamp. It is like a building erected on piles. The piles are driven down from above into the swamp, but not down to any natural or 'given' base; and if we stop driving the piles deeper, it is not because we have reached firm ground. We simply stop when we are satisfied that the piles are firm enough to carry the structure, at least for the time being.[18]

Status of models

One view of models, *literalism*, which is a characteristic of *naïve realism*, identifies the model with
reality. Another view, *instrumentalism*, regards
models as simply useful fictions. A softer form of
instrumentalism says simply that the principal
purpose of a scientific model is to provide predic-
tive control without prejudging whether there is
some kind of correspondence between features of
the chosen model and some reality. A middle way
between literalism and fictionalism is that of
critical realism, referred to in Chapter 2, from
which the softer form of instrumentalism may not
be far removed. This *via media* is expressed
elegantly by Barbour with reference to *theoretical
models* in science – the type chiefly concerned in
this study:

> . . . theoretical models in science . . . are mental
> constructs devised to account for observed phen-
> omena in the natural world. They originate in a
> combination of analogy to the familiar and creative
> imagination in the invention of the new . . . theor-
> etical models, such as the 'billiard ball model' of a
> gas, are not merely convenient calculating devices
> or temporary psychological aids in the formulation
> of theories: they have an important continuing role
> in suggesting both modifications in existing theo-
> ries and the discovery of new phenomena . . . such
> models are taken seriously but not literally. They
> are neither literal pictures of reality nor 'useful
> fictions', but partial and provisional ways of
> imagining what is not observable; they are sym-
> bolic representation of aspects of the world which
> are not directly accessible to us.[19]

In selecting a model, its likely fruitfulness in
generating further insights is a key criterion for
choice. This applies in a host of disciplines, among
which religion is a notable example. Despite its
problems, Ptolemy's astronomical model was
fruitful in that it was capable of indefinite refinement and enabled accurate predictions of astronomical phenomena to be made. However, some
models, like Rutherford's atom, though fruitful,
involve inconsistencies, as we shall see shortly.

Uses of models

We resort to 'model making' when we are con-
fronted with phenomena which are (1) too complex to handle by other means, (2) inaccessible to
our senses, (3) conceptually difficult or (4) novel.

Models and metaphors 'tease the mind into
action as one senses a tension and strange inter-
action of thought in the new use of language'.[20]
Ramsey illustrates this power in

> . . . a metaphor whose possibilities I first realized
> when Sir George Clark developed them in a
> humorous way in an informal speech at Oxford
> some years ago. The head of an Oxford college,
> said Sir George, is often thought of as a figure-
> head. Now what is a figurehead? It is a colourful,
> decorative but somewhat wooden personality, well
> to the front, representing the ship to the outside
> world. But it might be said that a figurehead is also
> virtually useless, needs pushing from behind if ever
> it is going to move at all; and yet everyone admits
> that if a storm breaks, it is the figurehead who
> bears the worst of it. In ways like this, even the
> most common metaphors can be seen to contain
> many unsuspected articulation possibilities. Here
> then is one way in which metaphors resemble
> models . . .[21]

He describes the function of models 'as builders of
discourse' which 'enable us to make sense of
discourse whose logical structure is so perplexing
as to inhibit literacy'.[22] As explanatory devices,
models can help in the teaching of science, but they
can also hinder; they offer benefits but they also
present pitfalls.

Limitations of analogies and models

> Like an understudy, it is never quite the same as
> the principal.[23]

To say that no analogy or model is perfect is
tautologous, for then it would cease to be an
analogy and become an *identity*. The point is
illustrated by R.V. Jones' account of British
attempts to deceive German radar in the Second
World War. Strips of tinfoil, cut to lengths which
resonated with German radar frequencies, were

dropped to give false echoes on the radar screens. Sufficient quantities gave the impression of a large bombing raid which drew off German fighters while the real raid was carried on elsewhere. The Germans countered the deception by using several stations operating on different frequencies. At frequencies other than the resonant frequency, the tinfoil gave a weak response, so genuine aircraft could be distinguished by giving echoes at all frequencies. But another difficulty for sustained deception was that fast-moving aircraft produced pronounced Doppler effects on the echoes, unlike the drifting tinfoil. So, Jones concluded:

> . . . against an omniscient controller, we have to make the decoy echoes move with the speed of aircraft, and reflect different frequencies in the same way. This is easiest done by making a glider of the same size as the bomber. Then if we allow the enemy controller to use sound and infrared detectors and other aids, we find that the only decoy which can mislead him into thinking that there is a British bomber flying through his defences is another British bomber flying through his defences.[24]

Some features of a chosen model will:

- provide helpful comparisons (positive features),
- appear to be unhelpful (negative features) and
- not obviously belong to either category (neutral features).

Positive features of models

The positive features are a prime *raison d'être* for models; but not only the positive features are useful:

Negative features of models

Sometimes, the places of disparity yield advances in understanding, through a creative insight or an intuitive leap. This feature of analogue models prompted Ramsey to label them *disclosure* models.[25]

An example of how *negative features* may advance our understanding is provided by Rutherford's atomic model. Geiger and Marsden's experiments showed that most alpha-particles passed straight through thin gold foil, while a few were deflected through large angles. A small fraction returned the way they came and Rutherford compared this to firing a fifteen-inch naval shell at tissue paper and finding it bounced back and hit you!

Rutherford's atomic model of a small, massive, positively charged nucleus surrounded mainly by space, apart from some circulating electrons, was fruitful in interpreting alpha-particle scattering. But the model was inconsistent with another well-accepted idea in physics, established by Hertz in 1887, that accelerating charges radiate energy. Circulating electrons are accelerating since their direction is changing. So they must radiate energy which could only come from the atom itself. So, on classical theory, all circulating electrons of all atoms should have spiralled into their nuclei by now.

But this negative feature prompted Niels Bohr to apply quantum theory so fruitfully to the energies of the electrons themselves.

Neutral features of models

Advances in understanding can also come by examining *neutral ground*, that area where there are no striking comparisons or differences, for:

> . . . as long as the model is under active consideration as an ingredient in an explanation, we do not know how far the comparison extends – it is precisely in its extension that the fruitfulness of the model may lie.[26]

The *extensibility* of models exemplifies the role of creativity in science, in contrast to a caricature of scientific discovery as the inevitable result of turning a handle called *The Scientific Method*.

Pitfalls of models

However, the *extensibility* of models presents hazards as well as helps, a point which could be brought out when teaching wave models. For the fruitful comparison of sound and light waves also

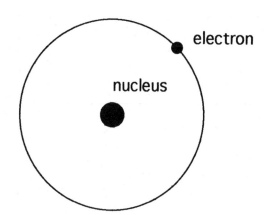

Fig. 3.3   Planetary model for a hydrogen atom

led to the mistaken hypothesis that light, too, must need a medium for its transmission – the 'aether'. This acts as a cautionary tale that there are

> . . . serious dangers in the use of models . . . that the theory will be identified with a model . . . Thinking of scientific theories by means of models is always *as-if* thinking; hydrogen atoms behave (in certain respects) as if they were solar systems each with an electronic planet revolving round a protonic sun. But hydrogen atoms are not solar systems; it is only useful to think of them as if they were such systems if one remembers all the time that they are not. The price of the employment of models is eternal vigilance . . .[27]

Boyle's clockmaker model provides another cautionary tale about the extensibility of models. The eighteenth-century deists believed God created everything and left it to its own devices. *They* used the clockmaker model to argue *against* the beliefs Boyle held. A perfect clock, once wound up, they reasoned, does not need a clockmaker in constant attendance. Furthermore, some of the deists argued, if God made the 'machine' perfect, there would be no need to 'intervene' to perform miracles – and Boyle believed in miracles – for that would suggest imperfections which needed to be rectified. Hence the mechanistic model, in the hands of the deists, overemphasised the *transcendence* (over and

above, 'otherness') of God at the cost of his *immanence* (presence, active involvement). In time, the deists credited so little activity to God, after creation, that their view virtually amounted to atheism.

Boyle's clockmaker model backfires

His last gesture in favour of Christianity was to leave in his will a sum sufficient to endow lectures for the defense of Christianity against its opponents; his intellectual legacy, however, was that mechanical interpretation of the world which deism took as its starting point.[28]

All this was far from Boyle's intention in developing the mechanistic model, although his description of the world as a 'self-moving engine' could be – and was – misread by some as support for deism.[29]

Atomic theory

The idea of things being 'self-moving' had other interactions with beliefs about the world, particularly in connection with the idea of atoms, something which could appropriately be introduced when teaching the particulate model of matter. During the seventeenth century, western science became very interested in the concept of particles, drawing on ideas gleaned from Aristotle and others. Pierre Gassendi (1592–1655), French sceptic and Epicurean philosopher, developed an atomic theory from the classical texts of Epicurus. He avoided committing himself to any possible metaphysical implications of his theory, which he claimed was compatible with a world which was divinely created and operated. He opposed those like Descartes (1596–1650), who claimed to have developed ways of knowing the true nature of things. Like other atomists, Gassendi was committed to the view that matter was not infinitely divisible. Descartes saw this as placing limits upon God's power. Furthermore, Cyrano de Bergerac (1619–55), Parisian freethinker and populariser of science, had conjectured that atoms, given chance and infinite time alone, would be bound to organise themselves into the world as we know it,[30] an idea commonly found today. So it seemed possible to identify atomic ideas with atheism – and some people did. There were, of course, other interpretations of the atomic picture which did not impute atheism. Indeed, by stressing God as *sustainer* as well as creator of their motion, atomism could be turned to theological advantage. Also, a mechanical philosophy could be seen as ridding the universe of a multitude of mystical, intermediate spiritual agents which appeared to detract from God's absolute power and control. Newton, who did more than many others to integrate science and religion in the same mind, said:

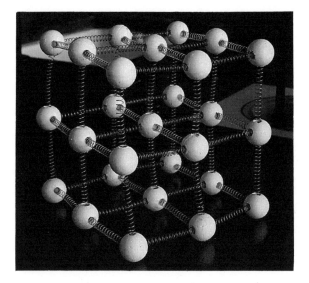

Fig. 3.4   Model for a crystal lattice

> . . . it seems probable to me, that God in the Beginning form'd Matter in solid, massy, hard, inpenetrable, moveable Particles, of such Sizes and Figures, and with such other Properties, and in such Proportion to Space, as most conduced to the End for which he form'd them; and that these primitive Particles being Solids, are incomparably harder than any porous Bodies compounded of them; even so very hard, as never to wear or break in pieces; no ordinary Power being able to divide what God himself made one in the first Creation.[31]

So the supposed indivisibility of atoms, which to Descartes had seemed to be a *limitation on God*, appears in Newton's comment as evidence of the *power of God*. In this and in other instances, there was cross-traffic between the science and beliefs of its practitioners. But lest we should fall into one particular historiographical trap, Brooke warns that 'one of the lessons of recent scholarship has been that to identify the mechanical philosophies with the triumph of rational over occult ways of thinking will not work'.[32]

But, like the mechanical model, the organismic model of the world had its associated sets of beliefs and values, as is evident over environmental matters.

Environment

Does it make any difference to the ways pupils treat the environment if they think about the world as a *machine* or an *organism*? Are there alternative models? Is the world semi-divine? How would it affect attitudes if it were? Lest this seems an irrelevant question today, there is a growing tendency to *re-deify* nature within the New Age movement.

These questions are the subject of the next chapter. The chapter after that concerns our not-so-immediate environment – the cosmos – so I shall only sketch a few points about cosmological models here.

Cosmology

Beliefs and values emerge over preferences for particular cosmological models when asking questions like, is the world *cosmos* (an orderly and harmonious system) or is it *chaos* (lawless, disorderly)? Why is there something rather than nothing? Does the world have any plan or purpose or was Monod right in the grand finale of *Chance and Necessity* that 'man at last knows that he is alone in the unfeeling immensity of the universe, out of which he emerged only by chance. Neither his destiny nor his duty have been written down'?[33]

Some scientists expressed disquiet on metaphysical grounds about Einstein's idea of a universe which was finite (though unbounded) in space. Metaphysical concerns were also voiced about a universe which was finite in time as indicated by the big bang theory; and some scientists opposed the theory for pointing too much towards a Creator. Pope Pius XII favoured it, claiming it 'postulates eloquently the existence of a Necessary Being'; while Bondi, Gold and Hoyle favoured a steady-state theory, which they claimed did not!

Astronomy

The extensibility of analogies led to a variety of astronomical and theological speculations about other worlds. Galileo argued from Jupiter being a planet and having moons to the possibility that Earth might be a planet. If so, since Earth is inhabited, might Jupiter also be inhabited? Furthermore, if so-called 'fixed stars' are suns, they too might have inhabited planets.[34] Such speculations were rife in the seventeenth century. Of particular fame was the *Discourses on the Plurality of Worlds* (1686) by Fontenelle, secretary of the French Academy of Sciences.

The *mechanistic* and the *organismic* models have affected astronomy as well as other sciences. Kepler, for all his mystical ideas, said 'My aim in this is to show that the Celestial machine is to be likened not to a divine organism but rather to clockwork'.[35] Geometric and mathematical models were more fruitful for Kepler's work on elliptical orbits than organismic ones. However,

> Where such organic analogies prevailed, it was common to suppose that there were sympathies,

special affinities, between physical objects. These allowed one body to affect another, even though they were not in contact. The most celebrated examples come from popular belief in the effect of the stars on human destiny, or from the belief of the alchemists that certain planetary conjunctions were propitious for the success of particular experiments.[36]

Today, the enormous popularity of horoscopes indicates how such ideas can still exist alongside a scientific world-view. Indeed, a central idea underlying the inhomogeneous collection of beliefs and values that goes under the umbrella title of the New Age movement is an astrological one.

Animal behaviour

In 1963 in the USA, a social-science curriculum, *Man: A Course of Study (MACOS)*, was launched, supported by a grant from the National Science Foundation. It used an ethological model to interpret human behaviour, which became a cause of popularist concern:

> The MACOS curriculum relies on studies of animal behaviour and of the culture of the Netsilik Eskimos to explore questions about the nature of human beings, patterns of social interaction and child rearing, and the development of a culture's total view of the world . . . the study of animal behaviour provided a provocative metaphor to illuminate features of human behaviour . . . in order for the Netsilik to survive in an environment with limited food resources they practiced infanticide and senilicide as means of controlling the population. MACOS suggested that in some societies such practices, disturbing as they would be in our own culture, were functional, and that neither behaviour nor beliefs have an absolute value apart from their social and physical context.[37]

Various misgivings were expressed about importing the unexamined beliefs and values of cultural relativism into the *descriptive* studies of what the Netsilik Eskimos actually *did*. Certainly an ethological model *is* useful for understanding aspects of human behaviour, since we are all part of the animal kingdom. But it does not follow that there is nothing distinctive about humankind, nor does it justify moral relativism. The usefulness, legitimacy and limitations of such comparisons could be explored when pupils consider the similarities and differences between themselves, plants and other animals and 'the uniqueness of humanity'.[38]

Similar disputes have arisen when particular beliefs and values have been presented as *entailed* by the science, when they have been covertly imported from the beginning. In few areas has this been more prevalent than in evolutionary theory, the subject of the final chapter. However, in this chapter, it is appropriate to consider some of the metaphors and models associated with evolution.

'Natural selection'

Darwin was more careful than many of his followers over possible implications of his theory. But even he came under criticism from Lyell and others for the way he wrote about his metaphor of natural selection:

> It may metaphorically be said that natural selection is daily and hourly scrutinizing, throughout the world, the slightest variations; rejecting those that are bad, preserving and adding up all that are good; silently and insensibly working, *whenever and wherever opportunity offers* . . . [Darwin's emphasis][39]

The problem of understanding Darwin's intentions in using this metaphor is compounded by the ambiguity of 'selection'. Darwin developed his metaphor from human intelligence operating the 'artificial selection' of variants under domestication. So, too, 'natural selection' could imply *Intelligence working through nature*.

Darwin's metaphor,[40] like many others, easily gets lost sight of and takes on a life of its own, for 'as soon as we begin to work with it its metaphorical character disappears, and it becomes intensely real, and is quite capable of doing anything. It has the character constantly ascribed to it both of a directing agency and of a presiding intelligence'.[41]

> **'Takes on a life of its own' – a contemporary example**
>
> Natural selection is like artificial selection, except that, instead of humans doing the choosing, nature does the choosing. Nature chooses which ones shall breed. Natural selection, nature, is constantly choosing which individuals shall live, which individuals shall breed . . .[42]

Darwin's chosen metaphor can be misleading in two ways: (1) 'nature' is not a conscious agent who 'selects', and (2) the process is not a 'selection' of certain characteristics but an 'elimination' of others. Darwin admits, 'It is difficult to avoid personifying the word Nature; but I mean by Nature, only the aggregate action and product of many natural laws'.[43] Nevertheless, the reification[44] of nature in Darwin's use of phrases like 'Nature may be said to have taken pains to reveal her scheme of modification'[45] easily leaves the impression that 'Old Mother Nature' is an active, personal being. It also conceals the fact that 'the frightful ambiguity of the word "nature" . . . according to hair-splitting philosophers, can have no less than one hundred meanings'![46] Darwin himself recognised the care that was necessary with analogical arguments: 'Analogy would lead me one step farther, namely, to the belief that all animals and plants are descended from some one prototype. But analogy may be a deceitful guide'.[47] Although Darwin's theory and its underlying metaphor were at variance with Paley's 'watchmaker' metaphor for design in nature, both writers used analogical arguments. With Paley it was a comparison of the world to a watch; with Darwin it was between artificial selection and natural selection.

What is particularly ironical about the Darwinian controversies is that evolutionary ideas should have been thought to be atheistic. There were those who saw the evolutionary model as providing a healthy re-emphasis on the *immanence* of God, underplayed by the clockmaker model, which in the hands of the deists over-emphasised divine *transcendence*. After all, it could be said that evolution stressed God's *continuous* activity, not the occasional rewinding of a clock. The Revd Charles Kingsley, Professor of Modern History at Cambridge, was pleased by the success of Darwin's theory, giving as his reason: 'they find that now they have got rid of an interfering God – a master-magician, as I call it – they have to choose between the absolute empire of accident, and a living immanent, ever-working God'.[48] One clergyman, who 'more than any other was responsible for breaking down the antagonism toward evolution then widely felt in the English Church', pointed out that 'Those who opposed the doctrine of evolution in defence of "a continued intervention" of God, seem to have failed to notice that *a theory of occasional intervention implies as its correlative a theory of ordinary absence*', an idea which 'fitted in well with the Deism of the last century'.[49] Frederick Temple, Headmaster of Rugby School and later Archbishop of Canterbury, made the point, in his 1884 Bampton Lectures, that:

> What is touched by this doctrine [of Evolution] is not the evidence of design but the mode in which the design was executed . . . In the one case the Creator made the animals at once such as they now are; in the other case He impressed on certain particles of matter . . . such inherent powers that in the ordinary course of time living creatures such as the present were developed . . . He did not make the things, we may say; no, but He made them make themselves.[50]

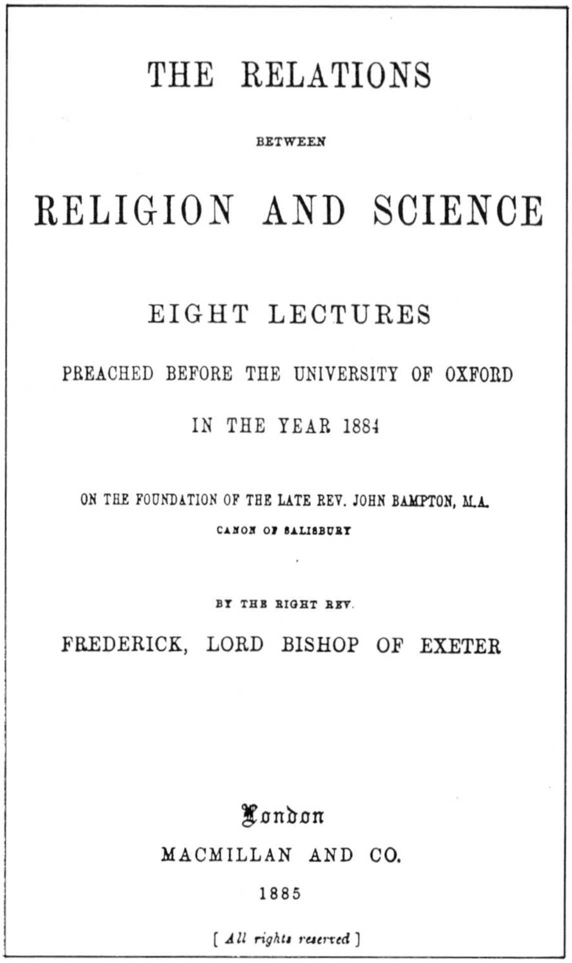

Charles Kingsley approved of this idea and used it in *The Water Babies*: Tom says to Mother Carey, 'I heard, ma'am, that you were always making new beasts out of old', to which she replied, 'So people fancy. But I am not going to trouble myself to make things, my little dear. I sit here and make them make themselves'.[51] Darwin also warmed to the idea and included an extract from a letter from Kingsley in the last chapter of *The Origin*:

> A celebrated author and divine has written to me that 'he has gradually learnt to see that it is just as noble a conception of the Deity to believe that He

THE RELATIONS

BETWEEN

RELIGION AND SCIENCE

EIGHT LECTURES

PREACHED BEFORE THE UNIVERSITY OF OXFORD

IN THE YEAR 1884

ON THE FOUNDATION OF THE LATE REV. JOHN BAMPTON, M.A.
CANON OF SALISBURY

BY THE RIGHT REV.

FREDERICK, LORD BISHOP OF EXETER

London

MACMILLAN AND CO.

1885

[*All rights reserved*]

Fig 3.5 Frederick Temple's Bampton Lectures

created a few original forms capable of self-development into other and needful forms, as to believe that he required a fresh act of creation to supply the voids caused by the action to His laws'.[52]

Henry Drummond, a Scottish Free-Churchman, ardently advocated Herbert Spencer's ideas of evolutionary progress in books like his *Natural Law in the Spiritual World* (1883) and *The Ascent of Man* (1884). However, although there were influential churchmen who saw no necessary conflict between evolution and Christian belief,[53] others found difficulties, including Darwin himself, as he wrote in 1876 of

> . . . the extreme difficulty or rather impossibility of conceiving this immense and wonderful universe, including man with his capacity for looking far backwards and far into futurity, as the result of blind chance or necessity. When thus reflecting I feel compelled to look to a First Cause having an intelligent mind in some degree analogous to that of man: and I deserve to be called a Theist . . . But then arises the doubt, can the mind of man, which has, as I fully believe, been developed from a mind as low as that possessed by the lowest animals, be trusted when it draws such grand conclusions.[54]

Could one still think of humans as made 'in the image of God' if they had such lowly origins? One reply was that the Bible itself put human origins even lower, 'for dust you are and to dust you will return'! (Genesis 3:19). Many people saw a problem, not so much in evolution, but the mechanism of natural selection, which they deemed out of keeping with divine providence.

The study of evolutionary biology is permeated by models and metaphors, with their beliefs and values, powers of persuasion, possibilities for misleading and potentialities for illumination. Asa Gray's raindrop metaphor asks whether the fact that 'multitudes of raindrops fall back into the ocean', and there are 'incipient varieties which come to nothing', means that rain was 'not designed to support vegetable and animal life?'[55] Other metaphors used in connection with Darwin's theory at the time include 'Streams flowing over a sloping plain by gravitation (here the counterpart of natural selection)' (Asa Gray); a stone house, crafted out of uncut stones, shaped by natural laws (Charles Darwin); a nautical metaphor in which 'Natural selection is not the wind that propels the vessel, but the rudder which, by friction, now on this side and now on that, shapes the course' (Asa Gray); and a saw mill, in which the final cause of the wood slabs are part of a larger system in which they may serve in many different ways towards a larger end (George Wright).[56]

The 'selfish gene'

A provocative metaphor in the study of evolutionary biology has been Dawkins' 'selfish gene'. *Selfishness* cannot, of course, be attributed directly to a gene because a gene does not have a personality which can be accused of 'concentrating on one's own advantage, pleasure, or well-being without regard for others'. But how about the idea of selfishness as a metaphor? Dawkins maintains that:

> The metaphor of the intelligent gene reckoning up how best to ensure its own survival . . . is a powerful and illuminating one. But it is easy to get carried away, and allow hypothetical genes cognitive wisdom and foresight in planning their 'strategy'.[57]

> If we allow ourselves the licence of talking about genes as if they had conscious aims, always reassuring ourselves that we could translate our sloppy language back into respectable terms if we wanted to, we can ask the question, what is a single selfish gene trying to do?[58]

Such statements are reassuring and suggest that here is a legitimate use of figurative language. But the 'selfish gene' metaphor, like the 'natural selection' metaphor, once brought to birth, takes on a life of its own. It has been criticised on the grounds that the force of the habitual usage of the word 'selfish' is much too strong to allow it to be given a new definition which is simply repeated from time to time.[59] In reply to this criticism, Dawkins says:

> When biologists talk about 'selfishness' or 'altruism' we . . . do not even mean the words in a *metaphorical* sense. We *define* altruism and selfishness in purely behaviouristic ways . . . I assume that an oak tree has no emotions and cannot calculate, yet I might describe an oak tree as altruistic if it grew fewer leaves than its physiological optimum, thereby sparing neighbouring saplings harmful overshadowing . . . words may be redefined for technical purposes. In effect I am saying: 'Provided I define selfishness in a particular way an oak tree, or a gene, may legitimately be described as selfish'.[60]

Here there appears to be a shift of ground from

the earlier acknowledgement of 'the metaphor of the intelligent gene' to a disclaimer that 'selfishness' is being used in a metaphorical sense. Nevertheless, the phrase 'selfish gene' *is* metaphorical, since 'a word or phrase denoting one kind of object or action is used in place of another to suggest a likeness or analogy between them'.

The 'selfish gene' is an essential component of Dawkins' world-view[61] about the purpose of living. A discussion of some of his claims might provide a way of fulfilling the recommendation that 'In most aspects of the curriculum pupils should encounter questions about . . . the purpose of life . . . [and] the uniqueness of humanity'.[62] The following extracts from Dawkins' 1991 Royal Institution Christmas Lectures and the Study Guide provide some provocative discussion material:

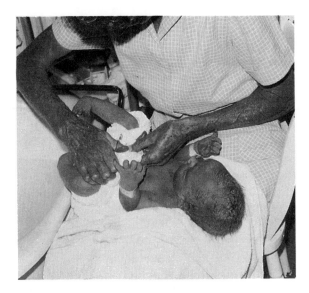

Fig. 3.6   What is the use of a baby?

[1] That is EXACTLY what we are for. We are machines for propagating DNA, and the propagation of DNA is a self sustaining process. It is every living objects' sole reason for living . . .[63]

[2] We can now see human purpose for what it really is. It is a product of our brains that has evolved by natural selection. Originally there was no purpose in the universe. For 3000 million years, life forms grew up on this planet dripping with designoid elegance and reeking with apparent purpose. Then, came along one species that was given, by natural selection, not digging claws like a mole or streamlining like a dolphin, but a powerful and flexible on-board computer. This computer is our brain and the nature and potential of our brain is the difference between us and every other living thing. It is our sense of purpose. [closing words of final lecture]

A 'sense of purpose' is not, of course, the same as a 'purpose'. A *sense* of purpose can be wholly illusory. In the first lecture, Dawkins quoted 'Faraday's reply to Sir Robert Peel's question, "what is the use of science?"' – the reply being, 'What is the use of a baby?' Dawkins said Faraday may have been referring to a baby's potential, and then went on:

[3] It's also possible that what Faraday meant was

there's no point in bringing a baby into the world if all that it's going to do is work to go on living to go on living and work to go on living again. If that's all the point of life, what are we here for? There's got to be more to it than that.

Some of life must be devoted to living itself; some of life must be devoted to doing something worthwhile with one's life, not just perpetuating it.

Pupils might consider whether Dawkins is claiming some privileged insight in declaring 'Originally there was no purpose in the universe' and 'the propagation of DNA . . . is every living objects' sole reason for living'. Whether he is or not, is the second of these assertions about purpose consistent with his other one, cited above, that 'some of life must be devoted to doing something worthwhile with one's life, not just be perpetuating it'?

Dawkins is committed to one of the most persistent models which has been claimed to represent the interplay of science with beliefs and values. That is the *warfare model* of science with religion, one which in particular needs examining if science education is to be related to the whole curriculum, including history and religious education.

Warfare model

This model is also known as the *military metaphor* and the *conflict thesis*. In its crudest form it juxtaposes *facts* (science) with *faith* (religion), usually portrayed as unevidenced belief. Science is alleged to be objective, religion subjective, even though there are subjective factors in science and objective ones in religion. The *conflict thesis* comes in several versions connected with (i) the *data* of science, (ii) the *nature* of science and (iii) rival struggles for power.

The metaphor of conflict is a nineteenth-century phenomenon, fostered by T.H. Huxley and those colleagues who were close to him in the struggle to wrest cultural supremacy from the Established Church and bestow it upon science. The concord between science and theology during the first three hundred years of modern science in Britain was conveniently forgotten.

The conflict thesis has persisted into the twentieth century, furthered by logical positivism. It is firmly entrenched in many pupils' world-views, despite research in the history of science which negates 'that popular but simplistic for-mula'. As a result of this research, there appear to be two pitfalls to be avoided:

1 Being seduced by the military metaphor on account of its resonance with folklore accounts of the meanings of the Galileo affair and the Huxley–Wilberforce confrontation. These events, which receive attention in Chapters 6 and 7, furnish insecure foundations for a warfare model. Cantor, writing from a non-Christian standpoint, comments:

> The various forms of the conflict thesis have attracted much support, but they are not adequate as general claims about how science and religion have been interrelated in history. To extend the military metaphor, the conflict thesis is like a great blunderbuss which obliterates the fine texture of history and sets science and religion in necessary and irrevocable opposition. Much historical re-search has invalidated the conflict thesis.[64]

2 Pursuing the strong form of the *revisionist thesis*,

Fig. 3.7 The main entrance of the new Cavendish laboratory with the 'research workers' text (Psalm 111:2) over it

which claims that Christianity *alone* provided the right climate for the growth of science. This tendency may have developed out of a quite proper reaction against the excesses of 'conflict' writers like J.W. Draper[65] and A.D. White,[66] whose polemical books on the subject are nowa-days often held up by historians of science as examples of how *not* to write history.[67] But what the strong version of the revisionist thesis does not account for is why it was that sixteen centuries elapsed between the birth of Chris-tianity's founder and the meteoric rise of science in the west. Nor does it adequately account for the contributions of Greek, Chinese and Islamic science. Historians are rightly suspicious of monocauses and are concerned to tease out the complex web of factors which gave rise to such a major phenomenon as the scientific revolution, of which Butterfield wrote, 'it outshines every-thing since the rise of Christianity and reduces the Renaissance and Reformation to the rank of mere episodes . . . .'.[68]

The important contributions of Judaeo-Christianity nevertheless need to be recognised. What *can* be said is that it provided fertile soil for the development of science, with its belief in a rational and orderly God, distinct from, yet involved with, creation – a creation which was itself intelligible. In addition, Judaeo-Christianity's concept of stewardship/managerial responsibility for maintaining the created order appeared to authorise science as a means of exercising that trusteeship. God, it appeared, could be glorified *both* by gaining knowledge about the world, knowledge that would help relieve suffering, *and* by acquiring knowledge that would reveal God's wisdom and power. Furthermore, the Christian belief that God was free to make any world of his choosing meant that one needed science to find out just what kind of a world he *had* made, rather than appeal to the writings of authorities like Aristotle. The ways such beliefs have affected attitudes to the environment is the subject to which we now turn.

CHAPTER 4

Wanted! Alive or dead
– environmental beliefs and values

What *is* it that is wanted? The answers people give are sometimes pragmatic ones, such as wanting the environment to be self-sustaining and renewable. These wants may express aesthetic factors like 'preserving the beauty of the countryside', while others may include both practical and aesthetic considerations like wanting to 'preserve endangered species'. Underlying these various wants, explicitly or implicitly, are beliefs and value judgements, which is what this chapter is about. To illustrate this, the chapter is structured around a provocative and hard-hitting paper which has since stimulated many debates about beliefs and the environment. It was given by Lynn White, Professor of History at the University of California, to the American Association for the Advancement of Science.

> What people do about their ecology depends on what they think about themselves in relation to things around them. Human ecology is deeply conditioned by beliefs about our nature and destiny – that is, by religion.
>
> Lynn White[1]

White's statement emphasises a recurring theme of this book, that it is people's world-views, their interpretations of the world, which shape their perceptions of desirable courses of action. Chapter 3 indicated how world-views affect the choice of preferred models, *organismic* or *mechanistic,* of the world. So, is the world best conceived of as 'alive', as some people now claim in the name of *Gaia,* or as 'dead'?[2] World-views are particularly

Fig. 4.1 'THE GROUND IS CONTAMINATED . . . LANDING IS PROHIBITED' – Gruinyard Island, recently reopened, was used for anthrax experiments during World War II

evident about the environment, one of five National Curriculum cross-curricular themes.

Beliefs about the environment take a number of different forms. Some people believe in the concept of wilderness, advocating a return to some primeval state, unsullied by *Homo sapiens*. Those who do so are not usually keen to forfeit the benefits of modern health care and civilisation in the process. Such is the *preservationist* agenda, concerned with saving (species and wilderness) from destruction. Then there is the *conservationist* agenda, concerned with saving such commodities as fossil fuels and metals for future use. The strategies employed to realise the desired goals are laden with underlying assumptions about *what* should be done, *why* it should be done and *who* should do it. Even a few phrases from science curricula indicate a multitude of 'shoulds' and 'oughts' about the environment, such as 'responsibility for the care of living things', 'pollution', 'disposal of waste products on the Earth, in its oceans and in the atmosphere', 'exploitation of resources', 'management [of ecosystems] imposes a duty of care', 'ways electricity is generated in power stations', 'greenhouse effect', 'improving the local environment' and 'exploitation of raw materials'. Such phrases all bear testimony to moral and aesthetic issues in science education which reflect people's world-views, their ideas about *nature*.

The idea of 'nature'

Two key meanings of 'nature' are:

1 *The collective total of natural things* – its meaning in most modern European languages.
2 *Some kind of a 'principle' acting within* – it is in the 'nature' of lions to kill, and poisonous snakes to bite. This is the original meaning of the Greek *phusis*, as well as the original sense of the English word 'nature'. It is in this sense that we encountered 'nature' in Chapter 1 when referring to 'human nature'.

Ancient Greek view of nature

The ancient Greeks saw the natural world as permeated by mind, which accounted for its orderliness. So the world was regarded as intelligent, as *semi-divine*, and since it exhibits ceaseless movement, it was also regarded as alive, as an *organism*.

Post-Renaissance view of nature

This view was shaped in the sixteenth and seventeenth centuries:

Instead of being an organism, the natural world is a machine: a machine in the literal and proper sense of the word, an arrangement of bodily parts designed and put together and set going for a definite purpose by an intelligent mind outside itself. The Renaissance thinkers, like the Greeks, saw in the orderliness of the natural world an expression of intelligence: but for the Greeks this intelligence was nature's own intelligence, for the Renaissance thinkers it was the intelligence of something other than nature. This distinction is the key to all the main differences between Greek and Renaissance natural science.[3]

A modern view of nature

The deficiencies of the machine model became apparent as historical studies developed which emphasised change, process and evolution in the context of the Victorian preoccupation with the concept of progress. A machine is a finished product, not something evolving, and therefore inadequate to typify a changing world. But 'change', which the Greeks viewed as cyclic, was now seen as progressive.

Three models for nature

The Greek view of nature as an intelligent organism was based on an analogy: an analogy between the world of nature and the individual human being . . . between the macrocosm nature and the microcosm man . . .

Renaissance natural science was based on the analogy between nature as God's handiwork and the machines that are the handiwork of man . . .

. . . the modern view of nature . . . is based on the analogy between the processes of the natural world as studied by natural scientists and the vicissitudes of human affairs as studied by historians.

R.G. Collingwood[4]

I have deliberately headed this section, *a modern view of nature*, rather than use the direct article as Collingwood did, writing thirty years ago. There are other modern views of nature, vying for position. One of these, to which we shall come shortly, *returns* to the idea of nature as an organism.

Popular views of nature

A variety of world-views and views about nature will be found in science classes. Rarely articulated, they nevertheless affect ways in which pupils – and adults – think about and treat the environment. Sometimes nature is personified, spelt with a capital 'N' and treated as though it were some benevolent, sentient agent, Mother Nature, brimming over with wisdom – 'Nature knows best' or 'Nature doesn't make mistakes'. Alongside this runs the idea, capitalised on by advertisers, that whatever is 'natural' is good – 'contains only natural ingredients', 'removes stains naturally', 'contains no artificial flavouring/colouring'.

However, deadly nightshade is *natural* and cornflakes are *artificial*! Furthermore, it is *natural* for a man to want sexual intercourse with a woman, but that does not make it right for him to violate her. Also, if Bill punches Ben on the nose it may be only *natural* for Ben to punch Bill back, but that does not make it right. He could forgive him. Finally, *natural* selection can be a bloody process, yet the idea of the virtue of the natural still persists, as though this were a perfect world, and Flew points to one of the consequences:

> . . . the fact that many people are inclined to believe, that whatever is in any sense natural must be as such commendable, and that Nature is a deep repository of wisdom, we need not be surprised to discover that for many the process of evolution by natural selection becomes a secular surrogate for Divine Providence.[5]

Evaluating the mechanistic and organismic models

Hooykaas devotes a chapter in his Open University Set Book, *Religion and the Rise of Modern Science*,[6] to examining the mechanistic and organismic models, their place in history and the beliefs and values inherent in each. He points out that,

whereas an *organism* suggests something self-contained, a *machine* has its reason for existing *external* to itself, in the plan of its maker. The machine, however, is an inadequate model for divine creativity, since the mechanician is limited by the materials, whereas the creator creates his own. The machine, once made, has a certain independence which does not mirror the idea of divine sustaining. Nevertheless, Hooykaas concludes that 'the idea of a world-machine, though not to be found in the Bible, fits in better with its spirit than the idea of "nature" as a world-organism'.[7]

However, the idea of 'Nature' as some sentient being was not easily dispelled and

> The notion of Nature outlived the 'vulgar philosophy', that is, the scholasticism of Boyle's time. In the nineteenth century Darwin spoke about natural selection in the same anthropomorphic way, saying, for example, 'Natural Selection picks out with unerring skill the best varieties', so that the geologist Charles Lyell felt obliged to ask him whether he was not deifying natural selection too much. Even today a reference to Nature serves as the invocation of a deity for many members of the church scientific, while an appeal to what is 'natural' still seems to have the force of divine command for some leading members of the church catholic. Deification of nature is still alive, and the fact that this deity has no special cult does not prove anything to the contrary. There was no special cult of Nature in Antiquity, and no temples were erected to it, yet it was adored under the names of other gods.[8]

So can the mechanistic model really be claimed, as Boyle did, to be more biblical? Certainly it *de-deified* nature. The question is still pertinent today, since there are those, like Atkins, who argue passionately for the demise of God *because of increasingly complete mechanistic accounts of origins*:

> I am developing the opinion that the only way of explaining the creation is to show that the creator had absolutely no job at all to do, and so might as well not have existed. We can track down the infinitely lazy creator, the creator totally free of any labour of creation, by resolving apparent

complexities into simplicities, and I hope to find a way of expressing, at the end of the journey, how a non-existent creator can be allowed to evaporate into nothing and to disappear from the scene.[9]

I shall have occasion to refer to this passage again in Chapter 5.

A paradox

. . . the paradox is that among those seventeenth-century scholars who did most to usher in the mechanical metaphors were those who felt that, in so doing, they were enriching rather than emasculating conceptions of divine activity . . . Descartes mechanized the entire animal creation as a way of highlighting the spiritual uniqueness of humanity. However paradoxical it may seem, Robert Boyle compared the physical world with clockwork in order to emphasize, not detract from, the sovereignty of God. And, however strange, Isaac Newton saw in the very laws he discovered a proof, not of an absentee clockmaker, but of God's continued presence in the world.[10]

Fig. 4.2   God – the cosmic clockmaker?

A deficiency of the machine-model, particularly if applied to the environment, could be its impersonal nature. The organismic model might be considered more sensitive in expressing the care needed in looking after the environment. But this may have a touch of the 'rose-coloured spectacles' about it. There are those who will hit the beast of burden as well as kick the machine which fails them. The differences between attitudes engendered by the two models could be discussed during pupils' studies of topics like the exploitation of raw materials, exploitation being a charge which Lynn White has laid at the door of Judaeo-Christian teaching.

The Lynn White thesis

What did Christianity tell people about their relations with the environment? . . .
Man named all the animals, thus establishing his dominance over them. God planned all this explicitly for man's benefit and rule: no item in the physical creation had any purpose save to serve man's purposes . . .
Christianity . . . also insisted that it is God's will that man exploit nature for his proper ends . . .
By destroying pagan animism, Christianity made it possible to exploit nature in a mood of indifference to the feelings of natural objects.[11]

The sweeping nature of White's claim has generated a lot of lively debate. It raises three quite distinct questions:

Q1 Have those who held Judaeo-Christian beliefs exploited the natural world?
Q2 Is an exploitative attitude taught within Judaeo-Christianity?
Q3 How does the thesis stand up to the canons of historical tests?

The answer to question 1 must be 'yes', something which is widely admitted within the ranks of Christendom. For instance, Professor Ghillean Prance, Director of the Royal Botanic Gardens, Kew, gives as his answers to questions 1 and 2:

Many of White's allegations are true. The church shares the blame for the exploitation of nature that is so ingrained into our western society. However, by no means all of the church has endorsed such things and the biblical text upon which the church is based never endorses the exploitation of nature for the selfish benefit of mankind . . . The more closely I examine the foundation of the Christian faith in the biblical text, the more I am convinced that the problem is not a lack of an environmental ethic, but rather an under-emphasis on certain parts of the Judeo-Christian teaching . . . the world around us is not ours, *God* created it, and found that it was good, and to be enjoyed and protected. Humankind was given dominion over the rest of creation. 'Dominion' means 'lordship', implying caretaking, ownership or trusteeship, not wanton destruction.[12]

As Prance indicates, White was actually incorrect in claiming that Christianity taught that 'no item in the physical creation had any purpose save to serve man's purposes . . . [and] Christianity . . . also insisted that it is God's will that man exploit nature for his proper ends'. Nowhere in the Bible are these taught, rather the contrary. True the Stoics had concluded that 'whatever exists was made for men'. However, 'The Stoics knew no Revelation, no "sacred books". So they had to seek philosophical premises for their conclusion'.[13] But such an idea is not found in the Bible. The early instructions which were given to the ancient Hebrews about the use of the land were 'work it and take care of it', or, more literally, 'serve' it and 'preserve' it (Genesis 2:15). Land was to be left fallow every seventh year, 'Then the poor among your people may get food from it, and the wild animals may eat what they leave. Do the same with your vineyard and your olive grove' (Exodus 23:11). A similar point is made in Leviticus 25 with the addition that the land was to be redistributed every fifty years in order to reduce the inequalities of ownership, in line with the divine command, 'The land must not be sold permanently, because the land is mine and you are but aliens and my tenants' (v. 23). So the answer to question 2 must be 'no'.

The third question concerns the historicity of White's main thesis, that blame for exploiting earth's resources belongs to Judaeo-Christianity. Having made his damaging indictment, White graciously adds, 'When one speaks in such sweeping terms, a note of caution is in order', saying that one cannot tar all Judaeo-Christianity with this brush.

However, it is also true that peoples and nations whose belief systems represent a wide range of non-Christian world-views have mistreated the environment, sometimes knowingly, sometimes through sheer ignorance. In pre-Christian times, huge areas of forest were deliberately destroyed by fire for land clearance and in hunting. In India, the sacred River Ganges is heavily polluted, while Russia and Japan have huge environmental problems. In the Gulf War, an enormous environmental catastrophe was created when Iraq set fire to the Kuwait oil wells.

As a generalisation, White's thesis is flawed and has been criticised for exaggeration. But its value has been, 'if the cap fits, wear it' – and there *are* places where the cap fits. So White's censure has drawn timely attention to environmental abuses and sparked off fresh environmental initiatives within a Christendom[14] which had not hitherto been noted for being in the vanguard of environmental concern.

Although White directed his accusation of environmental exploitation at religion in its Judaeo-Christian form, he also asserted:

Since the roots of our trouble are so largely religious, the remedy must also be essentially religious, whether we call it that or not.[15]

What we do about ecology depends on our ideas of the man–nature relationship. More science and more technology are not going to get us out of the present ecologic crisis until we find a new religion, or rethink our old one.[16]

White's declaration of the need to 'find a new religion, or rethink our old one' points to two responses to the ecologic crisis which have arisen, partly out of his throwing down the gauntlet in the anti-science milieu of the 1960s. These two responses can be used to illustrate to science classes how factors other than scientific ones inform and affect scientific policies and attitudes to science. An examination of these two responses will form the substance of the rest of this chapter.

Response 1: '. . . find a new religion . . .'

The revival of the organismic model of the Earth has been favoured and indeed promoted by the New Age movement. Its concerns go deeper than sensitive handling of the ecosystem. It revives an ancient pantheistic doctrine that the Earth and God are one and goes with a belief in the demise of Christianity, supposedly heralded by events within the Zodiac and the dawning of a New Age.

New Age movement

As indicated in the previous chapter, a central idea behind the New Age movement is an astrological one. In the 1970s, the position of the sun in the Zodiac at the spring equinox began to move from the constellation of Pisces (The Fishes) where it has been for the last 2000 years, to Aquarius (The Water Carrier). This was claimed by astrologers to signify a transition from the dominant spiritual influence of Christianity (sign of the fish) to one which was new and was claimed to be more universal.

The significance of the New Age movement for this study is that the beliefs and values referred to are evident in educational theory and attitudes to science, as well as in cosmology and aspects of the Green movement. Although New Age ideas are heterogeneous, there are common ones which can be summarised as *monism, relativism, autonomy* and *pantheism.*[17] The movement is:

1 *Monist*, i.e. believing there is only one kind of substance or ultimate reality, as distinct from *dualism* or *pluralism*. It uses terms like 'collective consciousness' and sees the cosmos as 'pure, undifferentiated, universal energy'. Some try to justify their beliefs in 'wholeness' from ideas about non-locality in quantum mechanics. The writings of Capra and Zukav[18] have been influential. One attempt to justify the notion that the totality of reality is in every part appeals to the fact that every part of a hologram contains information about the whole.[19] The attempt provides an interesting example of trying to argue from analogy.

Fig. 4.3 'A central idea behind the New Age movement is an astrological one'

2 *Relativist* in claiming there are no absolute truths, a claim which suffers from the problem of *reflexivity*, encountered in Chapter 1. Its slogan, 'You create your own reality', finds echoes in the constructivist phrase 'constructing reality', examined in Chapter 2. An overemphasis on *autonomy*, where everyone does their own thing, goes hand in hand with relativism. The requirement of justifying beliefs has received insufficient attention.

Morality became internalised, a matter of individual choice, which hardly justified making anyone else's minority choice illegitimate. Virtues became values to be 'played on the Walkman of the mind: any tune we choose so long as it does not disturb others'. The central character in the moral drama became the free self, unencumbered by duties or responsibilities. Making moral judgements became judgemental. Educating our children in our moral codes became indoctrination.[20]

3 *Pantheistic* in declaring God is everything and everything is God. If, however, there is nothing that is *not* God, the term 'God' becomes vacuous. As in ancient Greece, 'nature' is again vested with the properties of an organism. Even the ancient Greek Earth Mother Goddess, *Gaia*, is invoked.

Fig. 4.4 A full-scale engineering model of the Viking lander against a Marscape, 1975

The Gaia hypothesis

During the 1960s, James Lovelock was employed by the National Aeronautics and Space Administration (NASA) to investigate the possibility of life on Mars. He theorised that the absence of life would result in an atmosphere near chemical equilibrium. The presence of life would result in the atmosphere being drawn upon by living things for raw materials and being a depository for products of their metabolism. Infra-red spectroscopy indicated an atmosphere dominated by carbon dioxide and near to chemical equilibrium. From this Lovelock concluded, the planet was lifeless, a prediction confirmed by the 1975 Viking mission to Mars. His prediction and conclusion could be used with classes as an illustration of generating and testing theoretical models.

Lovelock took up the view of the eighteenth-century geologist, James Hutton, that the world's self-repairing, self-regulating qualities made it more like an organism than a machine. Lovelock considered the fluctuations in our atmosphere, postulating his *Gaia hypothesis* in the early 1970s. It claimed that life does not simply adapt to its environment but *actually shapes the environment to its own advantage*. More audaciously he maintained, 'It is this persistent instability [of the Earth's atmosphere] that suggests that the planet is alive'; and so was launched, 'Gaia, the theory of a living planet'.[21] William Golding, author of *The Lord of the Flies*, suggested to Lovelock that anything alive deserves a name and proposed 'Gaia', a suggestion which had far-reaching effects. Naming ideas, claimed as scientific, after a Greek goddess introduced a cultic element which has become firmly entrenched. Ideas rooted in Greek mythology entangled themselves with scientific ones muddying the waters round Lovelock's hypothesis.

'Gaia' is used to designate several distinct claims concerning Earth's suitability for sustaining carbon-based life. These claims are paralleled by ones about the suitability of the universe for giving rise to life in the first place – the so-called *anthropic principle*, addressed in the next chapter. As we shall see, a number of the forms of the anthropic principle, of increasing generality, can be designated as 'weak', 'strong' and 'final', a nomenclature which also lends itself to the Gaia hypothesis.[22]

Weak form of Gaia:

There are complex interactions between living matter, earth, air and sea

This statement is uncontentious and will not detain us here. Pupils will encounter some of these interactions when considering the disposal of waste products on the Earth, in the oceans and in the atmosphere.

Strong form of Gaia:

The Earth is alive and Gaia's 'unconscious goal is a planet fit for life'

Is Lovelock's statement that 'The Gaia hypothesis supposes the Earth to be alive'[23] just a harmless metaphor? In Lovelock's hands and certainly in those of some of his followers who advertise themselves as being able to 'talk about Gaia from a mythological and theological point of view', 'Gaia' seems to be much more than an organismic metaphor. 'The concept of Gaia', says Lovelock, 'is entirely linked with the concept of life. To understand what Gaia is, therefore, I first need to explore that difficult concept, life'.[24]

> . . . we all know intuitively what life is. It is edible, lovable, or lethal.[25]

But when Lovelock tries to go further than intuition, he runs into definitional difficulties, which is not surprising! Science teachers distinguishing between living and non-living things will remember the MR GREEN mneumonic for Movement, Respiration, Growth, Reproduction, Excitability, Excretion and Nutrition, as characteristics of living things. They will also remember how well 'fire' appears to fit these characteristics. Yet despite the solid fuel advertisement for 'The Living Fire', we do not count fire as 'alive' in any other than a metaphorical sense. The MR GREEN criteria for the characteristics of life are *necessary*, but not *sufficient*. This is also true of Lovelock's defining characteristics, which include 'incessantly act', 'bounded', 'grow', 'change', 'reproduce' and exhibit 'homeostasis' (tendency for a body to maintain a relatively stable internal environment).[26] Consequently, the case for regarding the Earth as alive in any other than a metaphorical sense is unproven.

Lovelock attempts to defend the counterintuitive idea that the Earth is alive by appealing to the persuasive analogy of a giant redwood tree, cited in the previous chapter. But an analogy does not prove something. It may illuminate; it may mislead. Lovelock employs the analogy but does not establish the necessary *isomorphism*, discussed in Chapter 3, which would justify using it. By claiming Gaia's 'unconscious goal is a planet fit for life', Lovelock is introducing a teleological[27] element, even though he denies doing so.

'Mother Earth'

Far back into antiquity, movement manifest in volcanoes, earthquakes, rolling oceans and mighty winds, prompted the idea that the Earth was alive. The dominant image was female, Earth *Mother*. This image, in the Middle Ages and later, was associated with mining, alchemy and the technology of furnaces:

Fig. 4.5 Clouds forming over remote oceans

A widespread belief throughout the Middle Ages was that metals contained the seeds of their own development, while some saw their transmutation into one another as a real process taking place within the womb of 'Mother Earth'. There were all kinds of speculation as to how subterranean transformations occurred, including changes to the 'mix' of the Aristotelian elements earth, air, fire and water (or of the later Paracelsian 'principles', salt, sulphur and mercury). As each metal was linked to a planet, the influence of these heavenly bodies was also sometimes supposed to be at work.[28]

Metals came from the 'bowels of the earth' and the aspect of alchemy which was concerned with their extraction and refinement was seen as imitating what was already happening within 'Mother Earth'. The internal heat of the Earth could be imitated using a furnace, an 'artificial uterus' to complete the 'gestation' of the ore. Some of this background from the history of science could be incorporated when teaching pupils about the extraction of metals.

'Mother Earth' and the related 'Mother Nature' image have been revived by the New Age movement. The female image has proved attractive to the feminist movement and, when combined with ecological concerns, has resulted in the politics of *ecofeminism*.

Lovelock says, rather naïvely, 'When I wrote the first book on Gaia I had no inkling that it would be taken as a religious book'.[29] However, his willingness to speculate about such matters as the possible identification of Gaia with the Virgin Mary[30] indicates the quasi-religious nature of the Gaia concept. While Lovelock claims, 'In no way do I see Gaia as a sentient being, a surrogate God',[31] his way of speaking about 'Gaia' is highly religious.

Final form of Gaia:

The whole self-regulating system is maintained in homeostasis by the biota[32]

> The Gaia hypothesis . . . the temperature, oxidation state, acidity, and certain aspects of the rocks and waters are at any time kept constant, and that this homeostasis is maintained by active feedback processes operated automatically and unconsciously by the biota.[33]

If Lovelock's claim is a scientific one, it must be empirically testable. He claims it is, calling the 'science of Gaia geophysiology'[34] and citing its prediction of a lifeless Mars. But while this example is *consistent* with 'the complex interactions which take place between living matter, earth, air and sea', it does not indicate *unambiguously* that balance in the atmosphere is 'operated automatically and unconsciously by the biota'. Lovelock cites other examples of what he considers to be testable consequences of his hypothesis. An important one is that many species of plankton in the sea produce a chemical, dimethyl sulphide, which provides most of the condensation nuclei that encourage clouds to form over remote oceans. Certainly, it seems that some atmospheric conditions are *correlated* with oceanic algal activity, but it does not follow that algae *control* these changes, nor that such a system operates on a global scale.[35] Both these examples could be discussed when teaching how the atmosphere evolved and its composition remains broadly constant.

Although testing such aspects of the Gaia hypothesis are difficult, they appear in principle to be open to empirical tests of a scientific kind.

Objections to the Gaia hypothesis

Two principal objections have been made to Lovelock's hypothesis:

1 That it is teleological, requiring communication between species, as well as foresight and planning.
2 That the biological regulation is overstressed, the real world being a 'co-evolution' of life *and the inorganic*.

1 Is Gaia teleological?

Lovelock confesses 'I am happy with the thought that the Universe has properties that make the emergence of life and Gaia inevitable. But I react to the assertion that it was created with this purpose'.[36] To Lovelock, the charge of being teleological 'was a final condemnation'.[37] So he sought a way of showing the biological regulatory processes were 'an automatic, but not purposeful, goal-seeking system'.[38] Whether the provocative idea that 'automatic' processes provide a logical alternative to plan and purpose is one to which we must return.

Daisyworld

Lovelock appreciated the extreme difficulty of testing his hypothesis because of the complicated interactions between living things and their environment. So, in 1983, he suggested an ingenious model, 'The Parable of Daisyworld'. Daisyworld is an imaginary planet, about the size of Earth, which spins and orbits a star similar to our sun. Daisyworld's sun, like ours, has increased in luminosity by about a quarter since life began on earth. Daisyworld is so-called because its principal plant species are daisies of different shades – some dark,

some light and some in between. Daisyworld has more land and less sea than our planet and is well watered by rain at night, but cloudless during the day. The average temperature of Daisyworld is determined by the mean shade of colour – the albedo – of the planet. The daisies grow best at about 20°C; below 5°C and above 40°C, they will not grow. Lovelock argues convincingly,[39] using computer modelling, that given these constraints, from the time when the Daisyworld sun was less hot to the time when its brilliance would scorch even the white daisies, the daisies would achieve automatic temperature-control of the environment. So Lovelock seeks to escape the charge of being teleological on this count. But Gaia's 'unconscious goal is a planet fit for life'[40] is certainly a teleological statement.

Gaia's teleology

. . . when teleology is located within the Gaia theory a profound difference is noted. Gone is an Earth made for man. In Lovelock's Gaia the converse is true: man (and the rest of the biota) exists for Earth. Humanity's own future may well be in doubt, but in the event of catastrophe Gaia would survive our departure. It would just be different.

Thus Lovelock has retained teleology but with inverted priorities. This means that he has also stood conventional natural theology on its head – the argument for God from a 'designer universe' created with us in mind. In fact both forms of teleology are grossly at variance with the biblical picture, according to which humanity does not exist for Earth any more than Earth exists for humanity. The Judaeo-Christian vision is of both Earth and man existing for God.

Colin Russell, Professor of History of Science and Technology at the Open University[41]

The Daisyworld model does not, of course, *prove* Lovelock's hypothesis, only its feasibility. But the question arises whether processes being 'automatic' *does* provide a logical alternative to plan and purpose. If not, *purpose* might co-exist with automatic processes.

'Automatic' processes and 'self-regulation'

The language of 'automatic' processes, 'self-repair', 'self-regulation' and 'spontaneous' re-actions have sometimes been employed to assert the absence of any plan, purpose or divine agency behind the universe. Such expressions as 'it's spontaneous' and 'it happens automatically' have been used to imply 'therefore not God', as does Lovelock when he speaks of 'an automatic, but not purposeful, goal-seeking system'. But such expressions do not entail the absence of divine agency. Instruments of 'self-regulation', 'automatic' devices expressly planned with purposes in mind, are abundant – governors on steam engines, thermostats and ballcocks are just three such feedback devices.

> It would be as if the savage, who had marvelled at the steady working of the steam-engine, should cease to consider it a work of art, as soon as the self-regulating part of the mechanism had been explained to him.
>   William Whewell, Master of Trinity College, Cambridge, 1839[42]

The idea of purposeful 'self-repair' might be illustrated by attempts which have been made to make bicycle punctures self-repairing by having some form of rubber solution permanently inside the inner tube. All that such terms as 'automatic' and 'spontaneous' can justifiably be taken to say is that the properties of a system – inorganic or organic – are such that, given certain circumstances, something will happen without further action being required. Even 'spontaneous combustion', as sometimes happens in a heap of oily rags, could be used for a purpose by an arsonist!

In the organic world, the same point can be made about the automatic processes of evolution by natural selection. Charles Kingsley found it 'just as noble a conception of Deity, to believe that He created primal forms capable of self development . . . as to believe that He required a fresh act of intervention to supply the *lacunas* [gaps, missing parts] which He Himself had made'.[43] It has been argued that evolution by natural selection is an ingenious way of making sure that available ecological niches are occupied. It also ensures that if climate and food supplies change, provided the changes are not too rapid, populations of living things are likely to adapt to these changes rather than die out. To describe such processes as *automatic* – as Dawkins legitimately does – does *not*, however provide secure grounds for him to deny 'design' and substitute 'designoid':

> A designoid object is an object that LOOKS good enough for it to have been designed, but which in fact has grown up by an entirely different process, an automatic, unguided and wholly unthought-out process.[44]

'Automatic' is not a word which entails 'unguided and wholly unthought-out', as can be illustrated from an unlikely source. Mark's Gospel records that when

> a man scatters seed on the ground . . . the seed sprouts and grows, though he does not know how. All by itself [Gk. *automatos*; Eng. automatic] the soil produces grain – first the stalk, then the head, then the full kernel in the head. [4:27f. NIV]

Needless to say, the author of the second gospel did not intend 'all by itself' to be understood as denying God's activity!

2 Does Gaia overstress biological regulation?

The second criticism, that biological regulation is overstressed, is admitted by Lovelock as more difficult to rebut. Abiotic control mechanisms do also exist and the weathering of silicate-bearing rocks is the main abiotic way in which carbon dioxide is removed from the atmosphere. However, it has been suggested that enhanced microorganism activity may increase this rate of weathering. The question is whether biotic or abiotic control mechanisms predominate, an example of a scientific controversy which could be introduced to pupils when learning how the carbon cycle helps maintain atmospheric composition and the basic scientific principles associated with major changes in the biosphere.

The mixture of scientific claims and cultic elements provides an opportunity for pupils to distinguish between claims and arguments which are based on scientific and non-scientific considerations.

Responses to 'Gaia' within the New Age movement

1 Since much New Age thinking is anti-science, the scientific aspects of Gaia have not been generally welcomed.
2 On the other hand:

> The New Age movement has welcomed the idea in Gaian theory that diversity is an aspect of unity, and believes that Gaia is a scientific basis for New Age ideology. However, it has failed to recognize the inconsistency of Gaian thought with the New Age affirmation of human potential and individual self-improvement. The uncritical adoption of Gaian theory seems to depend on the mythical aspect of this theory, rather than its basis in science.[45]

The inconsistency referred to arises because, though Gaia might appear a little like a modern (or very ancient) version of divine providence, nevertheless with respect to the human race Gaia has no moral conscience. 'She' has no vested interest in 'human potential and individual self-improvement', only in the maintenance of life – and it does not have to be human!

3 Some environmentalists regard the idea of Gaia as a living, self-regulatory earth with distaste, since Gaia could then be expected to cope with human pollution, thereby underplaying its seriousness. Lovelock vehemently denies this:

> A frequent misunderstanding of my vision of Gaia is that I champion complacence, that I claim feedback will always protect the environment from any serious harm that humans might do. It is sometimes more crudely put as 'Lovelock's Gaia gives industry the green light to pollute at will.' The truth is almost diametrically opposite. Gaia, as I see her, is no doting mother tolerant of

misdemeanours, nor is she some fragile and delicate damsel in danger from ruthless mankind. She is stern and tough, always keeping the world warm and comfortable for those who obey the rules, but ruthless in her destruction of those who transgress. Her unconscious goal is a planet fit for life. If humans stand in the way of this, we shall be eliminated with as little pity as would be shown by the micro-brain of an intercontinental ballistic nuclear missile in full flight to its target.[46]

Beyond metaphor?

'Nature', which was *de-deified* by the mechanicians is becoming *re-deified*, thereby eclipsing possible benefits of an organismic metaphor. Gaia has taken on a life of its own, drawing forth a cry of protest:

> . . . there is nothing in the Gaia metaphor that has not been utterly familiar to biologists for the whole of this century – except the name . . . That is why most biologists remained politely silent when, more than a decade ago, Lovelock indicated, in his engaging way, that he, too, had grasped these ideas. After all, when someone rediscovers the wheel, rather than say, 'I told you so', the more courteous of us nod with satisfaction that enlightenment has spread to yet another colleague and quietly get on with our business. But when the colleague proposes a Goddess of Wheeliness to unify the global aptness of his newly discovered wheel, we shake our heads sadly; and when Wheely-Goddess worshippers start popping up all over, then it is definitely time to worry. A principle of wheeliness, like a planet-sized organism, may be fun as imagery; as anything more scientific it is silly . . . Lovelock's scientific achievements are tremendous and deserve our respect. It is gratifying to all of us that he found his Gaia metaphor stimulating and constructive. Let it remain a metaphor.[47]

So we have seen how the science of Gaia is intertwined with movements, as White puts it, to 'find a new religion' concerning the environment. But it turns out to be new only in outward presentation; in essence it is a revival of ancient pantheism.

White's alternative suggestion to finding a new religion for environmental needs was . . .

Response 2: '. . . rethink our old one . . .'

White reaffirms that 'modern Western science was cast in a matrix of Christian theology', and certainly these key verses about 'subduing' and 'ruling over' the earth, which have been occupying our attention, have been seen as powerful incentives to do science. As we noted in the previous chapter, the command to humankind to 'subdue' the earth and to 'rule over' it was taken to provide a biblical mandate for doing science, since in order to subdue nature you had to understand it. Moreover, since creation was seen as a free act of God, *contingent* (not *having* to exist; could have been otherwise) rather than *necessary* (*had* to be that way), then, rather than applying reason alone or appealing to recognised works of authority like Aristotle, one needed to go out and read the 'Book of Nature' to find out what was actually the case. But what exactly is meant by the 'Book of Nature'?

God's 'Two Books'

The 'Two Books' metaphor was widely used by Francis Bacon and others associated with the development of science in the sixteenth and seventeenth centuries and its ideas are germane to Chapters 2, 3, 6 and 7. God was seen as having

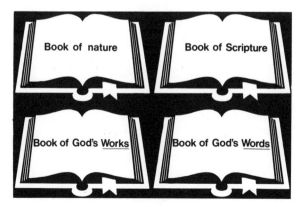

Fig. 4.6   'God's Two Books' metaphor

spoken to humankind in two great 'books' – the *Book of Scripture* and the *Book of Nature*; the first being the *Book of God's Words*, the second the *Book of God's Works*. The first was about the *creator*, the second about the *creation*; one was *verbal*, the other was *visual*. Charles Darwin prefaced the *Origin of Species* with one of Bacon's 'Two Book' passages:

> To conclude, therefore, let no man out of a weak conceit of sobriety, or an ill-applied moderation, think or maintain, that a man can search too far or be too well studied in the book of God's word, or in the book of God's works; divinity or philosophy; but rather let men endeavour an endless progress of proficence in both.
>
> Bacon: *Advancement of Learning*

But does the 'Book of Nature' metaphor have any mileage in it today? The constructivists Desautels and Larochelle say 'There is *no great book of nature* that can be consulted in order to check if the models or theories correspond to an ontological reality'.[48] If by this they mean the truth about the natural world cannot be 'read off' unambiguously, they are surely right to deny a 'book of nature'. At first sight, the metaphor certainly appears to be outmoded, for we have already articulated a view of science in which theory precedes observation. Simply claiming to read off the natural world like the pages of a book seems to do scant justice to 'seeing-as' and to prior theoretical commitments. Nevertheless, the 'Book of Nature' metaphor can still be useful, with one proviso which I shall develop.

In reading a book it is important to attend to the literary *genre* of the text. There were those in Galileo's day who tried to extract astronomical theories from Bible texts in ways that hardly did justice to the literary form. Such cavalier treatment prompted Galileo to quote Cardinal Baronius' words that 'the intention of the Holy Ghost is to teach us how one goes to heaven, not how heaven goes'. Galileo's contribution to the 'Two Books' metaphor, was an important one, for

> In [Galileo's] writings, a mutation occurred in the analogies customarily drawn between the two

books. The search for signs of God in nature had often been based on the assumption that the two books had been written in essentially the same language. Galileo however, achieved a telling differentiation when he argued that nature had a language all its own. The book of nature, he insisted, had been written in the language of mathematics. No amount of theologizing could be a substitute for mathematical analysis. In evaluating the Copernican system, for example, mathematical criteria should take precedence over interpretations of Scripture, which may have become normative but only through ignorance.[49]

The hermeneutical circle

Hermeneutics is a study of the methodological principles of interpreting and explaining the meaning of written texts, a study which is derived principally from biblical studies, but now used much more widely, as for example in understanding legal texts. It includes such matters as discerning authors' intentions and the social context and thought-forms of the time of writing. It is the interpretive aspect of reading the Book of Scripture which I wish to compare with 'reading' the Book of Nature, referring in particular to the *hermeneutical circle*.

Everyone studying a text comes with a set of presuppositions which affect what they 'see' and count important. Prior knowledge and theory result in selective perception in textual studies as in science. But the text itself plays back upon these prior theories, and in turn modifies *them*. So fresh insights may be gained on re-reading the text through theoretical spectacles whose lenses now have different optical characteristics – 'This situation underlies the idea of the "hermeneutical circle" in which the interpretative process is seen as flowing from subject to object, or indeed from object to subject, and back again, as the one interacts with the other'.[50] The hermeneutical circle may be entered at any place.

If the hermeneutical circle is acknowledged in reading the Book of Nature, a naïve realism is avoided. In the same way that we can never be entirely sure we possess the intended meaning of an ancient text, we can never be absolutely certain we have arrived at truth about the natural world. Like any metaphor, the Book of Nature is extensible. One extension is a possible connection between two aspects of a text and two aspects of the world. Some parts of a text appear to be transparent in the clarity of their message, while others are couched in language and thought-forms which make various interpretations seem possible to scholars of later centuries. This is not to say that even the apparently transparent parts are insulated from fresh insights, just that they seem largely unproblematic. So, too, in the natural world, our understanding of some things seems much less likely to be revised than others. Sometimes there appears to be a tendency to overplay the amount of uncertainty introduced by prior theoretical commitments and 'seeing-as'; the 'Two Books' metaphor might suggest a more balanced approach. But whether the metaphor is map-making, pile-driving or book-reading, creative insights exist alongside limitations.

Knowledge and control are closely connected and many natural philosophers of the sixteenth and seventeenth centuries saw reading the 'Book of Nature' as enabling them to fulfil their God-given, managerial responsibility of control. So White's second response – to rethink Christian attitudes to the environment – highlights the need to look carefully at what the biblical texts actually say about stewardship and managerial responsibility. It also suggests an answer to an earlier question about whether there are other possible models for nature than the *organismic* and *mechanistic* ones. Here is one which is not necessarily alternative to either of them (since an organismic view need not include the separate claim about nature being semi-divine), for it is a model which is concerned with responsibilities. The model can be variously described as a stewardship or managerial model, or that of a charitable trust.[51]

Charitable trust model

Trustees of a charity have responsibility for managing finances and resources according to the wishes of the creator of the trust, as set out in the trust deeds. Property is commonly held in trust for children who are yet unable to take responsibility for its management.

But can the world be thought of as an entrustment to each generation in turn? If we are trustees, to whom are we responsible? If we 'owe it as our duty' to do this or that, to whom do we owe it? – to other people?, to ourselves? (whatever that could mean), to God?, to the generation yet unborn? (can one owe something to those who do not exist?), and so forth. Are we the owners of the Earth or its tenants? Have we 'a freehold on our world' or 'only a full repairing lease'?

A trusteeship model of the Earth has deep roots in the divine command to serve and preserve. Managerial accountability is stressed in the Old Testament books of the Law and in the New Testament parables (Matthew 25:14–29; Luke 19:11–27). Servants are entrusted with money until the return of their master, when faithfulness is rewarded and prodigality punished. The emphasis of such stewardship models is that humans are the managers, not the owners.

Like the 'Two Books' metaphor whose theistic elements will be unacceptable to non-believers, so here, such elements are unlikely to find favour. Nevertheless, in a society holding many different world-views, some aspects of a 'charitable trust' model may still find general appeal. The idea of the management of Earth's resources as a trusteeship for our children – from wherever it comes – has much to commend it. Indeed, we reject such a policy at our peril.

This chapter has illustrated a few ways in which world-views shape beliefs and attitudes towards our immediate environment. But those same world-views also affect studies much further afield, as we shall see by shifting our attention from planet Earth to the myriad inhabitants of space.

CHAPTER 5

'In the beginning . . .'
– cosmology and creation

'The mind of God'?

> . . . we shall all . . . be able to take part in the discussion of the question of why it is that we and the universe exist. If we find the answer to that, it would be the ultimate triumph of human reason – for then we would know the mind of God.
>
> Stephen Hawking[1]

The closing words of Hawking's best seller, *A Brief History of Time*, are some of the most quoted in popular presentations about the origins of the universe. Hawking admits in 'A Brief History of *A Brief History*', 'In the proof stage I nearly cut the last sentence in the book . . . Had I done so, the sales might have been halved'.[2] Others have adopted his words and *The Mind of God*[3] became the title of another popular book on cosmology, whose appearance was marked by a debate at The Royal Society entitled, 'Has science eliminated the need for God?[4]

The word 'God' features frequently in this chapter, since it does in much current popular literature on cosmology and the search for Theories of Everything (TOEs). So something must be said about its meanings. Public opinion polls produce high ratings for belief in God, and reflect the wide variety of meanings assigned to the word. To one person it means some 'force' 'behind' the universe, to another it is used for phenomena currently inexplicable by science, while to yet others it refers to a personal Being. Within this book, I am taking for my meaning the so-called 'God of the philosophers', viz. *transcendent conscious agency*, a cumbersome phrase which needs unpacking:

- *transcendent* – greater than us, existing independently of the created world;
- *conscious* – indicating the most appropriate language for God is personal language;
- *agency* – an active cause through which power is exerted or purposes are achieved.

This somewhat clinical terminology is not intended to deny factors like relationships between God and people, but such considerations are not the concern of this book.

The chapter starts by looking at how beliefs, particularly about God – or the absence of God – are embedded in many discussions about origins. This is followed by an examination of whether particular theories of origins have any implications for or against such beliefs. This necessitates reflecting on 'creation' as used in popular language and by scientists and theologians. Then, since certain vocal popularisers of science have gone to some lengths to promote the idea that scientific explanations of origins displace divine agency and purpose, the nature of explanation needs examining in order to assess such claims. The chapter ends with a look at the anthropic principle.

Fig. 5.1   An artist's concept of the Cosmic Background Explorer (COBE) Satellite

'The three fundamental questions of cosmology'

How did the Universe begin? How did it get to the state we see it in today? And what is its likely fate?[5]

Hawking's question about 'why it is that we and the universe exist' serves as a reminder that 'why?' questions are ambiguous. They can refer to the mechanisms of the world's origins (physical) and they can refer to the possibility of a creator (metaphysical). Questions of both sorts stimulate interest inside and outside schools. This was evident from public interest in NASA's Cosmic Background Explorer (COBE) Satellite. From the *physical* point of view, detection of the tiny 'ripples' in the background microwave radiation provided further support for the big bang theory.[6] But it also fuelled popular interest in *metaphysical* questions about the origins of the universe. As Martin Ince, science correspondent for *The Times Higher Education Supplement*, remarked:

God has had a busy time lately. Astronomical observations of the radiation left over from the Big Bang that started the universe has, according to taste, either confirmed his ingenious approach to the complex task of being a supreme deity or,

Almighty boom in our beginnings

GEORGE SMOOT is a happy man today. Only last month he was a humble research physicist. Then his satellite experiments revealed the first evidence of matter coalescing in the universe and he became an international star. Now he is a millionaire as well.

This newly-acquired fame ~~~~l~

Hawking, whose *A Brief History of Time* is about to become Britain's best-selling book of all time (overtaking *The Country Diary of an Edwardian Lady*). Across the world sales are now approaching six million copies, a phenomenon that has transformed science as a literary ~~~~~. Today science 'is to ~~~~~~ T

Robin McKie, Science Correspondent, reports that a publishing Big Bang has revived the science versus God debate.

remark, for Hawking does not believe in God. Nevertheless, this single sentence has had extraordinary ramifications. For a start, it has spawned literary clones such as *The Mind* ~ (Simon and Schuster). This

port trounced a hapless Bryan Appleyard when they discussed, on TV, *Understanding the Present*, the latter's daffy tirade against science's impact on spiritual values.
~~~~~~~~~~~~ -vill

no He is not' school of discourse. For all their dissimilarities, God and science are reconcilable to a great many people. Look at the United States: scientists hold high-status jobs, technology is considered essential to economic success, and newspapers run countless science features. In short, American culture is a scientific one. Ours is ~
~~C ic c'

account for the secular nature of British society. Science is not primarily responsible.

Nor is it likely that science's exponents will change the nature of people's religious beliefs, should they wish to do so — and very few do. As cosmologist Dr Peter Atkins puts it: 'Science cannot displace personal faith. You cannot ~ ~ `L `bp

Fig. 5.2 A headline from *Observer*, 17 May 1992

perhaps, shown at last that he is completely unnecessary.[7]

Robin McKie, science correspondent of *The Observer*, wrote similarly in 'Almighty boom in our beginnings': 'The critical point is that people still want to talk about science and creation'.[8] 'People' of course includes pupils, and the NCC discussion paper on *Spiritual and Moral Development* responded to this enduring interest in a recommendation which I cited in the Preface.

Both physical and metaphysical questions can appropriately be raised when pupils examine ideas used in the past and present to explain the origin and future of the universe. In such ways, science lessons can make their contribution, so that 'all areas of the curriculum may contribute to pupils' spiritual development'.[9]

A root question, from which many others stem, is does the universe result from a cosmic accident or a purposeful creator? The first view was strongly advocated by Monod, who claimed 'Our number came up in the Monte Carlo game',[10] and more recently by Atkins – 'Ultimately there is only chaos, not purpose'.[11] So, do particular theories of origins shed light on the root question? Other allied questions are: 'What is meant by the "creation" of the universe?' 'Are scientific accounts of origins the only/the best accounts?, and 'Can science explain everything?'[12] Such questions, though of specific concern in cosmology, are also of importance for science education; they prompt reflection on the role and status of science as a social activity as well as the kinds of enquiries for which its procedures are inappropriate.

Preferred theories of origins?

On a realist view of science, preferred theories are those which most closely account for the world as it is. But some theories of origins have been preferred, not for *physical* but for *metaphysical* reasons. An example occurred over the issue of whether the universe had a beginning. Ideas of a static universe had to be radically revised when, in 1929, Hubble interpreted the 'red shift' in the spectra of distant stars as evidence for an expanding universe. The magnitude of the red shift indicated the recession of the furthest stars was a substantial fraction of the velocity of light (3×10^8 m/s).

Steady-state/ Continuous Creation

In 1948, a famous paper appeared, advocating a *Steady-State Theory of the Expanding Universe*.[13] The theory was put forward by Bondi and Gold, who were later joined by Hoyle. The outward movement of matter in the expanding universe was held to be compensated by the 'continuous creation' of matter in the form of one atom of hydrogen per cubic metre every 300000 years, giving a steady-state universe. The term 'continuous creation' was a misnomer, for the proposal can be regarded as an endlessly repeated *series* of creations. Those people who, like the theory's authors, regarded the doctrine of continuous creation as purging cosmology of metaphysics and theology soon had it pointed out to them that it did nothing of the sort. By spreading out the occasions of creation from one to many, no matter of principle was altered. It simply replaced one 'big bang' by a lot of 'little pops'.[14]

Big bang

The idea of an initial big bang, advocated by Gamow, stood in direct competition with the steady-state theory. In 1965, two scientists, Penzias and Wilson, were investigating the radiation coming from different parts of the heavens, when they encountered an annoying background radiation. It was faint, independent of time and came from every direction. The 'nuisance' heralded one of the important discoveries of the decade. The 2.7 K background radiation was interpreted as left over from an early hot stage of the universe, lending strong support to the big bang model. In 1992, further support came as the COBE satellite found slight differences ('ripples'), no bigger than 15 μK, in the radiation. These were consistent with local irregularities in the early universe, without which stars and galaxies would not have formed.

There was some opposition to the big bang theory, not based on scientific considerations, but because it suggested a beginning to the universe with implications of a creator, which some regarded as unacceptable.[15] Some others who considered it unacceptable clung to the idea of an oscillating universe, in which successive 'big bangs' were alternated with 'big bounces', in order to preserve the notion of an eternal universe and to try to avoid what they considered to be 'the problem' of the universe having a beginning. Hoyle vigorously opposed the big bang model for many decades, maintaining, even after the discovery of the 2.7 K radiation, that any theory which suggests a cosmic beginning cannot be a good one.

> Among cosmologists he has been distinguished on the one hand for his unyielding opposition over the last three decades to models of the Big Bang sort and on the other for the explicitness with which he introduces attacks on Christian religious belief into his cosmological works. It does not seem unreasonable to see the conjunction as significant, and thus to present him as our most colourful

example of the potential relevance of *anti*-religious views in the choice of cosmological models.[16]

On the other hand, the model was applauded in 1951 by Pope Pius XII in an address to the Pontifical Academy of Sciences in Rome, claiming that it should lead scientists with open minds to 'ascend to a creating Spirit'.[17]

Eternal universe

The belief underlying these views seems to be that a universe which starts with a big bang is more 'God-friendly' than an eternal universe. But is it? The big bang theory is of course consistent with the idea of a creator God, although it would be premature to conclude that the big bang was the beginning. But, as indicated, other interpretations are possible. How about the idea of an eternal universe, though? Is that contradictory to belief in creation? Hawking seems to think so:

> So long as the universe had a beginning we could suppose it had a creator. But if the universe is really self-contained, having no boundary or edge, it would have neither beginning nor end: it would simply be. What place, then, for a creator?[18]

But, at a time when the steady-state theory was a live contender for acceptance, it was argued that an eternal universe could still have been created:

> The difference between the creation of a world which had a beginning and the creation of a world which has always existed is not the difference between an act which began at a certain moment and an act which has always been going on. It is the difference between two acts which are both timeless: the act of creating a world whose temporal measure has a lower boundary and the act of creating a world whose temporal measure has not.[19]

Contemporary physics indicates that time itself is part of the creation. But the idea of time itself coming into being is far from new. Augustine (A.D.354–430) wrote that creation is '*with* time' not '*in* time'. So the story of creation does not start with 'Once upon a time . . .', for there was none, but 'in the beginning . . .'.

> **A scientific account of 'creation'**
>
> In the beginning there was nothing. Absolute void, not merely empty space. There was no space; nor was there time, for this was before time. The universe was without form and void.
>
> Peter Atkins[20]
>
> **A religious account of 'creation'**
>
> In the beginning God created the heaven and the earth. And the earth was without form, and void . . .
>
> Genesis 1:1f.

There is, accordingly, no one theory of the origins of the universe that is any more favourable to the idea of a creator than any other theory; and, conversely, there is no theory which can justifiably claim to rule out the idea of divine activity. Science can neither confirm nor disconfirm a creator.

But what about the allied claim that, *whatever* the theory, increasingly comprehensive scientific accounts of origins render theological ones redundant? In order to examine *that* claim, it is first necessary to understand something about the idea of 'creation', if pupils are to distinguish between scientific claims and arguments and other ones.

Creation

A key idea of 'creation' is 'bringing-into-being'. Something which was not there before is there now. The something can be an object, a concept, a trend and so forth. Thus one could speak of an *object* such as Babbage's calculating machine as his 'creation'. Similarly, de Bono could be referred to as the creator of the *concept* of lateral thinking and a clothes designer as the creator of a new *trend* in fashion.

It is in this common use sense of bringing-into-being that cosmologists speak of the *creation* of the world, without necessarily implying divine origins. In so doing, they are borrowing a word which has deep roots in theology, for there it carries the additional idea of *God's* activity. So it is odd that the term 'continuous creation', which last century would have embarrassed an agnostic or atheist cosmologist, was, in the middle of this century, enthusiastically claimed to herald the demise of God!

Traditionally, the creation of the universe has been expressed as *creatio ex nihilo* – 'creation-out-of-nothing' – not meaning there is some mysterious substance 'nothing' from which the world was created, but 'not-out-of-anything', a view echoed by current cosmology.[21] Thus while it would be appropriate to refer to Babbage's calculating machine as his *invention*, signifying his use of existing materials to make something new, theologians do not talk of the world as God's 'invention'.

The concept of creation is not identifiable with any particular scientific theory of origins. The *act* of 'bringing-into-being' belongs to a different category to the *processes* involved. So it is a form of *category mistake*[22] to claim that an *act* of creation has not occurred because the *process* has been explained. Such a claim would be *seen* as odd if applied to human agents and 'creations'. Imagine denying Whittle's *act* of creating an entirely new form of aircraft propulsion because the *process* of impelling air into flame-tubes, heating it and ejecting it at higher velocity had been explained! Yet a similar logical blunder appears to pass muster with surprising regularity in popular writings about the origin of the universe, as the three following quotations show:

> Perhaps it would be more accurate to say that Hawking has already indicated an end, not to physics but to metaphysics. It is now possible to give a good scientific answer to the question 'Where do we come from?' without invoking either God or special boundary conditions for the Universe at the moment of creation.
>
> John Gribbin[23]

> This [*A Brief History of Time*] is also a book about God . . . or perhaps about the absence of God. The word God fills these pages. Hawking embarks on a quest to answer Einstein's favourite question about whether God had any choice in creating the

Fig. 5.3 'Whittle's act of creating an entirely new form of aircraft propulsion'

universe. Hawking is attempting, as he explicitly states, to understand the mind of God. And this makes all the more unexpected the conclusion of the effort, at least so far: a universe with no edge in space, no beginning or end in time, and nothing for a Creator to do.

> Carl Sagan's Introduction to *A Brief History of Time*[24]

> My aim is to argue that the universe can come into existence without intervention, and that there is no *need* to invoke the idea of a Supreme Being . . .
> Peter Atkins[25]

The thought that improved *scientific* explanations explain away explanations about divine activity is also commonly found among pupils, a typical statement being:

> Genesis says the world was made by God, but we know it was made by the Big Bang.
> (Jayne, age 16)

The curiosity of having to choose between the two accounts becomes evident once commonplace terms are substituted to give a sentence with a similar logical structure:

Mum's letter says the cake was made by Anne, but we know it was made by cooking.

Nevertheless, a whole cluster of important issues for science education are implied by Jayne's statement and those above it. One which is crucial to locating the role of science education in a total curriculum is the need to recognise there are other *types* of explanation than scientific ones:

The nature of explanation

> . . . explanations answering different questions are not necessarily rivals . . . The first moral, therefore, is that there is not just one single, *the* explanation for anything which we may wish to have explained. There may instead be as many, not necessarily exclusive, alternative explanations as there are legitimate explanation-demanding questions to be asked.
> Anthony Flew[26]

The nature of explanation has an extensive literature. I shall use a typology which has been developed within an educational context by Brown and Atkins:[27]

Our typology consists of three main types of explanation. These may be labelled the Interpretive, the Descriptive and the Reason-Giving. They approximate to the questions, What?, How?, and Why? Interpretive explanations interpret or clarify an issue or specify the central meaning of a term or statement . . . Descriptive explanations describe processes, structure and procedures . . . Reason-giving explanations involve giving reasons based on principles or generalisations, motives, obligations or values.[28]

These different types of explanation can be illustrated by applying them to Harrison's prize-winning chronometer:

- *Interpretive explanation* (answers the question 'WHAT is it?'):
  – an instrument for telling the time very accurately, a special kind of clock.
- *Descriptive explanation* (answers the question 'HOW is it constructed?'):
  – from cog wheels, springs, pivots, hands and a balance wheel.
- *Reason-giving (scientific – 'principles or generalisations') explanation* (answering the question 'WHY does it keep time so accurately, even when the temperature changes?'):
  – the expansion of a lever with changing temperature causes a compensating change in the length of the hairspring.
- *Reason-giving (motives) explanation* (answering the question 'WHY was it invented?'):
  – (i) to determine longtitude accurately at sea in order to save sailors' lives and time; (ii) the attraction of the very large prize money offered.[29]

It is with reason-giving explanations that our present concerns lie. There is clearly no conflict between the scientific (reason-giving) explanation of why the chronometer keeps time so accurately and the (reason-giving) explanations of the purposes and plans of its creator. The two types of explanation are *compatible* with each other.

A similar logical point applies to the creation of the universe. A scientific (reason-giving) explanation of origins provides no grounds whatsoever for concluding that agency and purpose are not involved. Such statements as 'the universe was the result of a big bang' and 'In the beginning God created the heavens and the earth' are in no way competitors. They are different *types* of explanations; to confuse them is to commit an explanatory *type-error*.

Type-errors

Among the criteria for evaluating explanations, criteria which include truth and a proper level of sophistication, is the requirement that the explanation should be of the proper function and type.[30] An explanatory *type-error* occurs if an explanation of a different type is given to that required. If a detective asks a pathologist, as a pathologist, to explain why a murder victim died, the answer might be 'because she swallowed cyanide'. However, if the pathologist replied, 'because her husband hated her', though true, he would have made an explanatory type-error by giving a different type of explanation from that required of him as a pathologist. To confuse scientific explanations of origins with religious explanations of agency is also making a type-error, as in Atkins' comment about an 'infinitely lazy creator' on page 67–8. The paradigm case of a type-error has been given the doubtful honour of having its own name – 'God-of-the-gaps'.

'God-of-the-gaps'

This type-error involves plugging current gaps in scientific explanations with 'God'. It originated when certain theologians became anxious that new scientific discoveries might undermine God's position as maker of everything. They would point to what was currently unexplained and say, 'Ah, but you don't understand that; that's God'. It was a transparently self-defeating position – transparent except to those who held it – for a God who was confined to gaps in scientific knowledge would be squeezed inexorably out as the gaps closed! If science is compared to filling in the pieces of a jig-saw puzzle, then, on this view, as more pieces

Fig. 5.4a,b 'If science is compared to filling in the pieces of a jigsaw puzzle'

get slotted into place, 'GOD'S' space reduces – to 'god's' space. The small 'g' is to indicate that such a view is entirely alien to the Judaeo-Christian concept of God as being involved with both the known and the unknown.

Goodlad, in discussing science education for non-scientists, suggested that 'the theological position of the "god-of-the-gaps" has probably done more damage to theology than anything else'.[31] But, more relevant to our study here is the damage it can do to *science* by discouraging painstaking efforts to discover physical mechanisms. It fosters a restricted view of the scope of science whereby certain areas of scientific knowledge are held to be inaccessible to science because they belong to God:

> "They won't split the atom. You can't unmake what God has made" – but to-day transmuted atoms if not actually ten a penny are at least ten for a thousand pounds. "It's not gravity, it's God that keeps the planets in their courses. Man will never be able to conquer space" – yet with a puff and a roar of flame from the launching pads . . .[32]

Newton himself fell into 'God-of-the-gaps' thinking. In one letter to Richard Bentley about the ways in which science and religion interacted, he said 'that the diurnal [daily] Rotations of the Planets could not be derived from Gravity, but required a divine Arm to impress them'. Bentley,

however, took what would nowadays be considered an orthodox view, that the world depends moment by moment on a Superior Being and not on God giving a little 'shove' every now and again. Newton's view on the supposed indivisibility of atoms, about 'no ordinary Power being able to divide what God himself made one in the first Creation', has already been referred to in Chapter 3.

> I reprefented that the diurnal Rotations of the Planets could not be derived from Gravity, but required a divine Arm to imprefs them.

There may be sound *moral* reasons for not carrying out certain kinds of experiments, but that is a different matter from saying that some aspects of the physical world cannot in principle be investigated. The limitations of science are *methodological*, not *territorial*.

C.A. Coulson, at various times Professor of Theoretical Physics, Applied Mathematics and Theoretical Chemistry, coined the phrase 'God-of-the-gaps'. From his Christian standpoint he regarded the position as unbiblical and unscientific, so his counsel was 'When we come to the scientifically unknown, our correct policy is not to rejoice because we have found God; it is to become better scientists'.[33]

Fig. 5.5 S1F launch – a shining reflection of bright flames soar across marshes near Pad 39A at the Kennedy Space Center

There are two polar outcomes of holding a 'God-of-the-gaps' position. Those people who believe in a 'God-of-the-gaps' are likely to regard science as threatening their belief. Those who do not believe in God but hold that if God *did* exist he would be a 'God-of-the-gaps', may pursue science with additional enthusiasm. They may thereby hope to close any gaps in which God might be imagined to lurk, as Atkins does with his 'infinitely lazy creator'. In the end, Coulson's 'God-of-the-gaps' asymptotically approaches Atkins' 'infinitely lazy creator'!

It may appear that 'God-of-the-gaps' is simply another example of the *naming = explaining* fallacy. Hawking used the word 'God' in this way during an interview about a possible 'edge' to the universe, prompting the interviewer's summary, 'You are invoking God because we need an explanatory principle for the edge . . . You said that *if* there is an edge, then we'd have to invoke God'.[34]

This is pure 'God-of-the-gaps' talk. Of course if God does not exist, then '*God*' is a label and no more. But if there is such a Being, it needs to be recognised that the explanation of a phenomenon does not stand in logical contrast to any Ultimate Cause of that phenomenon's existence. Even if a satisfactory and exhaustive mechanistic explanation of the phenomenon of gravity *were* available, it would not form a rival account to a claim that God had made matter to function in this way. To claim that mechanistic explanations displace explanations about plan and purpose, is to commit the *explaining = explaining away* fallacy.

'Need' for God?

Atkins asserts 'there is no *need* to invoke the idea of a Supreme Being'. Julian Huxley claims that 'in the evolutionary pattern of thought there is no longer either need or room for the supernatural', while John Gribbin states:

> . . . there are many cosmologists who would take all these new developments, inflation theory, the identification of the moment of creation and Hawking's new work as ultimate proof that there was no 'first cause', and that science therefore has no need of the hypothesis of God.[35]

These assertions merit careful consideration of the idea of 'need' for God. In Newton's time, references to God were included in science texts – including the *Principia* – but the current convention is not to refer to First Causes. That being so, there is 'no *need* of God' in a scientific account of the physical world, any more than *I* am needed in a scientific account of this book, as carbon on cellulose. But that doesn't mean I don't exist!

Ockham's Razor has sometimes been invoked as a reason for admitting only scientific explanations. But this is a gross misapplication of William of Ockham's (*c.* 1285–1349) principle of the parsimony of causes. He was, after all, a *theologian* as well as a philosopher and was

certainly not implying that the explanations given in Natural Philosophy ruled out divine agency! Flew's comment, about there being 'as many, not necessarily exclusive, alternative explanations as there are legitimate explanation-demanding questions to be asked', applies here. To claim otherwise is to fall prey to another explanatory snare –

'Reductionism'

Some theorists make a distinction between *descriptions* and *explanations*. Others subsume descriptions under the umbrella of explanations as a type of explanation known as a *descriptive explanation*. Whichever procedure is adopted, it is a fruitful practice in science to *reduce* descriptions of solids, liquids and gases to accounts of atoms and molecules. Such *methodological reductionism*,[36] which treats the behaviour of gases as elastic collisions between molecules, is without metaphysical significance.

But care is needed, for not only the individual components, but their arrangement, is significant. The *emergence*[37] of new properties takes place as a result of the way the constituents fit together. Significant information may be lost if the system is scrutinised only at the *analytic* level; the *synthetic* level also needs to be considered. An electron and a proton in combination become an atom of hydrogen. With a large number of hydrogen molecules, a new property – 'gaseous' – emerges, a property of collections, a *colligative* property. The same applies with oxygen, but with a different combination of constituents. If the hydrogen is burnt in the oxygen, water results, having the emergent property of 'wetness', which is not possessed by either hydrogen or oxygen.

Biologists, perhaps, are less prone to reduce everything to atoms and molecules. Their discipline provides constant reminders of the importance of organisation. But they also need to recognise other higher-order categories of concepts than biological ones. Pair-bonding is a biological concept; love is not. To attempt to reduce the richness of the human experience of love to 'nothing but' pair-bonding is to leave a lot unsaid.

There is, however, another kind of reductionism, *ontological reductionism* (*ontology*, the study of *being*, of what *is*). It surfaces in assertions like, 'human beings are nothing but complex chemical mechanisms'. The claim is trivially true in the restricted sense that if you take all the atoms and molecules away, there will be nothing left! It is the give-away words 'nothing but' (or 'just', 'only' and 'simply') which make the claim metaphysical. They signal an imperialistic claim that the scientific account is *all* that there is to be said about *being* – matter is all there is and a spiritual dimension is denied. Ontological reductionism is sometimes called metaphysical reductionism and abbreviated to 'reductionism'. Dubbed with the appropriately disparaging label, 'nothing-buttery',[38] it fails to give an adequate account of the totality of human experience. Given that science involves the study of the natural world, *if*, as the positivists claimed, 'what science cannot discover, mankind cannot know', then the natural world is all that can be known. But that conclusion simply follows deductively from the positivist premises, whose inadequacies have been detailed in Chapter 2.

Eddington once compared science to casting a net into the sea. A three-centimetre net says nothing about whether there are creatures in the sea which are smaller than three centimetres. Science systematically leaves out anything which does not belong to the natural world.

Awe, wonder and the Earth in space

Teaching the Earth in space provides ample opportunity for encouraging awe and wonder as part of pupils' spiritual development. A Hebrew shepherd boy, later to become king, looked into the night sky and voiced his wonder –

> When I consider your heavens, the work of your fingers, the moon and the stars, which you have set in place, what is man that you are mindful of him, the son of man that you care for him?
>
> Psalm 8:3f

– and, like us, he could only see a few thousand stars with the naked eye. Modern astronomy

Fig. 5.6 It would be odd to argue the mountains pre-eminence for having been around longer

paints a breathtaking picture of some hundred thousand million stars per galaxy and something like the same number of galaxies!

With the age of the universe at something like fifteen thousand million years, the human lifespan of 'threescore years and ten' is, by comparison, very brief. If the age of the universe were represented by a year, then civilised humans would appear on the scene at about half a minute to midnight on 31 December. Both in space and time, people are dwarfs. But is size, age or position in the universe an indicator of importance? It would be distinctly odd to argue that Lovelock's giant redwood tree was more important than a human *because* it was bigger, or that a mountain was vastly more important than both for the same reason. It would also be odd to argue for that tree's superiority *because* of its longer lifespan, or the mountain's pre-eminence for having been around longer still! Matters of *value* are logically distinct from matters of *scale*.

In his work *Paradise Lost*, the poet John Milton, following his visit to Galileo, wisely questioned whether, from a religious point of view, the motion or the position of the earth matter:

> Consider first, that great
> Or bright infers not excellence: the earth
> Though, in comparison of heav'n, so small,
> Nor glistering, may of solid good contain

More plenty than the sun, that barren shines . . .
. . . What if the sun
Be centre to the world, and other stars,
By his attractive virtue and their own
Incited, dance about him various rounds?[39]

Copernicus realised his scheme meant the universe was much bigger than previously thought, as well as displacing humankind from the 'centre' of things. However, he recognised that 'as to the place of the earth; although it is not at the centre of the world, nevertheless the distance [to that centre] is as nothing, in particular when compared to that to the fixed stars'.[40] His words negate a common idea that Copernicus saw the displacement from the central position as threatening human uniqueness and importance to God in a world which, he believed, 'has been built for us by the Best and Most Orderly Workman of all'.[41] One could after all offer alternative (metaphysical) interpretations of the new view of the position of the earth:

> On one reading the new system had to be resisted because it implied the decentralisation of humanity – a degradation at odds with a being made in God's image. But a quite different reading was also possible. There was a sense in which man was moved upmarket. He was now among the planets – in the celestial region that had hitherto been associated with perfection and immutability. No longer a central cesspit, into which everything fell, the Earth was described by Kepler as at last enjoying legal citizenship in the heavens.[42]

In Chapter 3 we saw how speculation about the plurality of worlds followed from analogies drawn between Jupiter and Earth, raising theological and other questions about the status of humankind. Apart from those who took the traditional Christian view that only Earth was inhabited, there were others of the Christian faith who found the plurality of worlds an attractive doctrine. The mathematician and physicist Christian Huygens (1620–95) could not conceive the Creator had put all his plants and animals on one planet alone leaving all others destitute of creatures who might adore him.[43] The physicist David Brewster argued for the plurality of worlds on both philosophical and theological grounds.

On the other hand, there were those unsympathetic to Christianity who claimed the *uniqueness* of our world supported their case against God. If this planet is the only one of its kind to be inhabited by living things, they said, it must have been an unlikely cosmic accident. Others, equally unsympathetic, claimed the very opposite – that the *plurality* of worlds buttressed their argument against God. If there are many inhabited planets, they maintained, human beings could not claim to be uniquely created and visited by God in the Incarnation. Although it sounds a bit like 'heads I win; tails you lose', these opposing views could be used as catalysts for a class debate.

Alternative interpretations of cosmological data are a feature of some of these metaphysical questions. A more recent example is the matter of the size and the antiquity of the universe. Its vastness, both in space and time, have been cited as showing human insignificance. But the same data have more recently been used to infer the opposite conclusion, expressed in the Anthropic Cosmological Principle, popularly called the *Goldilocks Effect*.

The 'Goldilocks Effect'

The technical name stems from *anthropos,* Greek for 'man'. The popular name comes from the fact that the conditions for humankind to exist, like Baby Bear's porridge, chair and bed, are 'just right'. The anomalous properties of water, having its maximum density at 4°C, with all the implications *that* has for life on earth, have long been known. What has been more recently realised is that minute changes in certain constants of nature would have made *Homo sapiens* impossible. The universe seems 'fine-tuned' for our being here.

There appears to have been an excess of matter over antimatter of one part in a thousand million, without which we would not be here, since equal quantities of matter and antimatter would have annihilated each other.[44]

Then again, our bodies contain a lot of carbon. According to our current understanding, carbon is made within vast nuclear furnaces – stars – over a period of thousands of millions of years. Certain stars, whose masses are greater than ten times our sun's mass, end their lives in gigantic explosions – supernovae. In the final death-throes of these stars, carbon, nitrogen, oxygen and phosphorus, key elements for life, are produced and scattered into space.

Our bodies are the 'ashes' of long-dead stars

Stars are born as hydrogen collects under gravity, becoming hot enough for its nuclei to fuse to form helium. Two helium nuclei (He^4) then fuse together to form an unstable nucleus of beryllium (Be^8). If this beryllium nucleus, before it decays, fuses with another nucleus of helium, carbon is formed and the process continues as elements are 'cooked further up the periodic table'. The two-step process of helium to carbon might be expected to be highly improbable and only to give rise to minute amounts of carbon. But some remarkable coincidences about the energy levels of the processes involved give a different result.

Furthermore, the balance between the outward explosion of the big bang and the attraction of gravity drawing it together again is also critical, and Hawking makes the following interesting conjecture:

> If the density of the universe one second after the big bang had been greater by one part in a thousand billion [10^{12}], the universe would have re-collapsed after ten years. On the other hand, if the density of the universe at that time had been less by the same amount, the universe would have been essentially empty since it was about ten years old.[46]

Even if the density differences had been very much smaller than these virtually infinitesimal figures, the universe – and therefore ourselves – would not be here. If the universe had recollapsed before the fifteen thousand million years needed for carbon to be synthesised in stars, and for chemical and organic evolution to take place, we should not be here. If the expansion of matter into space had

Cosmic coincidences

. . . remarkably the last step happens to possess a rare property called 'resonance' which enables it to proceed at a rate far in excess of our naïve expectation. In effect, the energies of the participating particles plus the ambient heat energy of the star add to a value that lies just above a natural energy level of the carbon nucleus and so the product of the nuclear reaction finds a natural state to drop into. It amounts to something akin to the astronomical equivalent of a hole-in-one. But this is not all. While it is doubly striking enough for there to exist not only a carbon resonance level but one positioned just above the incoming energy total within the interior of the star, it is well-nigh miraculous to discover that there exists a further resonance level in the oxygen nucleus that would be made in the next step of the nuclear reaction chain when a carbon nucleus interacts with a further alpha particle. But this resonance level lies just *above* the total energy of the alpha particle, the carbon nucleus, and the ambient environment of the star. Hence the precious carbon fails to be totally destroyed by a further resonant nuclear reaction. This multiple coincidence of the resonance levels is a necessary condition for our existence.

John Barrow, Professor of Astronomy, University of Sussex[45]

been minutely greater, there would not be time for stars and galaxies to form, so again, we would not be here. Davies theorises about just how precise the matching of the outward exploding force and the inward gravitational attraction had to be:

> At the so-called Planck time (10^{-43} seconds) (which is the earliest moment at which the concept of space and time has meaning) the matching was accurate to a staggering one part in 10^{60}. That is to say, had the explosion differed in strength at the outset by only one part in 10^{60}, the universe we now perceive would not exist. To give some meaning to these numbers, suppose you wanted to fire a bullet at a one-inch target on the other side of the observable universe, twenty billion light years

away. Your aim would have to be accurate to that same part in 10^{60}.[47]

Guth has theorised that the delicate balance between the expansive energy and the force of gravity can be accounted for by postulating an 'inflationary' universe, that is one which underwent an initial exponential expansion until it reached the size of a grapefruit. However, this interesting idea leaves untouched the curious fact that the constants of nature and the fundamental laws of physics still happen to be precisely what is needed for inflation to take place.[48] These constants are not the result of a process of natural selection, as in biology:

> Twentieth-century physics has discovered there exist invariant properties of the natural world and its elementary components which render inevitable the gross size and structure of almost all its composite objects. The size of bodies like stars, planets and even people are neither random nor the result of any progressive selection process, but simply manifestations of the different forces of Nature.[49]

It is a consequence of the weakness of the force of gravity that stellar evolution takes so long. So, then, if the universe were not very old we should not be here. But since the most distant stars are receding at nearly the velocity of light, an old universe also means a vast universe.

Instead of claiming humans are insignificant because of the vastness of space and time, it can be argued that the universe needs to be as big as it is, and as old as it is, in order for us to be here at all.

Barrow and Tipler, in a *magnum opus*, discuss the various forms of the anthropic principle: weak (WAP), strong (SAP), participatory (PAP) and final (FAP). All go farther than simply saying that conditions are just right for our being here. They are steeped in beliefs and values, which raises questions about the authors' provocative disclaimer that:

> . . . the authors are cosmologists, not philosophers. This has one very important consequence

which the average reader should bear in mind. Whereas philosophers and theologians appear to possess an emotional attachment to their theories and ideas which require them to believe them, scientists tend to regard their ideas differently. They are interested in formulating many logically consistent possibilities, leaving any judgement regarding their truth to observation.[50]

Those who wish to leave the detail until later can go straight to the 'Summary of the Goldilocks Effect'.

1 Weak anthropic principle

> *The observed values of all physical and cosmological quantities are not equally probable but they take on values restricted by the requirement that there exist sites where carbon-based life can evolve and by the requirement that the Universe be old enough for it to have already done so.*[51]

In stating that the requirements of carbon-based life *restrict* the values of the constants, rather than the values of the constants restrict what can exist, they are 'putting the cart before the horse'. Doing this makes it a *teleological* statement; but the next variant is even more teleological:

2 Strong anthropic principle

> *The Universe must have those properties which allow life to develop within it at some stage in its history.*[52]

As Barrow and Tipler acknowledge, this interpretation 'does not appear to be open either to proof or disproof and is religious in nature'. It amounts to one form of the Design Argument for the existence of God. Fred Hoyle, cited earlier in this chapter for his former intense opposition to teleological views of the universe, later altered his views, impressed by this string of coincidences:

> I do not believe that any scientist who examined the evidence would fail to draw the inference that the laws of nuclear physics have been deliberately designed with regard to the consequences they produce inside the stars. If this is so, then my apparently random quirks have become part of a

deep-laid scheme. If not then we are back again at a monstrous sequence of accidents.[53]

The next two variants also appear to be standing causality on its head.

3 Participatory anthropic principle

Observers are necessary to bring the Universe into being.[54]

This is another interpretation of the SAP, arising out of attempts to interpret quantum mechanics. An allied variant is that 'an ensemble of other different universes is necessary for the existence of our Universe'. This statement draws upon Everett's 'Many-Worlds' interpretation of quantum mechanics, in which all possible quantum worlds are considered to be realised and to exist 'in parallel' with each other. Thus for every quantum state in our world which exists in a certain way, there is postulated another world in which it exists in the opposite way. Thus universes are continually bifurcating, producing a nearly infinite number of them in which every possible configuration of matter/energy exists somewhere; but no cross-traffic between these parallel universes is possible. The idea raises the semantic difficulty of the significance of the word 'universe', a common meaning being 'the totality of material entities'. But on 'Many-Worlds' theory there is nothing particularly remarkable about our world being just right for life. If all possible worlds co-exist, then there is bound to be one where life exists – the only one we know. So to return to the earlier quotation about the physical constants not being a matter of natural selection as in biology, some kind of selection argument *might* be considered to apply in which our universe is one possible universe that can support carbon-based life out of a near-infinity of other 'universes'. The 'Many-Worlds' theory has no testable consequences due to the impenetrability of information from one universe to another.

Barrow and Tipler argue that if the SAP is true and intelligent life must come into existence somewhere in the world's history, then if it dies out before it has had any measurable non-quantum influence on the world, it is difficult to see why it must have come into existence in the first place. This leads them to formulate a generalisation of the SAP which they call the Final Anthropic Principle.

4 Final anthropic principle

Intelligent information-processing must come into existence in the Universe, and, once it comes into existence, it will never die out.[55]

Barrow and Tipler 'warn the reader . . . that both the FAP and the SAP are quite speculative', but warm to the theme of their grand concluding paragraph:

> . . . if life evolves in all of the many universes in a quantum cosmology, and if life continues to exist in all of these universes, then *all* of these universes, which include *all* possible histories among them, will approach the Omega Point.[[56]] At the instant the Omega Point is reached, life will have gained control of *all* matter and forces not only in a single universe, but in all universes whose existence is logically possible; life will have spread into *all* spatial regions in all universes which could logically exist, and will have stored an infinite amount of information, including *all* bits of knowledge which it is logically possible to know. And this is the end.[57]

It is tempting to slip in an exclamation mark after the final sentence.

In a television series, *Soul*,[58] Tipler took his ideas even further and claimed that the Christian hope of eternal life and of resurrection could now be understood as all our life, hopes and thoughts being encapsulated in a computer program so that, as the commentator put it, eventually 'we shall be perfect simulations living in a perfectly simulated world'.

But such a speculation raises a number of questions. How about the mentally handicapped who cannot encapsulate their thoughts in a computer program or, who, if they could, would only find a re-run in the next 'life'? The Christian

Fig. 5.7 Everything about us encapsulated in a computer program

resurrection, it must be remembered, also promises transformation. So how would *this* idea mesh in with Tipler's 'resurrection'? And would one want his kind of resurrection anyway – something which, at best, seems to offer little more than a repeat performance? Midgley concludes that:

> . . . there is, anyway, no nourishment in these fantasies. Even if their scientific support were stronger, they would still have no moral or spiritual consequences. The promise of immortality as an unenlightened computer program in a remote galaxy cannot restore meaning to life, because it is a prospect without meaning. Indeed, it might well be a form of hell.[59]

Summary of the Goldilocks effect

So what of the apparent 'fine-tuning' of the universe? Does it provide a watertight argument for the existence of God? It is certainly congruent with divine purpose and will be seen by the believer as such. But it does not force the non-believer into a corner in which there is no room to wriggle. There are possible physical explanations, such as the 'Many-Worlds' theory of *parallel universes* – albeit a prime candidate for Ockham's Razor! Another possibility is that of *serial universes* of 'big bangs' interposed by 'big bounces' in which each new universe has different constants of nature, one eventually arising which is favourable

to our existence. A further suggestion, due to Smolin *et al.*, is a combination of series and parallel universes: since the equations of the big bang expansion are the time-reverse of the collapse of a black hole, black holes might be the 'seeds' of new, mutated universes, each in their own 'dimensions'. By analogy with biology, successful universes would be those which leave the most offspring, prompting a new metaphor, 'Is the Universe alive?' – not to be confused with the one raised in the previous chapter, 'Is the Earth alive?'

Although the ideas are novel and speculative, it is perhaps not surprising that the old philosophical points about *type-errors* and *God-of-the-gaps* should rear their heads again. Gribbin concludes a *New Scientist* article with these words:

> The apparent unlikelihood of the Universe has . . . led some people to suggest that the big bang may have resulted from supernatural intervention . . .
>
> But if Smolin is right, there is no longer any basis for invoking the supernatural . . .[60]

All my earlier comments about '*need* for God' apply here, too. Atkins does something very similar:

> That such a universe as ours did emerge with exactly the right blend of forces may have the flavour of a miracle, and therefore seem to require some form of intervention. But nothing intrinsically lacks an explanation. We cannot yet see quite far enough to decide which is the right explanation, but we can be confident that intervention was not necessary.[61]

The confidence is misplaced, resting insecurely, as it does, on a monolithic notion of explanation. The matter of possible divine action is left untouched by these matters.

'The mind of science'?

Midgley, as already seen, makes sharp comments about unrealistic claims concerning the competence of science, saying that 'British scientific education is now so narrowly scientistic that many scientists simply do not know that there is any organised, systematic way of thinking besides their own'.[62] She comments on Hawking's words, with which this chapter opened, about knowing 'the mind of God':

> . . . in recent months the pressing issue has been what such statements reveal about the mind of science – as is evident from the rash of books and newspaper articles questioning the cultural ascendancy and function of science . . . triggered by the increasingly strident claims of cosmologists that they are close to understanding creation and providing a 'theory of everything'.[63]

For example, Atkins concludes his book *Creation Revisited* with the grand claim, 'We are almost there. Complete knowledge is just within our grasp. Comprehension is moving across the face of the Earth, like the sunrise'.[64] But is it true? Rather it seems that the more we find out about the world, the more there appears to be to investigate – something to which the history of elementary particle physics bears abundant testimony. But even if Atkins' lofty claim were true at a mechanistic level, there remain those questions referred to in Chapter 2, which science is not competent to answer.

It is important that pupils should be helped to realise that science, while important, is not the only way of thinking about experience. If this is done, it may go some way towards rectifying the state of affairs which prompted Midgley's indictment of 'British scientific education' as 'narrowly scientistic'.

CHAPTER 6

'Publish and be damned'?
– the Galileo affair

Superficially it all looks like a paradigm case of what nineteenth-century rationalist historians liked to call the warfare between science and religion . . . that popular but simplistic formula. The historical reality was much more fascinating and instructive than so crude a polarity would suggest.

John Brooke, Professor of History of Science, University of Lancaster[1]

Galileo Galilei

. . . the fame of this outstanding genius rests mostly on discoveries he never made, and on feats he never performed. Contrary to statements in even recent outlines of science, Galileo did not invent the telescope; nor the microscope; nor the thermometer; nor the pendulum clock. He did not discover the law of inertia; nor the parallelogram of forces or motions; nor the sun spots. He made no contribution to theoretical astronomy; he did not throw down weights from the leaning tower of Pisa, and did not prove the truth of the Copernican system. He was not tortured by the Inquisition, did not languish in its dungeons, did not say 'eppur si muove' [nevertheless it moves]; and he was not a martyr of science.[2]

So, what *did* he do?

The 'Galileo affair' offers a wealth of material for helping pupils understand the nature and history of scientific ideas,[3] so essential in studying science. It provides both background and fore-ground material for a study of the Earth in space. It underlines the limitations of scientific evidence and the provisional nature of proof, as well as illustrating the formulation of testable hypotheses and theoretical models. The events provide pupils with examples of scientific controversies, how scientific ideas change, and how they are affected by social, moral, spiritual and cultural factors. The episode also highlights the distinction between scientific and other claims and arguments and shows that science, while important, is not the only way of thinking about experience.

Star wars!

A God's-eye view?

He His fabric of the heav'ns
Hath left to their disputes, perhaps to move
His laughter at their quaint opinions wide
Hereafter, when they come to model heav'n
And calculate the stars; how will they wield
The mighty frame, how build, unbuild, contrive,
To save appearances; how gird the sphere
With centric and eccentric scribbled o'er,
Cycle and epicycle, orb in orb.

Paradise Lost[4]

So wrote the poet John Milton after visiting the ageing Galileo. But our story starts with the young Galileo, then in his twenties, being attracted by ideas in Copernicus' book, *On the Revolution of the Spheres of the Universe* (1543).

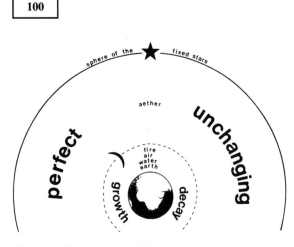

Fig. 6.1 Geocentric world-picture

priori[5] reasoning, Plato came to certain general conclusions regarding the shape and motions of the universe. These conclusions, of paramount importance for everything which follows, were that *the shape of the world must be a perfect sphere, and that all motion must be in perfect circles at uniform speed*. [So, Ptolemy believed] . . . 'the object which the astronomer must strive to achieve is this: to demonstrate that all the phenomena in the sky are produced by uniform and circular motions.'6

Theory and practice

The simple picture of a central Earth did not fit well with observations. The Sun appeared to move faster at different parts of its orbit and the planets seemed to be different in size at different parts of *their* orbits. But this should not be so if their distances from the Earth remained the same. However, by placing the Earth at an excentric point 'E' (Fig. 6.2), this difficulty could be reduced. The angular velocity is then uniform with respect to the centre 'C', but not with respect to 'E'.

At that time, university philosophers accepted the ideas of Aristotle and Ptolemy on physics and astronomy. Any disagreement with those ideas was seen as threatening their professional standing, as well as creating the social disquiet occasioned by any major upheaval in views about the cosmos. Society was still unsettled in the aftermath of the Reformation and Counter-Reformation. Pupils need to see the Galileo affair against this background.

On Ptolemy's geocentric *world-picture*, the heavenly bodies were considered perfect, moving in perfect circles with uniform speed round the Earth. Apart from this circular motion, the heavens themselves – what lay above the Moon's orbit – were changeless (Fig. 6.1).

The Ptolemaic scheme illustrates the difference between scientific and non-scientific arguments, for it was founded upon Plato's beliefs that the heavenly bodies were but dim and distorted shadows of the real world of ideas.

Plato's contribution to astronomy – which insofar as concrete advances are concerned, is nil . . .
However, by a process of metaphysical and *a*

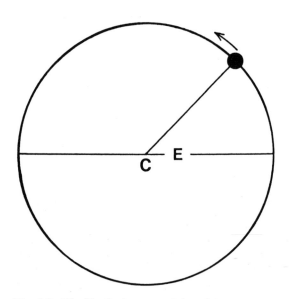

Fig. 6.2 The Earth at an excentric point

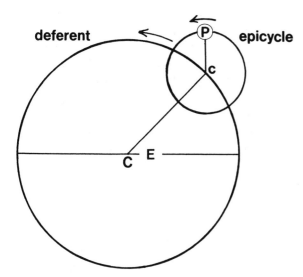

Fig. 6.3 Epicycles maintained the circular dogma

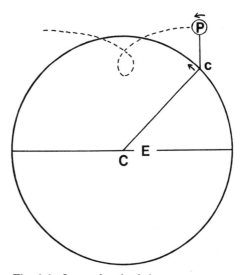

Fig. 6.4 Looped path of planet

The most difficult of the heavenly bodies to account for by this scheme of uniform circular motion were the six (known) planets (Gk. *wanderers*). Their motion appeared to be progressive, then stationary and then retrograde. However, by an ingenious system of circles (epicycles) upon circles, and even epicycles upon epicycles, even this could be accommodated. The path traced out by the planet 'P' as it moves round the epicycle (Fig. 6.3), whose centre moves uniformly round the large circle called the *deferent*, is shown by a dotted line in Fig. 6.4. This path approximates to the series of loops traced out by the apparent forward and backward motion of the planets against the background of the 'fixed' stars.

By adjusting the number and the radii of the circles, as well as the rotational speeds, one could *save the appearances*, i.e. match experiment with theory. Greater accuracy could be achieved by Ptolemy's introduction of a dodge called the *equant point*, which was the same distance from the centre 'C' as the Earth 'E', but on the opposite side to it (Fig. 6.5). But there was a price to pay – the violation of the Platonic dogma of uniform circular motion which, by definition, must be with respect to the centre of the circle (deferent), rather

than the equant point. This made the equant point unpopular but, notwithstanding, astronomical events like eclipses could be predicted with great accuracy. Ptolemy's theory held sway for about thirteen hundred years.

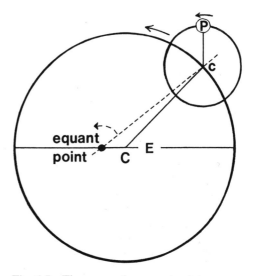

Fig. 6.5 The unpopular equant point

But even before the invention of the telescope, Greek astronomy was starting to crumble. A number of observations contradicted the belief that the heavenly bodies were perfect and unchanging:

- sunspots were visible through a dark filter, appearing and disappearing;
- in 1572 a Danish astronomer, Tycho Brahe, saw a new star which lasted for eighteen months;
- five years later, Tycho saw a comet *above* the moon's orbit, cutting through the 'crystalline spheres' thought to hold the planets.

The Copernican scheme

Contrary to one popular view, that Copernicus' system simplified the complicated system of circles, it actually made matters worse. For Copernicus was still committed to *circular* motion; the idea of ellipses did not come in until Kepler's work at the beginning of the seventeenth century. So although Copernicus made it sound simple with a central sun, his calculations had planets rotating about the *centre of the Earth's orbit*, which did not coincide with the centre of the Sun. So it required many circles to approximate to elliptical orbits and account for three movements of the Earth (orbiting, spinning and precessing on Copernicus' theory), rather than one on Ptolemy's scheme. John Milton cleverly incorporated the technicalities in *Paradise Lost*:

Their wand'ring course now high, now low, then hid,
Progressive, retrograde, or standing still,
In six thou seest; and what if sev'nth to these
The planet earth, so steadfast though she seem,
Insensibly three different motions move?
Which else to several spheres thou must ascribe.[7]

Copernicus was not driven to his conclusions simply from observations. They were not for those times particularly accurate and the astronomical tables he had would equally well have supported Ptolemy's theory. His reasons for suggesting a central sun were in part mystical. He considered it more fitting that everything should be lit up from a central position, citing the words of a legendary Egyptian mystic, *Hermes Trismegistus*, in support:

> In the middle of all sits Sun enthroned. In this most beautiful temple [the world] could we place this luminary in any better position from which he can illuminate the whole at once? He is rightly called the Lamp, the Mind, the Ruler of the Universe; Hermes Trismegistus names him the Visible God . . .[8]

Reasons for believing in a stationary Earth and a moving Sun

- The Earth seems big and there is no feeling of movement.
- The Sun looks small and appears to move.
- If the Earth moves fast enough to get round the Sun in a year, such a wind would surely be created that it would blow everything moveable off the Earth.
- It was believed that all bodies fall to the centre of the universe. So, since falling objects were seen to fall towards the centre of the Earth, it was argued that the Earth must be at the centre of the universe.
- Distant stars did not appear to change position, relative to each another, at different times of the year, when a moving Earth would be at different parts of its orbit (it was 1832 before the minute *stellar parallax* was actually detected).

Reasons for believing the Earth does not spin

- A spinning Earth, like a roundabout, seems likely to fling off any unsecured object, contrary to what happens.
- An arrow, fired vertically, appears likely to fall to the west of the firing point, because the Earth would continue spinning while the arrow was in the air. But this does not happen.
- Birds and clouds seem likely to drift westwards for the same reason.

'. . . whether heav'n move or earth'

In those days there seemed more evidence for a moving Sun than a moving Earth, which counted against the Copernican scheme. There also seemed good evidence against a spinning Earth – also part of Copernicus' theory.

The absence of noticeable stellar parallax, combined with the Sun's position near the centre of the world, meant the 'fixed stars' must be very far away and enormous in size to be visible, which Copernicus realised. Parallax can be demonstrated by having an individual walk across the front of a class of (preferably) standing pupils. As the observer crosses, individuals appear to change their relative positions.

Copernicus was reluctant to publish, not for fear of religious persecution, but ridicule, confessing that 'The scorn which I had to fear on account of the novelty and absurdity of my opinion almost drove me to abandon a work already undertaken'.[9] Thirty-five years after his death, a satirical poem was published in France and later in England. Here are a few lines of this popular poem:

> Those clerks who think (think how absurd a jest)
> That neither heav'ns nor stars do turn at all,
> Nor dance about this great round earthly ball;
> But th'earth itself, this massy globe of ours,
> Turns round-about once every twice-twelve hours:
> And we resemble land-bred novices
> New brought aboard to venture on the seas;
> Who, at first launching from the shore, suppose
> The ship stands still, and that the ground it
> goes . . .

After rehearsing the (spurious) arguments about arrows fired vertically, strong winds and birds drifting westwards, the writer concludes his jesting:

> Arm'd with these reasons, 'twere superfluous
> T'assail the reasons of Copernicus;
> Who, to save better of the stars th'appearance,
> Unto the earth a three-fold motion warrants.[10]

The mismatch between what common sense dictated and what Copernican theory suggested is an example of something more widely recognised today, the counterintuitive nature of much of science.

However, despite the apparent difficulties of Copernicus' scheme, it removed the unpopular equant point and suggested a comprehensive system, by contrast with the piecemeal nature of Ptolemy's. Ptolemy's system treated each planet separately by trial and error, giving it as many circles as the required accuracy demanded.

An important invention

In 1609, Galileo heard about the invention of the telescope by a Dutch spectacle maker. He constructed one for himself with a magnification of about 30× and turned it on the heavens. On 7 January 1610, he saw three small, bright 'stars' near the planet Jupiter and sketched their positions in his diary:

East   *   *   J   *   West

He thought they were fixed stars, but the following night showed:

East   J   *   *   *   West

His curiosity aroused, he waited for the next night – but it was cloudy! The night after, only two 'stars' were visible:

East   *   *   J   West

On 13 January, Galileo saw four 'stars' for the first time:

East   *   J   *   *   *   West

After many observations, Galileo concluded that the 'stars' revolved round Jupiter. He became convinced that Jupiter's moons answered the criticism of Copernican theory, which said it was impossible for the Moon to go round the Earth at the same time as the Earth went round the Sun. Here were four moons orbiting Jupiter while it went round the Sun. As seen in Chapter 3, an analogy could be drawn between the behaviour of

Jupiter and its moons, and the behaviour of the Sun and the planets, something which Galileo did. He published his discoveries in *The Starry Messenger* along with his observations that the Moon had blemishes and the Milky Way consisted of myriads of stars. Although Galileo may not have been the first to observe some things he reports, he was first to publish. His book was short, easily read, and consequently the ideas spread rapidly. Only five years afterwards, a Jesuit missionary published some of Galileo's ideas in Chinese.

Galileo's growing fame enabled him to achieve his ambition of gaining a post at the court of Cosimo II De Medici. Galileo wrote to the Grand Duke saying he had named the four 'stars' of Jupiter the 'Medicean Stars' after him, even claiming that God had told him to do so! So he became Chief Mathematician and Philosopher to the Fourth Grand Duke of Tuscany.

Farewell to Ptolemy

Copernicus' scheme led to a testable hypothesis for, if Venus went round the Sun, it should show phases like our Moon. But this would not occur according to Ptolemy's system. Just after *The Starry Messenger* was published, Galileo observed Venus' phases, showing Ptolemy's scheme was wrong – but *not* that Copernicus' was right. Venus should also show phases on some other theories, like that of the Danish astronomer, Tycho Brahe. Tycho's scheme retained a central Earth, with the Sun and Moon circling it, but all the other planets circled the Sun (Fig. 6.6). A comparison of the Ptolemaic, Tychonic and Copernican schemes can help pupils evaluate the validity of different interpretations of experimental evidence.

Galileo commits the fallacy of affirming the consequent

Premiss 1   If our planetary system is heliocentric, Venus will show phases.
Premiss 2   Venus does show phases.
Conclusion Our planetary system is heliocentric.

Only six planets were then known: Mercury, Venus, Earth, Mars, Jupiter and Saturn. Apart from possible confusion due to both Mercury and Mars beginning with 'M', I suggest the following mnemonic for the order of all nine planets:

Many Valiant Explorers Make Journeys Seeking Undiscovered New Planets

---

The *Undiscovered New Planets* were those found later, namely Uranus (1781), Neptune (1846) and Pluto (1930).

Tycho Brahe rejected Ptolemy's scheme because the supernova and the comet he saw showed the heavens *did* change. But Tycho did not accept Copernicus' scheme, partly because he could not detect stellar parallax and partly because he thought the Bible taught otherwise, providing another example for pupils of the distinction between views held for scientific and non-scientific reasons. Tycho's aesthetic sense was also offended, because the vast distance of the stars implied a great gulf between the furthest planet in our system and the first star. It did not seem fitting that God should have created such a barren space, and 'such aesthetic considerations played a decisive role in early modern science. Without them, it is not clear how mathematical elegance could ever have become a touchstone of truth'.[11] In class, this point about the vastness and apparent barrenness of space could lead on to a discussion of the 'Goldilocks Effect'.

Popular and unpopular astronomer

Galileo made a successful visit to Rome and was warmly received by Pope Paul V. The astronomers of the Jesuit Roman College had initial difficulties checking Galileo's findings, reported in *The Starry Messenger*, because his latest telescope was better than theirs. It was also known that curved glass could distort objects and, lens-grinding being in its infancy, distortions were inevitable. Some people thought what Galileo saw was due to optical

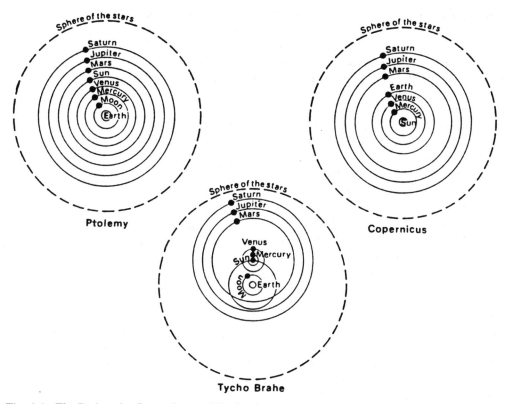

Fig. 6.6   The Ptolemaic, Copernican and Tychonic systems

defects and a few even refused to look through a telescope for this reason. But the Jesuits finally assured the head of the College, Cardinal Bellarmine, that Venus' phases *did* falsify Ptolemy's scheme. The Jesuits preferred the Tychonic system to the Copernican one since it kept the Earth central, yet fitted in with the new astronomy – a further example of arguments based on non-scientific considerations. Galileo returned home, pleased with the public honour accorded him.

Soon afterwards he became involved in some acrimonious arguments with a famous Jesuit astronomer, Father Scheiner. Both claimed priority in discovering sunspots, though neither was first to publish news of the discovery. A modern example for pupils of the cut and thrust of real science, and the race for priority, is the discovery of the

structure of DNA.[12] Galileo made enemies of two other Jesuits by making bitter attacks on their views. Unfortunately, one of them, a quarter of a century later, would turn out to be the Inquisition's Commissary-General at Galileo's trial. Galileo's regular strategy in controversy was to amplify and strengthen the arguments used against him and then to demolish them contemptuously at a blow. It made him a lot of unnecessary enemies, particularly among the Jesuits, who had been friendly earlier on. Indeed, one said later:

> If Galileo had only known how to retain the favour
> of the Jesuits, he would have stood in renown
> before the world, he would have been spared all
> his misfortunes, and he could have written what he
> pleased about everything, even about the motion
> of the Earth.[13]

Rumour, gossip and opposition

News of opposition reached Galileo. Later, a Dominican called Caccini preached on the text 'Ye men of Galilee, why stand ye gazing up into heaven?' (Acts 1:11). Caccini is said to have made a pun on the text, so as to make it, 'Ye men of Galileo, why stand ye gazing up into heaven?' Galileo eventually received an apology from an official of the Dominican Order.

Some followers of Aristotle banded together in Rome under the leadership of a layman, 'Colombe' (meaning 'dove'), to oppose Galileo. Others whom Galileo had offended joined the 'Pigeon League'. Opposition on religious grounds first arose through Colombe's influence. He maintained some biblical passages taught a central Earth, for during the thirteenth century, a Catholic theologian and philosopher, St Thomas Aquinas, had made a detailed attempt to link Greek science to particular Bible texts. So any attack on Aristotle's physics might be seen as attacking the Bible. The problem of 'sanctified science' – trying to read transient scientific theories out of Bible texts – was in evidence and Galileo warned against the practice.

In 1613, Galileo published his *Letters on Sunspots*. Like Copernicus, he feared ridicule if he openly endorsed a heliocentric system, but now he publicised his belief in his new book. This time he wrote in Italian, giving it a much wider readership. Among those who expressed their admiration was Cardinal Barberini, later to become Urban VIII – the Pope at the time of Galileo's trial. Barberini *even* composed a poem in praise of Galileo!

Table talk

The following year, an apparently trivial dinner-party conversation triggered a chain of events leading to Galileo's trial twenty years later. The Grand Duchess of Tuscany was present, as were Dr Boscaglia, Professor of Philosophy and Father Castelli, Professor of Mathematics at the University of Pisa – a former pupil of Galileo. Dr Boscaglia planned to discredit Galileo before the Duchess, saying a moving Earth contradicted Holy Scripture. The Duchess was worried, but eventually seemed satisfied by Castelli's answers. Castelli told Galileo about the incident. Galileo was furious and wrote back to Castelli.

Galileo's views on the Bible

In the following year (1615), Galileo expanded what he had written to Castelli, in a long *Letter to the Grand Duchess Christina, 'Concerning the Use of Biblical Quotations in Matters of Science'*. The letter, which Galileo also intended to be read by others, was meant to dispel theological anxieties about Copernicanism. It was also intended to caution the Roman Catholic Church against tying particular astronomical theories to Bible texts, since the theories might subsequently turn out to be wrong. Here are some extracts:

> . . . in expounding the Bible if one were always to confine oneself to the unadorned grammatical meaning, one might fall into error . . . Thus it would be necessary to assign to God feet, hands and eyes . . .

> . . . since the Holy Ghost did not intend to teach us whether heaven moves or stands still . . . nor whether the earth is located at its centre or off to one side, then so much the less was it intended to settle for us any other conclusion of the same kind . . . Now if the Holy Spirit has purposely neglected to teach us propositions of this sort as irrelevant to the highest goal (that is, to our salvation), how can anyone affirm that it is obligatory to take sides on them? . . . I would say here something that was heard from an ecclesiastic [Cardinal Baronius] of the most eminent degree: 'That the intention of the Holy Ghost is to teach us how one goes to heaven, not how heaven goes'.

> I should think it would be the part of prudence not to let anyone usurp scriptural texts and force them in some way to maintain any physical conclusion to be true, when at some future time the senses . . . may show the contrary.[14]

Far from allaying fears, Galileo's letter caused trouble. Some considered it presumptuous for

Fig. 6.7 Galileo Galilei

Galileo, a layman, to interpret scripture. However, Church officials generally wished to avoid making official pronouncements on Copernicus' scheme until more evidence was available. They told Galileo to produce conclusive evidence, and although he agreed to, he never did.

Other issues

Galileo continued to commit a fallacy in reasoning – the *Fallacy of the Excluded Middle* – by presenting only two alternatives, where others, like Tycho's, were possible. After falsifying Ptolemy's system he *assumed* Copernicus' system was true. Pupils can be given this illustration to show the tentative nature of conclusions and how they may be invalid unless a fair test is carried out.

Galileo regarded Tycho's scheme as just another device, like Ptolemy's, to 'save the appearances', but not saying anything about reality. The issue of whether astronomical theories were claiming to say how the heavens *actually* behaved (*physical* theories) or were simply calculating devices (*mathematical* theories) was central in Copernicus' day and in Galileo's. The authorities did not mind a new calculating device. Their objection was to a new theory, conflicting with the received view, which claimed to describe how things actually were. The difference between these two positions can be illustrated by showing pupils extracts (i) from the preface which Copernicus wrote to his book and (ii) from the anonymous preface preceding Copernicus' preface. The latter, headed 'Concerning the Hypothesis of the Work', was inserted without Copernicus' knowledge by Andreas Osiander. He had been entrusted with seeing the book through the press and, anticipating trouble for Copernicus, had tried to defuse a potential problem. Copernicus dedicated his book 'To The Most Holy Lord, Pope Paul III' and wrote:

> **Extract from Copernicus' preface**
> **– a realist position, advancing a physical theory**
>
> I may well presume, most Holy Father, that certain people, as soon as they hear that in this book *On the Revolutions of the Spheres of the Universe* I ascribe movement to the earthly globe, will cry out that holding such views, I should at once be hissed off the stage . . . How I came to dare to conceive such motion of the Earth, contrary to the received opinion of the Mathematicians and indeed contrary to the impression of the senses, is what your Holiness will rather expect.[15]

> **Extract from Osiander's (anonymous) preface**
> **– an instrumentalist position, claiming a mathematical theory**
>
> The author of this work has done nothing blameworthy, for it is the duty of an astronomer to . . . conceive and devise, since he cannot in any way attain to the true causes, such hypotheses as, being assumed, enable the motions to be calculated correctly from the principles of geometry . . .
>
> . . . they are not put forward to convince anyone that they are true, but *merely to provide* a correct basis for calculation.[16]

Copernicus received a copy of the published book on his death-bed and was very concerned to see the additional preface.

Now, some seventy years later, a different Pope, Paul V, ordered an investigation into the relationship between Copernicus' ideas and the Church's current understanding of the scriptures. It reported:

> [The claim that] The sun is the centre of the world and completely immovable by local motion . . . was declared unanimously to be foolish and absurd, philosophically and formally heretical inasmuch as it expressly contradicts the doctrine of Holy Scripture in many passages, both in their literal meaning and according to the general interpretation of the Fathers and Doctors.[17]

> [Secondly, the claim that] The earth is not the centre of the world, nor immovable, but moves according to the whole of itself, and also with a diurnal [daily] motion [was said] to deserve the like censure in philosophy, and as regards theological truth, to be at least erroneous in faith.[18]

As a result, Copernicus' book was temporarily suspended, pending a few small changes, particularly to the preface. The matter of censorship of scientific work and the ownership of intellectual property could be raised for class discussion. The issues could be broadened out and explored with respect to political ideology – such as in the Lysenko affair; religious beliefs – as above; public availability of information – for instance in war-time; and the destiny of discoveries, inventions and written materials produced while employed by others.

A crucial report

Cardinal Bellarmine was instructed by the Pope to persuade Galileo to abandon his views, or risk imprisonment. Much of what happened at their meeting remains a mystery. But rumours began to circulate soon afterwards and Galileo asked Bellarmine for a written report to use in his own defence. The report confirmed that Galileo had not been made to renounce his ideas on oath, nor do penance, but simply told:

> . . . that the doctrine of Copernicus, that the earth moves around the sun and that the sun is stationary in the centre of the universe and does not move from east to west, is contrary to Holy Scripture and therefore cannot be defended or held.[19]

Galileo trod carefully for about seven years and then, in another book, *The Assayer*, he started another bitter dispute with a Jesuit, about comets.

Good prospects ahead?

Just before publication of *The Assayer*, Galileo heard what seemed good news. Cardinal Barberini, an admirer of Galileo who had spoken up for him earlier, became Pope Urban VIII. The events which followed and eventually led to the trial of Galileo are inextricably linked with the personalities of Galileo and Urban VIII, and the relation between them.

> [Urban VIII] . . . was the first Pope to allow a monument to be erected to him in his lifetime. His vanity was indeed monumental, and conspicuous even in an age which had little use for the virtue of modesty. His famous statement that he 'knew better than all the Cardinals put together' was only equalled by Galileo's that he alone had discovered everything new in the sky. They both considered themselves supermen and started on a basis of mutual adulation – a type of relationship which, as a rule, comes to a bitter end.[20]

It needs to be borne in mind that for much of the time the Pope was Galileo's friend and ally. Also, Galileo affirmed he was a loyal member of the Catholic Church.

Self appraisal

No saint could have shown more reverence for the Church or greater zeal.

Galileo[21]

When Galileo heard about the new Pope, there was just time to make the prudent move of dedicating *The Assayer* to him before it went to press. Urban VIII enjoyed the book. Galileo subsequently went to Rome and had several long audiences with him, hoping that earlier restrictions might be reversed. He said he would like to write a book on the Copernican system called *Dialogue on the Flux and Reflux of the Tides*. He was sure he could produce firm evidence that the Earth moved, incorrectly reasoning that the Earth's motion caused the tides – even though Kepler said it was the Moon's attraction. The Pope said Galileo's proposed title implied the Copernican scheme could be shown to be true and insisted on the alternative title, *Dialogue Concerning the Two Chief World Systems*. Again no reference was made to Tycho's system. The Pope also insisted on Galileo's ideas being treated as a hypothesis. He also stipulated the inclusion of his own 'unanswerable argument' that, since God was able to do anything, he could produce the tides any way he chose and was not obliged to use the motion of the Earth.

Sharp practice?

The book took the form of a series of conversations, over four days, between three people. The names of two of them, *Salviati* and *Sagredo*, were those of friends of Galileo:

- *Salviati* argues the Copernican position and is clearly the mouthpiece of Galileo;
- *Sagredo* represents the open-minded layman, ready to be convinced by argument;
- *Simplicio* takes the orthodox Aristotelian position. His name results from making a small, but highly significant change in *Simplicius* – the name of an earlier commentator on Aristotle. *Simplicio* translates as 'simpleton'!

The way Galileo obtained the *Imprimatur* – the official licence to print – is open to question. Furthermore, it was clear on reading the book that it did *not* treat the issues hypothetically, as instructed. In his characteristic way, Galileo amplified his opponent's arguments and then demolished them – and there was a sting in the tail, a humiliating sting. Whether or not it was intentional is open to debate. But the Pope's so-called 'unanswerable argument' was relegated to the very end of the book and put into the mouth of none other than Simplicio! As the Pope said later, Galileo 'did not fear to make game of me'. It was not a move calculated to 'win friends and influence people'!

Backlash!

. . . it did not require much Jesuit cunning to turn Urban's perilous adulation ['Perilous Adulation' is a translation of the title of the poem that Barberini had written in praise of Galileo] into the fury of the betrayed lover. Not only had Galileo gone, in letter and spirit, against the agreement to treat Copernicus strictly as a hypothesis, not only had he obtained the *imprimatur* by methods resembling sharp practice, but Urban's favourite argument was only mentioned briefly at the very end of the book, and put into the mouth of the simpleton who on any other point was invariably proved wrong.[22]

The mystery minute

Galileo was summoned before a special commission in Rome in 1633. He was not confined to dungeons but stayed in comfortable apartments. However, events took a frightening turn when Galileo was interrogated about his 1616 meeting with Cardinal Bellarmine, for an alleged minute of that meeting was produced from Vatican files. The minute was unknown to Galileo and remains surrounded by mystery to this day. It was unsigned, which was irregular, and it differed in small, but significant respects from that given to Galileo by Bellarmine, who was now dead. Galileo produced Bellarmine's report which said Copernicus' ideas 'cannot be defended or held'.[23] But the Vatican minute said Galileo had been commanded

> . . . to relinquish altogether the said opinion that the Sun is the centre of the world and immovable and that the Earth moves; nor further to hold, teach, or defend it in any way whatsoever, verbally or in writing; otherwise proceedings would be taken against him by the Holy Office; which . . . Galileo . . . promised to obey.[24]

This wording is much stronger than Bellarmine's. The handwriting and the watermark of the Vatican minute have been subjected to recent scrutiny, showing it corresponds with other documents in the file and does not appear to be a later forgery. The discrepancy between the two documents is a key factor in the whole affair.

'Oh what a tangled web we weave . . . !'

Galileo was questioned about the devious way he had obtained permission to print and about the restrictions placed on him by the Pope. He replied:

> I have neither maintained nor defended in that book the opinion that the Earth moves and that the Sun is stationary but have rather demonstrated the opposite of the Copernican opinion and shown that the arguments of Copernicus are weak and not conclusive.[25]

This was an outrageous claim and its falsity was obvious to anyone, like Galileo's inquisitors, who read the book:

> By a long list of quotations they proved beyond doubt that Galileo had not only discussed the Copernican view as a hypothesis, but that he had taught, defended, and held it, and that he had called those who did not share it 'mental pygmies', 'dumb idiots', and 'hardly deserving to be called human beings'.[26]

Galileo's claim was ludicrous; it would never stand up in court. Attempts were made 'to deal leniently with the culprit' and arrange an out-of-court settlement. Galileo attempted to wriggle out of the predicament caused by his lying, saying:

> . . . it occurred to me to reperuse my printed *Dialogue*, which for three years I had not seen . . . it presented itself to me, as it were, like a new writing and by another author, I freely confess that in several places it seemed to me set forth in such a form that a reader ignorant of my real purpose might have had reason to suppose that the arguments brought on the false side, and which it was my intention to confute, were so expressed as to be calculated rather to compel conviction.[27]

Galileo also offered to add to his book, to *disprove* the Copernican scheme more fully!

Shock turn of events in court!

Then came the staggering news that Galileo was to be interrogated about the Copernican scheme under threat of torture. Although Galileo and his inquisitors knew it was illegal to torture a man of seventy, so the threat could not be carried out, it was still an alarming turn of events. Galileo denied holding Copernican views four times under oath and could easily have been convicted of perjury by quoting from his book. The decision to threaten Galileo with torture was probably taken by the offended Pope Urban VIII, in order to humiliate him and show he could not play fast and loose with the authorities. The Pope's nephew seems to have suspected it was more from personal vengeance than doctrinal defence. Despite the Pope's anger,

and no doubt remembering their friendship, he said they would 'consult together so that he may suffer as little distress as possible'.

Sentence passed

The trial stopped at that point. Galileo was sentenced to read a recantation of his Copernican opinions, saying that 'with sincere heart and unfeigned faith I abjure, curse, and detest the aforesaid errors and heresies'.[28]

He was placed under house arrest and required to recite the seven penitential Psalms once a week for three years. His 'formal prison' was initially a sumptuous apartment at the villa of the Grand Duke. Then he was moved to his own farm and finally back to his own house in Florence. He was even allowed to delegate the reciting of the penitential Psalms to one of his daughters – a nun, one of three children Galileo had by his mistress, whom he left on moving to the Medicean Court in Florence.

Hindsight

Galileo contended for a heliocentric universe (approximately); the Roman Catholic Church for a geocentric one. How does their dispute appear in the light of current ideas of spacetime and what were the key issues? Some verdicts are given in the box on page 112.

Galileo was concerned the Church should not lock its teachings to a changing science. But a key issue in the aftermath of the Reformation was the highly sensitive matter of who was authorised to interpret the Bible. The Roman Catholic Church was still smarting from the effects of a movement which challenged its authority by direct appeals to the Bible. Subsequently, the Council of Trent (1545–63) decreed that the ultimate authority for biblical interpretation belonged to the Church Fathers. But Galileo was presuming to interpret the Bible himself, in the light of the world around him! Many other issues were involved but 'the scientist's vanity, quarrels over priority of

There would now be almost universal agreement, first, that the Church sought to maintain an untenable doctrine of geocentrism that was quite unnecessary to its fundamental beliefs, and, second, that Galileo's theory, too, was mistaken, because we would not now recognize *any* spatial point as the absolute centre of the universe, but would measure all positions and motions relatively to some point chosen for our own convenience.

Professor Mary Hesse[29]

Galileo said that the earth moves and the sun is fixed; the Inquisition said that the earth is fixed and the sun moves; and Newtonian astronomers, adopting an absolute theory of space, said that both the sun and the earth move. But now we say that any one of these three statements is equally true, provided that you have fixed your sense of 'rest' and 'motion' in the way required by the statement adopted. At the date of Galileo's controversy with the Inquisition, Galileo's way of stating the facts was, beyond question, the fruitful procedure for the sake of scientific research. But in itself it was not more true than the formulation of the Inquisition. But at that time the modern concepts of relative motion were in nobody's mind . . .

Professor A.N. Whitehead[30]

We are not dealing with conflict between two abstract forces 'science' and 'religion', but with an internecine conflict within the Roman Catholic Church. Galileo did not belong to some detached and alien 'scientific culture'. Many of his methods were extensions of those employed by the Jesuits. If they fell out it was largely because they had so much in common! . . .
    . . . in the last analysis Galileo was disciplined as a member of the Church, not as an outsider.

Professor John Brooke[31]

Galileo's trial of 1633 was not the simple conflict between science and religion so commonly pictured. It was a complex power struggle of personal and professional pride, envy and ambition . . .

Dr Charles Hummel[32]

. . . the tragedy was the result of a plot of which the hierarchies themselves turned out to be the victims no less than Galileo – an intrigue engineered by a group of obscure and disparate characters in strange collusion who planted false documents in the file, who later misinformed the Pope and then presented to him a misleading account of the trial for decision.

Dr Giorgio de Santillana[33]

It is my conviction that the conflict between Church and Galileo (or Copernicus) was not inevitable; that it was not in the nature of a fatal collision between opposite philosophies of existence . . . but rather a clash of individual temperaments aggravated by unlucky coincidences. In other words, I believe the idea that Galileo's trial was . . . a showdown between 'blind faith' and 'enlightened reason', to be naively erroneous.

Arthur Koestler[34]

discovery, contemptuous attitude and effective sarcasm cost him dearly in the long run'.[35] It is ironical that 'The views concerning the interpretation of Scripture contained in Galileo's theological letters have become the official doctrine of the [Roman Catholic] Church since Leo XIII's encyclical *Providentissimus Deus* of 1893'.[36]

It was during the closing years of his life that Galileo made his most outstanding contribution to science – *Discourses Concerning Two New Sciences* – a treatise on falling bodies and projectiles. So although the quotation at the beginning of this chapter listed things Galileo did not do, what he *did* was to lay the foundation of dynamics.

During his last years, Galileo received many visitors, including the young English poet, John Milton. Galileo died in Florence in 1642, the year that Isaac Newton was born. By a coincidence, a teenage boy from Ireland happened to be staying in Florence when the 'great star gazer' died. The boy, too, was destined to play an important part in debates about matters of science and religion when he grew up. His name was Robert Boyle.

A teaching point

The problem is how to present the case in a way that does not caricature a complex historical situation. The temptation is to present the case as an illustration of some general thesis about conflict between science and religion. The assumption of some essential incompatibility between these two aspects of human aspiration does of course run very deep in our culture. To assert that the findings of science have gradually eroded or disproved the cherished dogmas of the church is one of the ways by which a secular society justifies its unbelief[37]

Galileo's star will shine once again in God's heaven

To bring the story up to date, under this headline *The Times* (31 October 1992) reported:

MORE than 359 years after he was condemned by the Inquisition, the astronomer Galileo is expected to be rehabilitated today by Pope John Paul II . . .

The closing words shall go to the historian Geoffrey Cantor as an appropriate summary of this chapter and as an introduction to the equally intriguing subject of the next:

Galileo can no longer be portrayed as the harbinger of truth and enlightenment who was pitted against reactionary priests who refused to look through the telescope. Instead he counted many Jesuits among his supporters, but his censure resulted partly from his mishandling of a sensitive diplomatic situation. The other paradigmatic conflict concerns the Darwinian theory of evolution . . .[38]

CHAPTER 7

'God knows what the public will think' – the Darwinian controversies

Part 1. Historical background

'I saw two very bad operations but I ran away before they were completed', wrote Charles Darwin about his days as a medical student in Edinburgh. Troubled by having to dissect dead bodies and distressed by seeing operations performed without anaesthetics on people who were gagged to stifle their screams, he left the course.

The personal story of Charles Darwin, told in Part 1, is a deeply poignant one, enacted within a web of political turmoil and the power struggles of a growing scientific professionalism. It is rich in material for teaching how science interacts with spiritual, moral, social and cultural factors – a bonus to its importance in teaching biology. Some associated philosophical issues which may arise in class are discussed in Part 2.

Outcome of a friendship

After leaving Edinburgh, Darwin went to Christ's College Cambridge to study for ministry in the Church of England, though his heart was not really in his studies. He liked collecting living things and became friendly with a proctor, Revd John Henslow, Professor of Botany. As a result, Darwin, aged nearly twenty-three, sailed from Plymouth in 1831, for a five-year voyage round the world.

The voyage of *HMS Beagle* was to improve Admiralty charts of the South American coast and the fixing of longtitude. Darwin went as gentleman companion to Captain Fitzroy, in command at the exceptionally early age of twenty-three. Everywhere they landed, Darwin collected specimens of rocks, fossils and wildlife, which he sent back to Britain.[1] When Darwin returned to England in

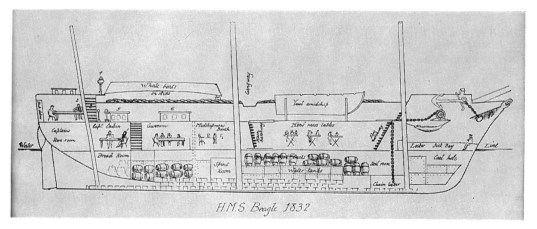

Fig. 7.1 Elevation of HMS Beagle

October 1836, it was to a country in social turmoil. He went to lodge in London, ambitious to make a name for himself.

Genesis of a theory

When Darwin set sail he shared the common belief – Special Creation – that God had created each species separately. During the voyage, he later said, 'vague doubts occasionally flitted across my mind' as to whether species *were* fixed. One factor was the sheer variety of living creatures occupying similar habitats, such as those in the Galapagos Islands off the Equador coast. Contrary to one version of how Darwin's theory developed, he did not recognise the finches of the Galapagos as coming from a common stock and continued to believe in the immutability of species for another year and a half. His switch to an evolutionary theory probably took place in the second week of March 1837, triggered by a meeting with the eminent ornithologist, John Gould, at the Zoological Society of London.[2] Gould identified all the birds as finches and Darwin saw the implications of his Galapagos collection:

> Seeing this gradation and diversity of structure in one small, intimately related group of birds, one might really fancy that from an original paucity of birds in this archipelago, one species had been taken and modified for different ends.[3]

Darwin realised too late he should have labelled his finches by island. He tried to rectify the omission from memory and by reference to collections made by other shipmates, but with limited success. In January 1844 he wrote: 'I am almost convinced (quite contrary to the opinion I started with) that species are not (it is like confessing a murder) immutable'.[4]

Stephen Jay Gould argues that Darwin's memories of the development of his theory were, in certain respects, deceptive:

> In an autobiography, which was written as a lesson in morality for his children and not intended for publication, he penned some famous lines that misled historians for nearly 100 years. Describing

his path to the theory of natural selection, he claimed, 'I worked on true Baconian principles, and without any theory collected facts on a wholesale scale'.[5]

But the (then) 'received wisdom' of *inductivism* as describing scientific discovery is inadequate to chart Darwin's pilgrimage. But some who rightly recognise its inadequacies promote 'eurekaism' as the alternative. Certainly Darwin *records* a 'eureka' experience:

> In October 1838, that is, fifteen months after I had begun my systematic enquiry, I happened to read for amusement Malthus on *Population*, and being well prepared to appreciate the struggle for existence which everywhere goes on, from long-continued observation of the habits of animals and plants, it at once struck me that under these circumstances favourable variations would tend to be preserved and unfavourable ones to be destroyed. The result of this would be the formation of a new species. Here, then, I had at last got a theory by which to work.[6]

But this record occurs, not in Darwin's contemporary notebooks on Transmutation of Species (1837–9), but in what Stephen Jay Gould calls Darwin's 'maddeningly misleading autobiography', begun in 1876, long after the event.

> Yet, again, the notebooks belie Darwin's later recollections – in this case by their utter failure to record, at the time it happened, any special exultation over his Malthusian insight. He inscribes it as a fairly short and sober entry without a single exclamation point, although he habitually used two or three in moments of excitement.[7]

Darwin did not drop everything to concentrate on this supposed flash of inspiration. He wrote in his diary the following day a longer passage on something entirely different. Gould concludes:

> The theory of natural selection arose neither as a workmanlike induction from nature's fact nor as a mysterious bolt from Darwin's subconscious, triggered by an accidental reading of Malthus. It emerged instead as the result of a conscious and productive search, proceeding in a ramified but ordered manner, and utilising both the facts of natural history and an astonishingly broad range of

insights from disparate disciplines far from his own. Darwin trod the middle path between inductivism and eurekaism. His genius is neither pedestrian nor inaccessible.[8]

Struggle in society

It is important for pupils to understand something of the backdrop against which Darwin's ideas took shape and to realise no scientific discoveries take place in a social vacuum. In 1798, the Revd Thomas Malthus, an economist, published his *Essay on the Principle of Population*. A central theme of his book was there would always be struggle and competition because populations tend to increase faster than available resources. Malthus' ideas were affecting Victorian society. The Elizabethan Poor Laws and subsequent welfare policies increasingly drained the public purse and, two years before Darwin docked at Falmouth, the Poor Law Amendment Act (1834) was passed, based upon harsher principles than its predecessor. Pauperism among able-bodied workers was regarded as moral failing, handouts to the poor as encouraging fecundity, making further demands on scarce resources. The resultant policy of the workhouse aggravated the social unrest, as did the economic depression and high unemployment of the late 1830s. Out of this social milieu, Chartism was born – a British working-class movement for parliamentary reform which attracted nationwide support. Its demands included universal manhood suffrage, payment for parliamentary members, vote by ballot, equal electoral districts, annually elected parliaments and the abolition of the property qualifications for membership.

The Whigs had replaced the Tory Anglicans and the Established Church was losing both privileges and power. In contrast to advantages exclusively offered to Anglicans at Oxbridge, the establishment, in 1826, of a new university in London offered to all the benefits of higher education, regardless of class or creed – but at what some regarded as a price:

> What was disturbing . . . was the fact that the institution situated in Gower Street, Bloomsbury,

which was known as 'the University of London', and which had been brought into being in 1826 through the efforts of Jeremy Bentham and his secularist friends Henry Brougham, James Mill, and Joseph Hume, had been deliberately founded on conditions which excluded the provision of a chapel, as well as religious instruction and theological teaching of any kind. Small wonder therefore that churchmen should be moved to take counter-action.[9]

The 'counter-action' led to a resolution in June 1828 'that there should be founded in London a College [King's College] where the pursuit of knowledge and the practice of religion should be joined in indissoluble union'.[10] The *Evening Standard* of 19 June 1828 declared

> With such a seminary in a prosperous position there will be neither motive nor excuse for any parent to inflict upon his offspring the disgrace of education in the infidel and godless college in Gower Street.[11]

At the 'godless college', occupying the Chair of Zoology, was Darwin's former tutor from his Edinburgh days, Robert Grant. Grant was an ardent secularist and pro-evolution. But evolution was regarded as bordering on atheism, especially in the aftermath of the French Revolution (1789–94), with the developing doctrines of human perfectibility and progress. Comte's three stages, theological–metaphysical–scientific, referred to in Chapter 2, taught that scientific ideas displaced theological ones. So within this social milieu, Darwin, a Whig gentleman living on a private fortune, found himself under pressure from rival factions. In May 1839, riots broke out in Birmingham; in July, Parliament rejected a petition presented by the Chartists; in November, an armed uprising in Newport was quickly put down.

In January that year, Charles married his cousin Emma, a member of the Wedgwood family, noted for fine pottery. Emma's devout religious beliefs and her concern for Charles' spiritual health are part of the poignant human story. In 1842, Charles and Emma moved out of Gower Street to the quiet Kent village of Downe, away from the civil unrest

On the Tendency of Species to form Varieties; and on the Perpetuation of Varieties and Species by Natural Means of Selection. By CHARLES DARWIN, Esq., F.R.S., F.L.S., & F.G.S., and ALFRED WALLACE, Esq. Communicated by Sir CHARLES LYELL, F.R.S., F.L.S., and J. D. HOOKER, Esq., M.D., V.P.R.S., F.L.S., &c.

[Read July 1st, 1858.]

London, June 30th, 1858.

MY DEAR SIR,—The accompanying papers, which we have the honour of communicating to the Linnean Society, and which all relate to the same subject, viz. the Laws which affect the Production of Varieties, Races, and Species, contain the results of the investigations of two indefatigable naturalists, Mr. Charles Darwin and Mr. Alfred Wallace.

Fig. 7.2 Introduction to Darwin and Wallace's joint paper

of central London and fears of a general uprising, where Darwin wrote down a short version of his 'species Theory'. He expanded his ideas in 1844, the same year that an anonymous book appeared under the title of *Vestiges of the Natural History of Creation*. The author, later identified as the publisher, Robert Chambers (of Chambers' Encyclopedia note), described a story of cosmic evolution, from planets to people. It was a popular work, liberally sprinkled with mistakes, but quickly proved a best seller. It was presented as a treatise on natural theology[12] and in it Chambers argued that evolution could be seen as a law of divine activity. But transmutationist views were not widespread within the Anglican establishment and there were those, like Adam Sedgwick, Professor of Geology at Cambridge, who saw Chambers' book as disguised atheism rather than as natural theology. Even T.H. Huxley disliked the book.

Charles Lyell tried to persuade Darwin to publish, lest he should be pre-empted, but Darwin wanted more time. The outcry about Chambers' book may have deterred him from going public.

A black June

On 18 June 1858, Darwin heard from a fellow naturalist, Alfred Russel Wallace, working in Malaya. He too had read Malthus, hit on a similar idea to Darwin about mechanisms for evolution

and wanted Darwin's help over publication. It was a severe blow, exacerbated by acute family worries. Darwin's daughter Etty was very ill with diphtheria and, five days later, baby Charles went down with scarlet fever which had already claimed several lives in Downe village. Darwin sent Wallace's letter to Lyell saying:

> Your words have come true with a vengeance – that I should be forestalled . . . I never saw a more striking coincidence; if Wallace had my MS. sketch written out in 1842, he could not have made a better short abstract![13]

Lyell and another friend, Hooker, acted rapidly to save Darwin from being pre-empted in publishing his theory. They arranged for Wallace's paper and one by Darwin to be read jointly at a meeting of the Linnean Society on 1 July 1858. The papers attracted little interest and the President later reported, 'The year . . . has not been marked by any of those striking discoveries which revolutionise the department of science on which they bear'![14]

Charles Darwin was not present. He was attending the funeral of baby Charles.

Struggle for survival

It was urgent for Darwin to publish in more detail, and in 1859 he produced a substantial volume, *The Origin of Species*. Evolutionary ideas had been around for a long time, but now Darwin set out a plausible mechanism, together with supporting evidence. He was familiar with the *artificial selection* of racehorses, dogs and pigeons to breed strains with better endurance and faster speeds. By analogy with artificial selection, Darwin decided upon a name:

> The preservation of favourable individual differences and variations, and the destruction of those which are injurious, I have called Natural Selection.

Darwin's theory can be summed up in four words: *multiplication*, *struggle*, *variation* and *heredity*. It was based on certain reasonable assumptions:

Darwin's assumptions

Multiplication and struggle:

- Living things reproduce freely in the wild, resulting in more than can be supported by available resources. Consequently, there is competition.
- There is predation. Living things feed on other living things.
- The longest living members of species are likeliest to reproduce most.

Variation:

- Offspring are not exactly like their parents. There may be differences in colour of eyes, shape of beaks, lengths of legs, etc.

Heredity:

- Many characteristics seem to be transferred from one generation to another, although Darwin had no idea how (the idea of genes came later).

Darwin's theory

- Some variations may offer better chances of survival against predators or food scarcity. Longer legs help in a chase; 'camouflage' reduces detection.

- If the last two assumptions are true, more of the population will possess such characteristics, resulting in a gradual change, or 'evolution'. Darwin called this change 'descent with modification'.

Darwin's theory presented numerous problems which pupils could discuss. One was why characteristics, which artificial selection enhanced by selective breeding, did not get diluted in the wild by indiscriminate mating; for new varieties produced under domestication tended to revert to type. Darwin held to a theory of *blending inheritance*, by which, if one of a pair had a certain characteristic and the other did not, the resulting offspring would each have a reduced amount. It could be compared to mixing some clean water with some red ink. The resulting liquid is pink.

The development of the idea of genes and the science of genetics changed this perception and, linked with Darwin's ideas, led to the New Synthesis of the 1930s and 1940s, or Neo-Darwinism.[15] On this theory, mating could be compared to mixing the contents of two vessels full of differently coloured balls (genes). The offspring – a new set of vessels – either contain particular coloured balls or they do not. Where the genetic information enhances survival and reproduction, the genes are carried on into future generations.

Another problem was that if individual changes from generation to generation were small, many were needed, requiring a longer time-scale than was thought to be available. A useful link with earth sciences could be to make pupils aware of the time-scales of geological processes and help them evaluate earlier ideas, like those below, about the Earth's age:

'The poor world is almost six thousand years old'

– or so said Rosalind in Shakespeare's *As You Like It*.[16] The Revd Thomas Sprat, writing a history of the Royal Society, formed 'in the wonderful pacifick year, 1660', said 'they have fram'd such an assembly in six years, which was never yet brought about in six thousand'.[17]

CHAPTER I.

1 *The creation of heaven and earth*, 3 *of the light*, 6 *of the firmament*, 9 *of the earth separated from the waters*, 11 *and made fruitful*, 14 *of the sun, moon, and stars*, 20 *of fish and fowl*, 24 *of beasts and cattle*, 26 *of man in the image of God.* 29 *Also the appointment of food.*

BEFORE CHRIST 4004.

a John i. 1, 2; Heb. i. 10.

Fig. 7.3 4004BC in the margin of an old Bible

The figure of six thousand arose because a number of people, notably James Ussher, Archbishop of Armagh, thought the age of the Earth could be calculated by adding up all the ages in the (incomplete) family trees in the book of Genesis. Then, if the 'days' of Genesis were consecutive twenty-four hour periods, it seemed the age of the Earth could be estimated. The procedure illustrates to pupils the difference between scientific and non-scientific considerations. An accepted date of creation of 4004 B.C., though no part of the original text, can be seen in the margins of old Bibles.

However, long before geology pointed towards an ancient earth, scholars like Augustine (A.D.354–430), as we saw in Chapter 5, argued that creation was not *in* time, but *with* time. He said the 'days of God' have no human analogies.[18] So the idea that the 'days' were not intended to be understood as twenty-four hour periods did not arise to get theologians out of geological difficulties! The Genesis text itself provided clues, for with the creation of the sun, moon and stars on 'day' four, the writer probably did not intend the preceding 'days' to represent 'twenty-four hour' periods. Without sun or stars for reference, *solar* or *sidereal* days would have no meaning. Furthermore, the absence of rain is given as the cause of

the absence of plants (Genesis 2:5), which does not fit in with the idea of a literal week. At a more sophisticated level, the whole argument Jesus develops in John chapter five about healing on the Sabbath, depends on the seventh 'day' *not* being twenty-four hours, but still continuing.[19]

Support from the geological column?

In the early nineteenth century, ideas about the age of the Earth were revised upwards. Fossils and rock strata exposed when digging canals, quarries and mines at the time of the industrial revolution suggested the Earth was much older than popularly believed.

The Scottish geologist, James Hutton, saw the Earth as having undergone a gradual development by cyclical processes of mountain building, erosion, soil formation and loss, over vast periods of time, a view which came to be known as *uniformitarianism*. Certain difficulties arise over two different meanings assigned to this word: (i) the belief that the rates of geological processes operating in the past were similar to those operating today, and (ii) the belief that the laws of nature which operated in the past are similar to those operating today. Hutton concluded from his view that the processes were cyclical, 'with respect to

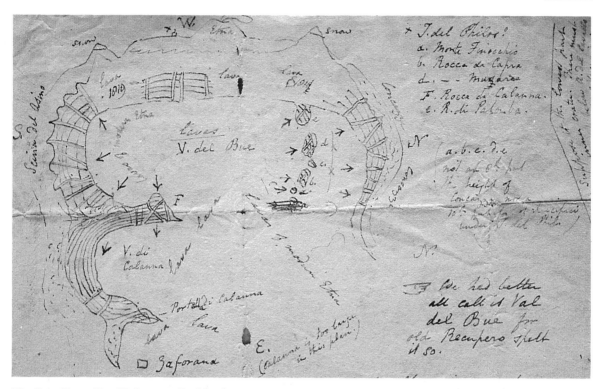

Fig. 7.4   Part of Lyell's letter to Buckland

human observations . . . we see no vestige of a beginning, no prospect of an end'. Some wrongly thought this meant Hutton denied any beginning or end to the Earth. But Hutton was a deist and wanted to show 'the globe of this earth is evidently made for man'.[20]

Hutton's uniformitarian ideas were taken up by the geologist Charles Lyell, who in 1830 published an important book, *Principles of Geology*, the year before Darwin set sail. Darwin took Volume One with him to help with his collecting. Lyell travelled to Mount Etna in Sicily and saw many remains of eruptions from the volcano. He knew something about their frequency. The many eruptions, separated by long time intervals, supported the theory of an ancient Earth. Lyell wrote to a fellow geologist, William Buckland at Oxford, about his findings.

Prior to this it had been commonly believed that catastrophic events like Noah's Flood played a large part in shaping the Earth's surface. Buckland's discovery of the remains of long extinct animals in mud in a cave in Kirkdale[21] seemed to support the idea and Buckland's opposite number at Cambridge, Revd Adam Sedgwick, also accepted a universal Noachian flood. So within the geological community, two pairs of disagreements existed. There were those who saw water as the primary geological agent (i.e. the Neptunists) and those who believed it was fire (i.e. the Vulcanists). Then there were those who saw the history of the Earth as largely quiescent, but punctuated by several catastrophic upheavals, the latest being Noah's Flood. These were the Catastrophists, who stood in contrast to Uniformitarians like Lyell – although to see the issues simply as a catastrophist/ uniformitarian antithesis is an oversimplification. Theological issues were involved but it would be wrong to portray the controversies as *science versus religion*.[22] Lyell's *Principles of Geology* brought to an end the widespread consideration of Noah's Flood as a major geological agent. Sedgwick announced his change of view in a remarkable Presidential Address to the Geological Society in 1831:

> Having been myself a believer, and, to the best of my power, a propagator of what I now regard as a philosophic heresy . . . I think it right, as one of my last acts before I quit this Chair, thus publicly to read my recantation. We ought, indeed, to have paused before we first adopted the diluvian theory, and referred all our old superficial gravel to the action of the Mosaic Flood.[23]

Russell, who furnishes this quotation, gives a necessary warning against misinterpreting Sedgwick's recantation:

> Sedgwick did not deny the historicity of Noah's Flood; he most certainly did not abjure a deeply-held faith in Scripture and a commitment to biblical doctrines that realistically can be termed evangelical. He simply abandoned an arbitrary determination that Genesis should be interpreted in certain specific ways.[24]

Lyell himself seems to have favoured the idea that Noah's Flood was a local event. The significance of his work in pointing to an ancient Earth was, for Darwin's needs, clear enough.

Later, in 1862, Lord Kelvin would estimate the habitable age of the Earth, from its rate of cooling, as not greater than two hundred million years, a figure he dropped in 1899 to twenty to forty million years, in contradiction to the geologists. The discovery of radioactivity by Becquerel in 1896 led to a realisation that the Earth had an internal supply of heat, making it necessary to revise Kelvin's estimates upwards. The discovery of radioactivity also led to a method for dating the Earth, substantially confirming the estimates of the geologists.[25] These events could be used to illustrate scientific controversies and change.

The reception of the 'Origin'

Darwin was quite ill by the time he finished proof-reading the *Origin* and retired to the Yorkshire moors, apprehensively awaiting the reception of his book. He sent anxious notes out with the complimentary copies; one to Wallace read, 'God knows what the public will think'.[26] But he need not have been fearful. The social climate at the time of publication was very different from what it had been twenty years earlier. The Great Exhibition of 1851 symbolised a rising national pride as free trade and *laissez-faire* brought prosperity to some and raised the expectations of others. Evolution too had become a symbol – of Victorian belief in inevitable progress towards perfection. Competition in business – if one doesn't examine the argument closely – was seen as the natural outworking of competition in nature. So the Victorian capitalists would, within a few years, be holding out welcoming arms to an evolutionary theory fancied to support their cause. Nevertheless, there were those who *did* examine the argument closely, both then and now; and for those who imagine that ethical systems and political ideologies can be justified by appealing to evolutionary ideas – the fallacy of trying to derive OUGHT from IS – it may be salutary to remember that the mutually incompatible ideologies of Capitalism, Communism and Nazism have all at times claimed their justification from evolution!

The *Origin* was avidly read and different reactions to it soon appeared in reviews, lectures and papers. Although Darwin hardly mentioned humans in the *Origin*, the implications were obvious and were developed in Darwin's later book, *The Descent of Man* (1871). His ideas got a mixed reception from fellow scientists and from the public at large. Adam Sedgwick wrote strongly against the *Origin* in *The Spectator*. T.H. Huxley reviewed the *Origin* anonymously and favourably in *The Times*, defending it at one of the famous Friday Evening Discourses at the Royal Institution:

> Surely, it is the duty of the public to discourage everything of this kind, to discredit these foolish meddlers who think they do the Almighty a service by preventing a thorough study of his works.[27]

Legend has it that religious people opposed

Darwin's theory and scientists welcomed it. One difficulty about this folklore is that the scientists were in many cases religious believers, so any attempts to line up 'the scientists' on one side and 'the religious' on the other raises problems! Moore, in his magisterial study, *The Post-Darwinian Controversies*, responds to one writer who asserts 'many theologians and a few scientists rejected the hypothesis outright as "the latest form of infidelity"':

> The truth is nearer to the exact opposite: it was a few theologians and many scientists who dismissed Darwinism and evolution . . . a fair assessment is made only by comparing the more enlightened representatives of science and theology – a point consistently overlooked by authors addicted to counterposing Huxley's tirades with the outcries of ignorant clergymen . . .[28]

Another piece of folklore surrounding the reception of Darwin's ideas is that it was those who had a strong commitment to the authority of the Bible who were most against Darwin's ideas. History shows this generalisation to be misleading.[29]

'A legendary encounter'

Seven months later, at the AGM of the British Association for the Advancement of Science, a section meeting was held in the newly completed museum (Natural History) in Oxford. The 30th of June 1860 was hot and an audience of some seven hundred people necessitated moving to a larger room.

A popular version

. . . in 1860, Huxley came up against the Bishop of Oxford and his prompter Owen and smashed them both, thereby earning the title of 'Darwin's bulldog' and spoiling all attempts of the Church of England to discredit evolution.[30]

Most people know the *legendary* account of the afternoon's proceedings, prized in television[31] where confrontations are avidly sought. Records of the occasion are scarce – giving abundant scope

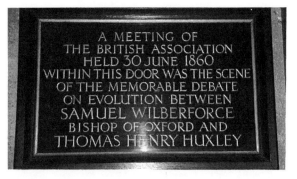

Fig. 7.5 Plaque outside the room where the Huxley-Wilberforce encounter took place

for the imagination – and they vary in reliability. Later exaggerations, aimed at portraying science and religion locked in deadly combat with science the inevitable winner, have muddied the waters further. A different and more interesting picture emerges from recent studies[32] in history of science.

John Draper, Professor of Chemistry and Physiology at the University of New York, spoke for something between sixty and ninety minutes about Darwin's views, and a lengthy and lively discussion followed. In view of the occasion, it is interesting that it was Draper who published (1875) the anti-Roman Catholic polemic *History of the Conflict between Religion and Science*, referred to under the 'warfare model' in Chapter 3.

Bishop Samuel Wilberforce, third son of the anti-slavery campaigner, William Wilberforce, was called upon to speak. Darwin's Cambridge mentor, John Henslow, took the chair; Darwin remained at Richmond, in poor health. 'Soapy Sam', as the bishop was called, explained his nickname by saying 'You see I am always in hot water and always come out with clean hands'.[33] The bishop was not a popular person and his slippery debating skills were the real reason for his nickname. However, he was 'not so soapy'[34] and, as an ardent naturalist, had reviewed the *Origin* for the *Quarterly Review*. The review was published in the month after the Oxford debate. Darwin himself referred to Wilberforce's critique as 'uncommonly clever; it picks out with skill all the most conjectural parts, and brings forward well all the difficulties'.[35] At the time, many good scientific reasons could be given for not accepting Darwin's theory, something which Darwin himself realised. He kept a list of these objections and tried to answer them.

Wilberforce's summary of his review paints a different picture to the popular one of an obscurantist bishop opposing science for religious reasons:

> we have objected to the views with which we are dealing solely on scientific grounds. We have done so from the fixed conviction that it is thus that the truth or falsehood of such arguments should be tried. We have no sympathy with those who object to any facts or alleged facts in nature, or to any inference logically deduced from them, because they believe them to contradict what it appears to them is taught by Revelation. We think that all such objections savour of a timidity which is really inconsistent with a firm and well-intrusted faith.[36]

The bishop spoke for about half an hour and almost certainly used arguments from his review in the debate. He had also probably been primed by Owen, some say inadequately, since Owen stayed with him the previous night. But Wilberforce committed what was seen by many as a social *gaffe*. It may simply have been a follow-on from Huxley's comment two days earlier that churchmen 'had nothing to fear even should it be shown that apes were their ancestors'.[37] But his flippant question as to 'whether Huxley was related by his grandfather's or grandmother's side to an Ape' (different accounts vary slightly), stung Huxley into action. Two months later, he wrote down what he *thought* he had said in reply:

> If then, said I, the question is put to me would I rather have a miserable ape for a grandfather or a man highly endowed by nature and possessed of great means and influence and yet who employs those faculties for the mere purpose of introducing ridicule into a grave scientific discussion – I unhesitatingly affirm my preference for the ape.[38]

'Storm in a Victorian teacup'?

There is some doubt about Huxley's audibility. Joseph Hooker, Assistant Director of Kew Gardens, was more fully reported in one journal than either Huxley or Wilberforce. But Huxley's name is the one associated with the episode. No official records of the meeting exist, most of the reports coming from Huxley's friends. A newspaper report suggests the exchange was not one-sided: 'One convert to Darwin's theory . . . was actually deconverted as he witnessed the debate!'[39] *The Athenæum's* summary was that Huxley and Wilberforce 'have each found foemen worthy of their steel, and made their charges and countercharges very much to their own satisfaction and the delight of their respective friends'.[40] Both parties, in later correspondence, spoke as though they won the 'debate' and their relationship remained civil:

> It is a significant fact that the famous clash between Huxley and the Bishop was not reported by a single London newspaper at the time, and that of the few weekly reviews that mentioned it none brought out the force of Huxley's remark.[41]

So, then, was the episode 'a storm in a Victorian teacup'?[42] Cantor's summary of the exchanges helps to demythologise

> the Huxley–Wilberforce confrontation in 1860. These opponents are now viewed as trading minor insults in the heat of debate and not as exemplifying the necessary conflict between science and religion. Moreover, in the latter nineteenth century Darwinian theory was not generally seen as antagonistic to scriptural religion.[43]

But despite this, the brief episode has become a legend.

A cultural myth

Among those who shared Huxley's views, any 'episcopophagous' ('bishop-eating' – Huxley's word!) encounter like the Oxford one, was both popular and symbolic. It symbolised a view of science and religion in conflict which one section of society wished to promote. The exchanges between Huxley and Wilberforce became elevated to a cultural myth, having tenuous contact points with history, as it has been endlessly manipulated to serve particular ends. Inconvenient details like the official sermon by Frederick Temple the day after the encounter get forgotten. It does not fit the legend to tell how another leading churchman supported Darwin's ideas and discerned God's activity in the laws of nature!

---

some myths need to be slain, not because they are unfashionable or fail to conform to contemporary ideologies, but because they are demonstrably false.

Colin Russell, Professor of History of Science and Technology at the Open University[44]

The potential value for classroom teaching of the 'legendary encounter' has been developed by Gauld.[45] But, at that time, the legend was developed for a very different purpose – as a weapon in another kind of Victorian struggle:

Struggle for cultural supremacy

The background of the Huxley–Wilberforce confrontation was one of a growing professionalism in science and the struggle for hegemony, or cultural supremacy. Contributions from outsiders like clerics were becoming less welcome, however keen such clerics might be as naturalists. A widespread dissatisfaction with Anglican privilege existed – Oxbridge's entry requirements, for example – something Huxley felt keenly after his own struggles to find a position within the scientific community. Huxley concluded his autobiography by declaring his 'untiring opposition to that ecclesiastical spirit, that clericalism, which in England, as everywhere else, and to whatever denomination it may belong, is the deadly enemy of science'.[46] Against this background, the potential of the 'legendary encounter' was exploited to the full by those who, in furtherance of their own ends of separating science from clerical interference, presented the episode as typical of the relationships between science and religion.

In this struggle, the concept of 'Nature' was spelt with a capital N and reified. Huxley, less scrupulous than Darwin in using the word, vested 'Dame Nature', as he called 'her', with attributes hitherto ascribed to God, a tactic eagerly copied by others since. The oddity of crediting *nature* (every physical thing there is) with planning and creating every physical thing there is, passed unnoticed. 'Dame Nature', like some ancient fertility goddess, had taken up residence, her maternal arms encompassing *Victorian scientific naturalism*.

The 'X-Club'

Among the alliances developed to promote *scientific naturalism* was the nine-man 'X-Club', founded in 1864. Eight, including Huxley, were Fellows of the Royal Society and three had been Presidents. Herbert Spencer, the author, was the only non-Fellow. They were a pressure group, 'of one mind on theological topics':[47]

Besides personal friendship, the bond that united us was devotion to science, pure and free, untrammelled by religious dogmas. Amongst ourselves there is perfect outspokenness, and no doubt opportunities will arise when concerted action on our part may be of service.[48]

Opportunities certainly did arise and Russell traces their strategy for promoting the *conflict thesis* as outlined in the box on page 126.[49] The perceived 'enemy' was not primarily religion or even the established church *per se*, but the church or its representatives *when they dared to interfere with science*:

In their bitter battles for scientific hegemony the Victorian scientific naturalists fought largely in vain. But in establishing their myth of an enduring conflict between religion and science they were successful beyond their wildest expectations.[50]

From one vantage point, the 'storming of the citadel', by conspiring to have Darwin buried in Westminster Abbey, might appear to be the X-Club's great triumph, for

Darwin had stormed the holy of holies with a naturalistic creed . . . Like the mind gone out within, the body now served them well, in a last

Four military tactics for success

(i) They tried to *undermine the defences* of the opposition by taking every opportunity to pour scorn on the defenders of orthodoxy by magnifying temporary disagreements about Darwinism.

(ii) They took active steps to *repel invaders* by discouraging any attempts, as they saw it, for incursions by ecclesiastics into science.

(iii) They attempted to *steal the uniforms* of the enemy by invading the territory of religion in disguise. A Sunday Lecture Society imitated the role of the Sunday School; hymns to creation were sometimes sung; Huxley gave 'lay-sermons', spoke of 'the church scientific' and referred to himself as its 'Bishop'. The Natural History Museum, whose architecture reflects an ecclesiastical style has been called 'nature's cathedral'.

(iv) They managed to *storm the citadel* of established religion in a clever manœuvre by having the body of Darwin buried, not in Downe, where Darwin and his family wished, but in Westminster Abbey itself.

symbolic rite testifying to their authority, the extreme unction of a rising secularity. No less significance should be attached to the simple irony that Charles Darwin lies in Westminster Abbey.[51]

. . . but from another standpoint it was ironic in quite a different way – as the X-Club's great inconsistency, since

It is ironic that those who insisted that science needed no external legitimation should seek the recognition of the state church for their greatest hero, or saint. For in editorials and sermons throughout the country, Darwin was presented as a middle-class saint. His impartiality, moderation, patient industry, calmness and domestic happiness were models to all. The sermons confirmed the consistency of Faith and Science, of Evolution and 'ancient belief' . . .

It was an irony of which they seemed unaware, that the greatest symbolic achievement of the X-Club was not the separation of theology from science, but a conflation of science, church and state in Darwin's burial in Westminster Abbey.[52]

Part 2. Evolutionary issues

The legendary nature of the conflict thesis does not mean evolution raised no religious questions. It did, and scholarly debate is very much alive within *academe* today,[53] as the recent endowment of the *Starbridge Lectureship in Theology and Natural Science*[54] at Cambridge indicates. Such issues also get raised in science classes and a likely one to surface is 'creationism'.

Creationism

The word 'creationism' obscures several distinct issues. The root word, *creation*, encountered in Chapter 5 as *bringing-into-being*, involves *some* process or other, whether creation concerns a universe or an entirely new design of car. The former may involve the processes of stellar, chemical and organic evolution; the latter the processes of automation. To present the *processes* of creation as alternative to the *act* of creation is to commit some kind of *category mistake*. Furthermore, it would be nonsense to deny agency in the *act* of creation, *because* the *processes* were understandable. It is patently obvious with respect to the car that the agency of car designers could not rationally be denied *because* automation was used.

Yet in a situation of similar logical form, it is sometimes claimed that divine agency was not at work in creating the world *because* evolutionary processes were involved. Even worse is the phrase, 'Evolution did it', in which evolution is reified and vested with the properties of a sentient agent. Imagine saying 'automation did it'! In any classroom discussion about creationism it needs to be made clear that, while evolution is incompatible with the idea of many separate creations of fully formed creatures – Special Creation – it *is* compatible with divine creation in general. Darwin himself made this point in a letter to Asa Gray: 'I can see no reason why a man, or other animal, may not have been expressly designed by an omniscient Creator, who foresaw every future event and consequence'.[55]

If 'creationists' were simply believers in divine

creation, then orthodox Jews, Moslems and Christians would all be 'creationists'. The word is unfortunate because it annexes *creation*, a word which others want to use, for a restricted interpretation of the Genesis text which, *in addition to* the root idea of bringing-into-being-by-God, insists on particular modes and timing. Of all the different forms of creationism[56] – and it is also an issue within Islamic education[57] – some variant of the *young Earth* kind is currently most likely to be encountered in the classroom.

With the revival of Flood geology[58] in Morris and Whitcomb's (1961) *The Genesis Flood*,[59] the 'young Earth' movement began campaigning in earnest, even though in the 1920s creationists happily conceded a great age. In general, *young Earth creationists* see the 'days' of Genesis as consecutive twenty-four hour periods, along with a belief that the Earth is a mere ten thousand years old, rather than about 4.6×10^9 years. The issue, however, cannot justifiably be presented as between 'evolution' and 'God' but between a short or lengthy time-scale.

A young Earth position commits its followers to reject huge areas of established biology, physics, geology and cosmology. While current science is not sacrosanct, the wholesale disruption of a vast, coherent picture to accommodate a particular reading of the Genesis text might suggest the interpretation is suspect. Problems are sometimes created by reading *into* the text (*eisegesis*) rather than determining the text's meaning (*exegesis*). For instance, 'kinds' in 'God created everything . . . according to their kinds', has been interpreted as 'species', necessitating a commitment to the *fixity of species*. But to superimpose the modern biological concept of *species* onto an ancient Hebrew word is to read the text through western scientific spectacles. 'According to their kinds' is probably simply saying the world is orderly, not capricious, so sheep have lambs rather than piglets. As in shadow-boxing, an imaginary opponent is created which someone then feels obliged to knock about. Vast amounts of time and energy have been expended trying to show *real* science supports a young Earth. I have examined the

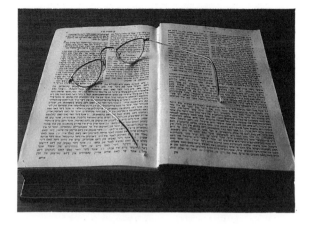

Fig. 7.6 Reading an ancient Hebrew text through western scientific spectacles

origins and status of much of this literature elsewhere,[60] and so have others, less sympathetically.[61]

However, despite inadequacies in a young Earth position, arguably on textual and scientific grounds, it will not do to dismiss its followers with a muttered, 'fundamentalists!' Creationists are making a sincere attempt to do justice to the meaning of an ancient text. Those who use 'fundamentalist' dismissively, like a theological swearword, overlook its historical roots. A series of tracts under the general title of *The Fundamentals* was published in America between 1910 and 1915, reasserting certain 'fundamental' doctrines of Protestant Christianity. 'Fundamentalist' was coined in 1920 by the editor of *The Watchman-Examiner*, as a term 'to be used in compliment and not in disparagement', to describe 'those who still cling to the great fundamentals'.[62] But, however ignorantly 'fundamentalist' is used today, it was not coined to describe mindless literalism. *Among the leading fundamentalists were those who accepted evolutionary biology.*

Evolutionism

If creationism is open to criticism, so too are some extravagant claims made for evolution which far exceed anything inherent in the biology – claims about progress towards moral perfection, ever onward and upward; claims about the justification of Capitalism, Communism and Nazism; claims that divine action is pushed out of the picture, and many others. Just as there is a distinction to be made between 'creation' and 'creationism', a clear distinction needs to be maintained between *evolution*, the biological theory, and *Evolution*ism, the philosophical system-building which has often been parasitic upon it.

Concern about the confusion between *evolution* and *Evolution*ism is not confined to religion. Indeed, from a secularist perspective, the philosopher, Anthony Flew, criticised the late Sir Julian Huxley, saying:

> There is, surely, something very odd, indeed pathetic, in Huxley's attempt to find in evolutionary biology 'something, not ourselves, which makes for righteousness'. For this quest is for him a search for something, not God, which does duty for Divine Providence. Yet if there really is no Divine Providence operating in the universe, then indeed there is none; and we cannot reasonably expect to find in the Godless workings of impersonal things those comfortable supports which – however mistakenly – believers usually think themselves entitled to derive from their theistic beliefs.[63]

At a British Society for the History of Science conference, commemorating the centenary of Darwin's death, Durant observed that:

> In the past, attempts to derive optimistic lessons from biology concerning the future of humankind have owed far more to prior religious or political convictions than they have to any independent insights derived from science; and as the case of Julian Huxley illustrates, this has been the case even where those involved have been major authorities on Darwinism. There is nothing in a scientific training, it would seem, that immunizes a person against their own prejudices.[64]

Sir Peter Medawar said in Huxley's obituary, 'so great was Huxley's enthusiasm for the idea of evolution that he came in his later years to treat evolutionism as a sort of secular religion'.[65] But it is not only Julian Huxley, among 'major authorities on Darwinism', who made these kinds of claims. The philosopher, Mary Midgley, has devoted a whole book to the phenomenon. *Evolution as a Religion: Strange Hopes and Stranger Fears*[66] is dedicated 'To the Memory of Charles Darwin Who Did Not Say These Things'.

It is precisely because one sometimes comes across the kind of teaching which led the sixth-former, quoted at the end of Chapter 1, to complain, 'Our biology teacher was an atheist and often implied that science has once for all disproved religion', that the foregoing points need making. The received views of biology and geology do not negate 'creation' and 'God' and it is important not to convey the impression they do. Darwin appreciated this point: 'In my most extreme fluctuations', he wrote, 'I have never been an Atheist in the sense of denying the existence of a God'.[67] A member of Charles' family was once asked to reply to a letter from a German student and say, 'He [Charles] considers that the theory of Evolution is quite compatible with the belief in a God; but that you must remember that different persons have different definitions of what they mean by God'.[68] So the statement made in a BBC schools biology series, that 'In his time, Darwin removed the idea of God as the Creator and gave a theory to enlightened and progressive thinkers',[69] was highly tendentious and ill-conceived. It is an example of bad practice in influential places.

Creationists have a legitimate complaint, Durant contends, when Evolution*ism* is wheeled in to make anti-religious capital:

> For much of the energy of the creationist movement arises from a sense of moral outrage at the advance of an evolution-centred world-view that has the audacity to parade its secular, liberal values as if they were the objective findings of science. Here at least, if not in matters of biological fact and theory, creationism has a point of which the scientific community might do well to take heed.[70]

Scientific naturalism

An example of what Durant refers to occurred in the 1991 Royal Institution Christmas Lectures.

The imaginative series, fascinatingly presented with the vast resources of the Royal Institution and the BBC, was given by Richard Dawkins, Reader in Zoology in the University of Oxford. But in addition to much excellent biological material, an intrusive anti-religious element was soon apparent, which was maintained throughout the five hours of programming.

My disquiet over these lectures was not simply concerning the philosophical *non sequiturs*, but over the way in which a world-view of *scientific naturalism* was promulgated to a philosophically untrained audience of young people as though it had secure foundations in science. Many were probably not in a position to assess the validity of the arguments, nor to know of alternative interpretations. As an educational series which involved controversial issues, it broke the conventional guidelines outlined in Chapter 1 and was another example of bad practice in influential places. The alleged implications of 'Growing up in the universe' – the title of the series – was baldly stated in the first of the programmes:

> Growing up in the universe . . . also means growing out of parochial and supernatural views of the universe, growing up to a proper scientific understanding of the universe, based upon evidence – public argument – rather than authority, or tradition or private revelation. Growing up means trying to understand how the universe works, not copping out with superstitious ideas that only seem to explain things but actually explain nothing.

From the start, the confusion between different compatible types of explanation, referred to in Chapter 5, was in evidence. Science alone was presented as omnicompetent to answer the whole range of questions which can be asked about life:

> So where does life come from? What is it? Why are we here? What are we for? What *is* the meaning of life? There's a conventional wisdom which says that science has nothing to say about such questions. Well all I can say is that if *science* has nothing to say, it's certain that no other discipline can say anything at all.

Argument from design?

The series appropriately included a look at the question of design in nature. William Paley, whose treatise on Natural Theology (1802) was studied by Darwin at Cambridge, said that if he found a stone on a heath he would attach no significance to it, but that if he found a watch he would conclude that he had found something that was designed for a purpose. So far, so good. But Paley then went on to argue from analogy – a perilous procedure – that, because a designed object like a watch points to a watchmaker, a world which bears many signs of apparent design must indicate the existence of God. Now while the person who already believes in God will see many signs of divine purpose and design in the world, Paley's analogical argument is logically faulty and does not drive the unconvinced person into a corner from which there is no escape. Dawkins recognised this *apparent* design, but then assured his audience it was not *actual* design, claiming to have 'explained it away' by natural selection.

> Living objects . . . look designed, they look overwhelmingly as though they're designed. But it's terribly, terribly tempting to use the word designed. Time and time again I have to bite my tongue and stop myself saying, for example, that this swift is designed for rapid, high speed, highly manoeuvrable flight and, as a matter of fact, when talking to other biologists, we none of us bother to bite our tongues. We just use the word designed. But I've told you that they are not designed and coined the special word 'designoid', and I said that there is a special process that brings designoid objects into existence and gives them their apparently designed look . . . [Lecture 2]

Dawkins rightly took creationists to task for claiming the eye is far too complex to have evolved. He described clearly, using excellent models, how variation plus natural selection can account for it. However, his assertion, 'I've told you that they are not designed', is one which goes beyond what the biology allows. Evolutionary theory certainly changed the Paleyean form of the design argument, but it did not banish the idea of design. People like Robert Chambers and Baden

Powell – and Darwin himself – saw evidence of design in the laws of nature rather than in specific adaptations.[71] Darwin experimented with 'his own variant of natural theology which was decidedly more positive than a mere negation of Paley'.[72]

Chance and randomness

Finally, on the subject of design, Dawkins' claim that the processes of *chance variations plus natural selection* rules out divine intelligence was negated by an interesting example he supplied himself in the second lecture. He told how 'Ingo Rechenberg from Germany . . . designs windmills and he claims that he designs his windmills by a kind of natural selection'. The process, which Dawkins referred to as 'Darwinian design' in the TV version of *The Blind Watchmaker*,[73] involves *randomising* certain parameters of aerofoil sections and discarding those which fail to meet chosen criteria. But here an intelligent agent is certainly employing *chance variations plus selection* in purposeful design. Dawkins too, as intelligent agent, employs *chance variations plus selection* in his fascinating computer program, *Biomorphs*, for the *purpose* of teaching the processes of evolution.

The distinction between the way the word 'chance' is used in popular speech and its meaning in technical language is beyond the scope of this present review and can be followed up elsewhere.[74] However, 'chance', along with 'nature' and 'natural selection', are not sentient agents which plan and *do* things. 'Chance' is often a subject for the 'fallacy of reification' – 'confusing a concept with a real object or cause'. The attendant problems can be light-heartedly illustrated, using the concept 'nobody', as does Lewis Carroll:

'I see nobody on the road', said Alice.
'I only wish *I* had such eyes', the King remarked in a fretful tone. 'To be able to see Nobody! And at that distance too! . . .'
'Who did you pass on the road?' the King went on, holding out his hand to the Messenger for some more hay.
'Nobody', said the Messenger.
'Quite right', said the King: 'this young lady saw him too. So of course Nobody walks slower than you'.
'I do my best', the Messenger said in a sullen tone. 'I'm sure nobody walks much faster than I do!'
'He can't do that', said the King, 'or else he'd have been here first'.[75]

A concluding comment

Throughout my life I have enjoyed being both on the receiving and the giving end of science education. My own beliefs as to where science's metaphysical foundations lie will have been transparent. I have argued in this book that science should be neither deified, denigrated, nor forced into demise. Rather it should be promoted as a fascinating and worthwhile human endeavour practised by fallible people.

Notes and references

Preface

1 National Curriculum Council (1993) *Spiritual and Moral Development*. NCC Discussion Paper, p. 6. York, NCC.

2 Russell, C.A. (1974) 'Some approaches to the history of science', Unit 1, p. 9, Open University Course AMST 283, *Science and Belief: From Copernicus to Darwin*. Milton Keynes, Open University Press.

Chapter 1: 'Everyone needs Standards'

1 Bain, quoted in Braithwaite, R.B. (1967) 'The nature of believing'. In Phillips Griffiths, A. (ed.), *Knowledge and Belief*, p. 31. Oxford, Oxford University Press.

2 Stevenson, L. (1987) *Seven Theories of Human Nature*, 2nd ed. Oxford, Oxford University Press. Complementary to Stevenson's book is *Ideas of Human Nature* by Trigg, R. (1988) Oxford, Blackwell.

3 *Penguin Dictionary of Modern Quotations*, revised 1980, p. 108, cited from Readers Digest 1977.

4 Siddons, C. and Spurgin, B. (1990) 'Beliefs and values in science education', *Forum, School Science Review*, 72(259), 145f.

5 The particular meaning of rationalisation here is of 'the provision of plausible reasons to explain to oneself or others behaviour for which one's real motives are different and unknown or unconscious' (*Webster's Third New International Dictionary*, 1971).

6 Huxley, A. (1937) *Ends and Means*, p. 273. London, Chatto and Windus.

7 Haldane, J.B.S. (1932) *Possible Worlds and Other Essays*, p. 209. London, Chatto and Windus.

8 Trigg, R. (1993) *Rationality and Science: Can Science Explain Everything?*, pp. 219ff. Oxford, Blackwell.

9 Open University Course A381, *Science and Belief: From Darwin to Einstein*, Unit 1, pp. 6ff. Milton Keynes, Open University Press (1981).

10 The following points are developed in Cook, D. (1983) *The Moral Maze*, pp. 18ff. London, SPCK.

11 Bentham, J., *The Commonplace Book* (Works, x.142), 268, 20.

12 Reiss, M. (1993) *Science Education for a Pluralist Society* is a title in this series.

13 Mitchell, B. (1973) *The Justification of Religious Belief*. London, Macmillan.

14 Edel, A. (1955) *Ethical Judgement: The Use of Science in Ethics*, p. 16. Glencoe, IL, The Free Press.

15 Cranston, M. (1972) 'Toleration', *The Encyclopedia of Philosophy*, 8, 143.

16 To deny that 'the genesis of a proposition is at all times irrelevant to questions of its truth or falsity' is to commit the genetic fallacy.

17 Gould, S.J. (1980) 'Darwin's deceptive memories', *New Scientist*, 85, 1195, 579.

18 Ibid.

19 Sutton, C. (1992) *Words, Science and Learning*, p. 86. Buckingham, Open University Press.

20 Cited in Jeeves, M.A. (1976) *Psychology and Christianity: The View Both Ways*, p. 133. Leicester, Inter-Varsity Press.

21 Flew, A. (1985) *Thinking about Social Thinking: The Philosophy of the Social Sciences*, p. 165. Oxford, Blackwell.

22 James, W. (1960) *The Varieties of Religious Experience*, p. 58. London, Collins/Fontana.

23 Lukes, S. (1970) 'Some problems about rationality'.

In Wilson, B.R. (ed.), *Rationality*, p. 208. Oxford, Blackwell.

24 Ibid., 'criterion of rationality' – a rule specifying what would count as a reason for believing something (or acting).

25 Ibid., p. 210.

26 Midgley, M. (1991) *Can't We Make Moral Judgements?*, p. 84. Bedminster, Bristol Press.

27 Bridges, D. (1986) 'Dealing with controversy in the curriculum: A philosophical perspective'. In Wellington, J.J. (ed.), *Controversial Issues in the Curriculum*, p. 33. Oxford, Blackwell.

28 Clark, C. (1981) 'The sociology of knowledge, what it is and what it is not', *Oxford Review of Education*, **7**(2), 148.

29 Wellington, op. cit., p. 1.

30 Bailey, C. (1975) 'Neutrality and rationality in teaching'. In Bridges, D. and Scrimshaw, P. (eds), *Values and Authority in Schools*, p. 122. London, Hodder and Stoughton.

31 Dearden, R.F. (1981) 'Controversial issues and the curriculum', *Journal of Curriculum Studies*, **13**(1), 38.

32 Ibid.

33 Gardner, P. (1984) 'Another look at controversial issues and the curriculum', *Journal of Curriculum Studies*, **16**(4), 381.

34 Warnock, M. (1975) 'The neutral teacher'. In Brown, S.C. (ed.), *Philosophers Discuss Education*, p. 169. London, Macmillan (cited in Gardner, op. cit.).

35 Gardner, op. cit., p. 384.

36 Stenhouse, L. (1970) *The Humanities Curriculum Project: An Introduction*, p. 6, London, Heinemann and, identically, in Ruddock, J. (1983) *The Humanities Curriculum Project*, p. 11. London, Schools Council.

37 Ibid., p. 10.

38 Dearden, op. cit., p. 40.

39 Stenhouse, op. cit., p. 6.

40 Dearden, op. cit., p. 37.

41 Bridges, op. cit., p. 21.

42 Stradling, R., Noctor, M. and Baines, B. (1984) *Teaching Controversial Issues*, pp. 3f. London, Edward Arnold.

43 Ibid., p. 6.

44 Stenhouse, op. cit., p. 7.

45 Stradling *et al.*, op. cit., p. 8.

46 Hulmes, E. (1979) *Commitment and Neutrality in Religious Education*, p. 9. London, Geoffrey Chapman.

47 In addition to those already cited, *The Teaching of CONTROVERSIAL ISSUES in Schools*, Advice from the Inspectorate, ILEA (undated).

48 Bridges, op. cit., pp. 24–36.

49 Reiss, M.J. (1992) 'How should science teachers teach the relationship between science and religion?', *Forum, School Science Review*, **74**(267), 126–9 and op cit., pp. 53–7.

50 Snook, I.A. (1975) *Indoctrination and Education*, p. 17. London, Routledge and Kegan Paul.

51 Snook, op. cit., p. 47.

52 Hulmes, op. cit., p. 8.

53 Mitchell, B. (1970) 'Indoctrination', *The Fourth R*, p. 355. London, National Society/SPCK.

54 Moore, W. (1965–6) 'Indoctrination as a normative conception', *Studies in Philosophy and Education*, **IV**(4), 402.

Chapter 2: 'What science cannot discover, mankind cannot know'

1 Hoffman, B. (1972) *Albert Einstein: Creator and Rebel*, p. 18. Viking, New York.

2 Polkinghorne, J. (1988) *Science and Creation*, p. xi. London, SPCK.

3 Whitehead, A.N. (1975) *Science and the Modern World*, p. 24. Glasgow, Collins.

4 Graham, L.R. (1981) *Between Science and Values*. Guildford, Columbia University Press.

5 Weinberg, S. (1993) *Dreams of a Final Theory*, pp. 141f. London, Hutchinson Radius.

6 Russell, B. (1970–2) *Religion and Science*, p. 243. Oxford, Oxford University Press.

7 Ayer, A.J. (1974) *Language, Truth and Logic*, 2nd ed., p. 12. Harmondsworth, Penguin.

8 Popper, K.R. (1959) *The Logic of Scientific Discovery*, p. 36. London, Hutchinson.

9 For example, in Stanesby, D. (1985) *Science, Reason & Religion*, pp. 28ff. London, Croom Helm.

10 Wittgenstein, L. (1968) *Philosophical Investigations* (trans. G.E.M. Anscombe), 3rd ed., pp. 51^e and 19^e. Oxford, Blackwell.

11 Atkins, P. (1992) 'Will science ever fail?', *New Scientist*, 1833, 8 August, pp. 33f.

12 Dawkins, R. (1991) *Growing Up in the Universe*, 1991 Royal Institution Christmas Lectures, Lecture 1, 'Waking up in the universe'.

13 Medawar, P. (1986) *The Limits of Science*, pp. 59f. Oxford, Oxford University Press.

14 Midgley, M. (1992) 'Can science save its soul?', *New Scientist*, 1832, 1 August, p. 26.

15 Office for Standards in Education (1993) (Including May 1994 supplementary material) *Handbook for the Inspection of Schools, Part 4: Guidance on the Inspection Schedule*, p. 17. London, HMSO.

16 Ibid., p. 86.

17 Ibid., *Part 2: Framework for the Inspection of Schools*, p. 21.

18 In addition to examples given in this book, other materials relating to the spiritual and moral dimensions of science education are given in Gosling, D. and Musschenga, B. (eds) (1985) *Science Education and Ethical Values*, Washington, Georgetown University Press, and in Frazer, M.J. and Kornhauser, A. (eds) (1986) *Ethics and Social Responsibility in Science Education*. Oxford, Pergamon Press.

19 Clifton, R.K. and Regehr, M.G. (1989) 'Capra on eastern mysticism and modern physics: A critique', *Science and Christian Belief*, 1(1), 53–74.

20 Speech to a Consultation at Westhill College on *Inspecting Pupils' Moral and Spiritual Development*, January 1993, by Professor Stewart Sutherland, H.M. Chief Inspector of Schools.

21 Flew, A. (1985) *Thinking about Social Thinking: The Philosophy of the Social Sciences*, p. 153. Oxford, Blackwell.

22 Trigg, R. (1989) *Reality at Risk*, 2nd ed., p. 139. Brighton, Harvester Press.

23 Barbour, I.G. (1974) *Myths, Models and Paradigms*, p. 37. London, SCM Press.

24 Helm, P. (1987) 'Why be objective?' In Helm, P. (ed.), *Objective Knowledge: A Christian Perspective*, p. 33. Leicester, Inter-Varsity Press.

25 Flew, op. cit., p. 143.

26 Dex, S. (1987) 'Objective facts in social science'. In Helm (ed.), op. cit., p. 179f.

27 Kuhn, T.S. (1962) *The Structure of Scientific Revolutions*, 2nd ed. (enlarged, 1970a). Chicago, IL, University of Chicago Press.

28 Masterman, M. (1970) 'The Nature of a Paradigm'. In Lakatos, I. and Musgrave, A. (eds) *Criticism and the Growth of Knowledge*, p. 61. Cambridge, Cambridge University Press.

29 The *perihelion* of Mercury is the point in its orbit at which it is closest to the sun. *Precession* is the slow gyration of the rotation axis of a spinning body, readily observed in a spinning top.

30 Siegel, H. (1980) 'Objectivity, rationality, incommensurability, and more', *British Journal for the Philosophy of Science*, 31, 361.

31 Kuhn, op. cit. (1970a), p. 204.

32 Kuhn, T.S. (1970b) 'Reflections on my critics'. In Lakatos and Musgrave (eds), op. cit., p. 234.

33 Siegel, op. cit., p. 366.

34 Kuhn's relativist claims lead relentlessly to the 'anarchistic theory of knowledge' developed in Feyerabend, P. (1975) *Against Method*. London, New Left Books.

35 Driver, R. (1989) 'The construction of scientific knowledge in school classrooms'. In Millar, R. (ed.), *Doing Science: Images of Science in Science Education*, p. 85. London, Falmer Press.

36 Driver, R. and Oldham, V. (1986) 'A constructivist approach to curriculum development in science', *Studies in Science Education*, 13, 106.

37 Matthews, M.R. (1992) 'Constructivism and empiricism: An incomplete divorce', *Research in Science Education*, 22, 303.

38 Millar, R. and Driver, R. (1987) 'Beyond processes', *Studies in Science Education*, 14, 57.

39 Russell, T. and Munby, H. (1989) 'Science as a discipline, science as seen by students and teachers' professional knowledge'. In Millar (ed.), op. cit., p. 85.

40 Ernst von Glasersfeld is one of constructivism's leading exponents. See his (1989) 'Cognition, construction of knowledge, and teaching', *Synthese*, 80(1), 122 and a critique of his position in Suchting, W.A. (1992) 'Constructivism deconstructed', *Science and Education*, 1(3), 223–54. Glasersfeld's reply is given in the following issue of the same journal.

41 Driver and Oldham, op. cit., p. 109.

42 See Harré, R. (1986) *Varieties of Realism*. Oxford, Blackwell.

43 Millar, R. (1989) 'Bending the evidence: The relationship between theory and experiment in science education'. In Millar (ed.), op. cit., p. 56.

44 It might simply refer to the truism that it is all-too-easy to get pupils to trot out the answer required for examinations without understanding it. But it is unclear from the passage.

45 Hawking, S.W. (1993) *Black Holes and Baby Universes and Other Essays*, p. 10. London, Bantam Books.

46 Matthews, op. cit., p. 305.

Chapter 3: 'Every comparison has a limp'

1 Lovelock, J. (1991) *The Ages of Gaia: A Biography*

of Our Living Earth, p. 27. Oxford, Oxford University Press.

2 *Virtuoso* – an experimenter or investigator in the arts or sciences.

3 See *Association for Science Education*, (1994) *Models and Modelling in Science Education*. Hatfield, ASE.

4 Sutton, C. (1992) *Words, Science and Learning*. Buckingham, Open University Press.

5 Bloch, F. (1976) 'Heisenberg and the early days of quantum mechanics', *Physics Today*, December, p. 27.

6 Sutton, C. (1993) 'Recovering the voice of the scientist', p. 10. Paper for the *Conference on Science Education in Developing Countries*, Jerusalem, 3–8 January.

7 Lovelock, J. (1986) 'Gaia: The world as living organism', *New Scientist*, 18 December, p. 28.

8 Barbour, I.G. (1974) *Myths, Models and Paradigms*, p. 6. London, SCM Press.

9 Honey, J. N. (1988) 'Models in biology, form and function', *Journal of Biological Education*, **22**(4), 295–300.

10 Barbour, op. cit.

11 Black, M. (1962) *Models and Metaphors, Studies in Language and Philosophy*. Ithaca, NY, Cornell University Press.

12 For example, Harré,R. (1967) *An Introduction to the Logic of the Sciences*, pp. 86ff. London, Macmillan.

13 Hesse, M.B. (1953) 'Models in physics', *British Journal for the Philosophy of Science*, **15**, 198–214; Hesse, M.B. (1966) *Models and Analogies in Science*. Indiana, University of Notre Dame Press.

14 Ramsey, I.T. (1964) *Models and Mystery*. Oxford, Oxford University Press; Ramsey, I.T. (1973) *Models for Divine Activity*. London, SCM Press.

15 Hutten, E.H. (1954) 'The role of models in physics', *British Journal for the Philosophy of Science*, **4**, 285f.

16 Thomson, W. [Lord Kelvin] (1904) Baltimore Lectures, p. 187. Baltimore, MD, Johns Hopkins University Press.

17 Toulmin, S. (1969) *The Philosophy of Science*, p. 94. London, Hutchinson.

18 Popper, K.R. (1974) *The Logic of Scientific Discovery*, p. 111. London, Hutchinson.

19 Barbour, op. cit., pp. 6f.

20 Sutton (1993), op. cit., p. 4.

21 Black, op. cit., p. 49.

22 Ramsey (1964), op. cit., pp. 14f.

23 Woods, G.F. (1966) 'The idea of the transcendent'. In *Soundings*, p. 51. Cambridge, Cambridge University Press.

24 Cited in Mendoza, E. (1974) *A Random Walk in Physics*, compiled by R.L. Weber, pp. 13f. London, Institute of Physics.

25 Ramsey (1964), op. cit., p. 48.

26 Hesse (1966), op. cit., p. 162.

27 Braithwaite, R.B. (1968) *Scientific Explanation*, pp. 93f. Cambridge, Cambridge University Press.

28 Passmore, J. (1972) 'Robert Boyle', *The Encyclopedia of Philosophy*, Vol. 1, p. 359. London, Collier Macmillan.

29 Brooke, J.H. (1991) *Science and Religion: Some Historical Perspectives*, p. 143. Cambridge, Cambridge University Press.

30 *The Encyclopedia of Philosophy* (1972), Vol. 1, p. 286. London, Collier Macmillan.

31 Cited in Scott, W.L. (1970) *The Conflict Between Atomism and Conservation Theory 1644–1860*, p. 5. London, Macdonald.

32 Brooke (1991), op. cit., p. 119.

33 Monod, J. (1974) *Chance and Necessity*, p. 167. Glasgow, Collins/Fontana.

34 Hooykaas, R. (1974) 'The impact of the Copernican transformation', Unit 2, p. 78, Open University Course AMST 283, *Science and Belief: From Copernicus to Darwin*. Milton Keynes, Open University Press.

35 Kepler, cited in Brooke (1991), op. cit., p. 120.

36 Brooke (1991), op. cit., pp. 119f.

37 Nelkin, D. (1976) 'The science-textbook controversies', *Scientific American*, **234**(4), 34.

38 National Curriculum Council (1993) *Spiritual and Moral Development – A Discussion Paper*, p. 6. York, NCC.

39 Darwin, C. (1906) *The Origin of Species* (6th [last] ed.), pp. 102f. London, John Murray.

40 Darwin's metaphor has been examined in a lengthy article: Young, R.M. (1971) 'Darwin's metaphor, does nature select?', *The Monist*, **55**, 442–503.

41 Iverach, J. (1894) *Christianity and Evolution*, p. 121. London, Hodder and Stoughton, cited in Moore, J.R. (1979) *The Post-Darwinian Controversies*, p. 256. Cambridge, Cambridge University Press.

42 1991 Royal Institution Christmas Lectures, 'Growing Up in the Universe', by Dr Richard Dawkins, BBC2, 2nd lecture, *Designed and designoid objects*.

43 Darwin, C., op. cit., p. 99.

44 '. . . "fallacy of reification" . . . confusing a concept

with a real object or cause'. Beck, L.W. (1952) *Philosophic Enquiry*, p. 35. Englewood Cliffs, NJ, Prentice-Hall.

45 Darwin, C. op. cit., p. 656.

46 Brooke, J.H. (1974) 'Natural theology in Britain from Boyle to Paley', Unit 9, p. 8. Open University Course AMST 283, *Science and Belief: From Copernicus to Darwin*. Milton Keynes, Open University Press.

47 Darwin, C., op. cit., p. 663.

48 Kingsley, F. (1877) *Charles Kingsley, His Letters and Memories of His Life*, Vol. 2, p. 171. London, cited in Meadows, A.J. (1975) 'Kingsley's attitude to science', *Theology*, LXXVIII(655), 20.

49 Moore, A.L. (1843–1890), cited in Moore, J.R., op. cit., pp. 263f.

50 Temple, W.F. (1885) *The Relations Between Religion and Science*, pp. 114f. The Bampton Lectures for 1884, London, Macmillan.

51 Kingsley, C. (1889) *The Water-Babies*, pp. 272f. London, Macmillan.

52 Darwin, C., op. cit., p. 658.

53 A detailed study of this subject appears in Livingstone, D.N. (1987) *Darwin's Forgotten Defenders*. Edinburgh, Scottish Academic Press/Eerdmans.

54 Darwin, F. (ed.) (1958) *The Autobiography of Charles and Selected Letters*, p. 66. New York, Dover.

55 Ibid., p. 67.

56 Moore, J.R., op. cit., pp. 274–6 and 292.

57 Dawkins, R. (1982) *The Extended Phenotype*, p. 15. Oxford, Oxford University Press.

58 Dawkins, R. (1989) *The Selfish Gene*, 2nd ed., p. 88. Oxford, Oxford University Press.

59 Midgley, M. (1983) 'Selfish genes and social Darwinism', *Philosophy*, 58, 369.

60 Dawkins, R. (1981) 'In defence of selfish genes', *Philosophy*, 56, 557.

61 I have examined Dawkins' world-view in 'A critique of aspects of the philosophy and theology of Richard Dawkins', *Science and Christian Belief*, 6(1), 41–59.

62 Op cit., National Curriculum Council.

63 *Growing Up in the Universe* (1991) BBC Study Guide to the Christmas Lectures, p. 21. London, BBC Education.

64 Cantor, G. (1991) *Michael Faraday, Sandemanian and Scientist*, p. 290. Basingstoke, Macmillan.

65 Draper, J.W. (1875) *History of the Conflict Between Religion and Science*. London, King and Co.

66 White, A.D. (1895) *A History of the Warfare of Science With Theology in Christendom*. London, Macmillan.

67 See, for example, Brooke (1991), op. cit., p. 35; Russell, C.A. (1985) *Cross-currents: Interactions Between Science and Faith*, p. 193. Leicester, Inter-Varsity Press; and Cantor, op. cit., p. 290.

68 Butterfield, H. (1973) *The Origins of Modern Science 1300–1800*, p. vii. London, Bell.

Chapter 4: 'Wanted! Alive or dead'

1 White, L., Jr. (1967) 'The historical roots of our ecologic crisis', *Science*, 155, 1205.

2 Not of course denying the world *contains* living and non-living things.

3 Collingwood, R.G. (1965) *The Idea of Nature*, p. 5. Oxford, Clarendon Press. He refers to the *Post-Renaissance* view as the 'Renaissance' view, for brevity.

4 Ibid., pp. 8f.

5 Flew, A.G.N. (1970) *Evolutionary Ethics*, p. 15. London, Macmillan.

6 Hooykaas, R. (1972) *Religion and the Rise of Modern Science*, Ch. 1. Edinburgh, Scottish Academic Press.

7 Ibid., p. 15.

8 Ibid., pp. 18f.

9 Atkins, P.W. (1981) *The Creation*, p. 17. Oxford, W.H. Freeman.

10 Brooke, J.H. (1991) *Science and Religion: Some Historical Perspectives*, p. 118. Cambridge, Cambridge University Press.

11 White, op. cit., p. 1205.

12 Prance, G., 'The environmental crisis: A challenge to the Judeo-Christian faith', unpublished paper, pp. 7f.

13 Passmore, J. (1974) *Man's Responsibility for Nature*, p. 15. London, Duckworth.

14 For example, Berry, R.J. (1991) 'Christianity and the environment: Escapist mysticism or responsible stewardship', *Science and Christian Belief*, 3(1), 3–14.

15 White, op. cit., p. 1207.

16 Ibid., p. 1206.

17 Lucas, E. (1992) 'A short introduction to the New Age movement', *Science and Christian Belief*, 4(1), 4.

18 Capra, F. (1975) *The Tao of Physics*. Aldershot,

Wildwood House; Zukav, G. (1979) *The Dancing Wu Li Masters*. London, Rider/Hutchinson.

19 Lucas, E. (1992) 'Scientific truth and New Age thinking', *Science and Christian Belief*, **4**(1), 18f.

20 Phillips, M. (1993) 'Don't damn the Pope out of hand', *The Observer*, 10 October.

21 Lovelock, J. (1986) 'Gaia: The world as living organism', *New Scientist*, 18 December, p. 25.

22 This usage for Gaia adopted from Russell, C.A. (1994) *The Earth, Humanity and God*, p. 117. London, UCL Press. The *Final Form* gets its name from the Aristotelian term 'Final Causes', which expresses a teleological idea of purpose and ends.

23 Lovelock, J. (1991) *The Ages of Gaia: A Biography of Our Living Earth*, p. 8. Oxford, Oxford University Press.

24 Ibid., p. 16.

25 Ibid.

26 Ibid., pp. 17f.

27 Teleology is the theory of purpose in nature by which certain phenomena appear best explained, not in terms of prior causes, but in terms of ends, purposes, aims or intentions.

28 Russell, op. cit., pp. 99ff.

29 Lovelock (1991), op. cit., p. 203.

30 Ibid., pp. 206, 222f.

31 Ibid., p. 218.

32 *Biota*: living things.

33 Lovelock (1991), op. cit., p. 19.

34 Ibid., p. 11 .

35 Deane-Drummond, C. (1993) *Gaia and Green Ethics*, p. 10. Nottingham, Grove Books.

36 Lovelock (1991), op. cit., p. 205.

37 Ibid., p. 33.

38 Ibid., p. 39.

39 Ibid., pp. 35ff.

40 Ibid., p. 212.

41 Russell, op. cit., p. 124f.

42 Cited in Brooke, J.H. (1991) 'Indications of a creator: Whewell as apologist and priest'. In Fisch, M. and Schaffer, S. (eds), *William Whewell: A Composite Portrait*, p. 151. Oxford, Clarendon Press.

43 Desmond, A and Moore, J. (1992) *Darwin*, p. 477. London, Penguin.

44 Dawkins R. (1991) *Growing Up in the Universe*, BBC Study Guide to the Royal Institution Christmas lectures, p. 11. London, BBC Education.

45 Deane-Drummond, C. (1992) 'God and Gaia: Myth or reality?', *Theology*, **95**, 283.

46 Lovelock (1991), op. cit., p. 212.

47 Postgate, J. (1988) 'Gaia gets too big for her boots', *New Scientist*, 7 April, p. 60.

48 Cited in Matthews, M.R. (1992) 'Constructivism and empiricism: An incomplete divorce', *Research in Science Education*, **22**, 300.

49 Brooke, J.H. (1991) *Science and Religion: Some Historical Perspectives*, p. 77. Cambridge, Cambridge University Press.

50 Bruce, F.F. (1977) 'The history of New Testament study'. In Marshall, I. (ed.), *New Testament Interpretation*, p. 52. Exeter, Paternoster Press.

51 Term used by Colin Russell on Radio 4's 'Start the Week' on 21 March 1994 at the start of Science, Engineering and Technology Week.

Chapter 5: 'In the beginning . . .'

1 Hawking, S.W. (1989) *A Brief History of Time*, p. 175. London, Bantam Press.

2 Hawking, S.W. (1993) *Black Holes and Baby Universes and Other Essays*, p. 37. London, Bantam Press.

3 Davies, P.C.W. (1992) *The Mind of God*. London, Simon and Schuster.

4 22 May 1992.

5 Gribbin, J. (1979) 'Taking the lid off cosmology', *New Scientist*, **83**, 506.

6 Silk, J. (1992) 'Cosmology back to the beginning', *Nature*, **356**(6372), 741f.

7 *The Times Higher Education Supplement*, 8 May 1992, p. 6.

8 McKie, R. (1992) *The Observer*, 17 May.

9 Office for Standards in Education (1993) *Handbook for the Inspection of Schools, Part 2: Framework for the Inspection of Schools*, p. 21. London, HMSO.

10 Monod, J. (1974) *Chance and Necessity*, p. 137. Glasgow, Collins/Fontana.

11 Atkins, P.W. (1992) *Creation Revisited*, p. 41. Oxford, W.H. Freeman.

12 Trigg, R. (1993) *Rationality and Science: Can Science Explain Everything?* Oxford, Blackwell.

13 Bondi, H. and Gold, T. (1948) 'The steady-state theory of the expanding universe', *Monthly Notices of the Royal Astronomical Society*, **108**(3), 252–70.

14 Mascall, E.L. (1956) *Christian Theology and Natural Science*, p. 162. London, Longmans, Green and Co.

15 Jaki, S.L. (1974) *Science and Creation*, pp. 336ff. Edinburgh, Scottish Academic Press.

16 McMullin, E. (1981) 'How should cosmology relate

to theology?' In Peacocke, A.R. (ed.), *The Sciences and Theology in the Twentieth Century*, p. 34. Stocksfield, Oriel Press.

17 Ibid., pp. 30ff.

18 Hawking (1989), op. cit., pp. 140f.

19 Mascall, op. cit., p. 135.

20 Atkins (1992), op. cit., p. 149.

21 The physics, in a form suitable for classroom use, is in Stannard, R. (1993) *Doing Away With God? Creation and the Big Bang*, Ch. 5. London, Marshall Pickering.

22 A *category mistake* is made if what can only appropriately be said about something in one category is said about something in another. For the original use of Gilbert Ryle's term, see his (1963) *The Concept of Mind*, pp. 17ff. Harmondsworth, Penguin.

23 Gribbin, J. (1986) *In Search of the Big Bang*, p. 392. Toronto, Bantam Books.

24 Hawking (1989), op. cit., p. x.

25 Atkins, P.W. (1981) *The Creation*, p. vii. Oxford, W.H. Freeman.

26 Flew, A. (1985) *Thinking About Social Thinking: The Philosophy of the Social Sciences*, p. 40. Oxford, Blackwell.

27 Brown, G.A. and Atkins, M.J. (1986) 'Explaining in professional contexts', *Research Papers in Education*, **1**(1), 60–86.

28 Ibid., p. 63.

29 Poole, M.W. (1995) *A Guide to Science and Belief*, 2nd edn. p. 37. Oxford, Lion Publishing.

30 Ennis, R.H. (1969) *Logic in Teaching*, p. 281. Englewood Cliffs, NJ, Prentice-Hall.

31 Goodlad, J.S.R. (1973) *Science for Non-scientists*, p. 24. Oxford, Oxford University Press.

32 Pilkington, R. (1961) *World Without End*, p. 12. Glasgow, Colins/Fontana.

33 Coulson, C.A. (1955) *Science and Religion: A Changing Relationship*, p. 7. Cambridge, Cambridge University Press.

34 Weber, R. (1990) *Dialogues with Scientists and Sages*, p. 209. London, Penguin/Arkana.

35 Gribbin, J. (1986) 'In the beginning, perhaps there was God', *The Guardian*, 25 April, p. 16.

36 Ayala, F.J. and Dobzhansky, T. (eds) (1974) *Studies in the Philosophy of Biology: Reduction and Related Problems*, p. ix. London, Macmillan. See also Peacocke, A.R. (1976) 'Reductionism: A review of the epistemological issues and their relevance to biology and the problem of consciousness', *Zygon*, **11**(4), 307–34.

37 Polanyi, M. (1967) *The Tacit Dimension*, pp. 29–52. London, Routledge and Kegan Paul.

38 MacKay, D.M. (1960) 'Man as a Mechanism', *Faith and Thought*, **91**(3), 149.

39 Milton, J., *Paradise Lost*, Book VIII, lines 90–4 and 122–5 (Raphael speaking to Adam).

40 Hooykaas, R. (1974) 'The impact of the Copernican transformation', Unit 2, p. 67, Open University Course AMST 283, *Science and Belief: From Copernicus to Darwin*. Milton Keynes, Open University Press.

41 Hummel, C.E. (1986) *The Galileo Connection*, p. 55. Leicester, Inter-Varsity Press.

42 Brooke, J.H. (1990) 'The Galileo affair: Teaching AT17', *Physics Education*, **25**(4), 201.

43 Hooykaas, op. cit., pp. 83ff.

44 Davies, P.C.W. (1984) *God and the New Physics*, pp. 29f. Harmondsworth, Penguin.

45 Barrow, J.D. (1992) *Theories of Everything*, p. 95. London, Vintage.

46 Hawking (1993), op. cit., p. 150.

47 Davies (1984), op. cit., p. 179.

48 Polkinghorne, J. (1986) *One World*, pp. 57f. London, SPCK.

49 Barrow, J.D. and Tipler, F.J. (1986) *The Anthropic Cosmological Principle*, p. 288. Oxford, Oxford University Press.

50 Ibid., p. 15.

51 Ibid., p. 16.

52 Ibid., p. 21.

53 Hoyle, F. (1959) *Religion and the Scientists*, p. 64. London, SCM Press. Cited in Barrow and Tipler, op. cit., p. 22.

54 Ibid., p. 22.

55 Ibid., p. 23.

56 A term borrowed from the theologian/philosopher Teilhard de Chardin.

57 Barrow and Tipler, op. cit., p. 677.

58 *Soul: The New Science and the Mind of God*, was a series of three 50-minute programmes, presented by Anthony Clare, broadcast on BBC2 during Holy Week, 1992.

59 Midgley, M. (1992) 'Free from the monster of science', *Life and Times*, 13 April, p. 1.

60 Gribbin, J. (1994) 'Is the Universe alive?', *New Scientist*, **141**, 40.

61 Atkins (1992), op. cit., pp. 153, 155.

62 Midgley, M. (1992) 'Can science save its soul?', *New Scientist*, **1832**, 1 August, p. 25.

63 Ibid., p. 24.

64 Atkins (1992), op. cit., p. 157.

Chapter 6: 'Publish and be damned'?

1 Brooke, J.H. (1990) 'The Galileo affair, teaching AT17', *Physics Education*, **25**(4), 198.
2 Koestler, A. (1969) *The Sleepwalkers*, p. 358. Harmondsworth, Penguin.
3 Honey, J.N. (1992) 'Progression in understanding history: Its effects upon understanding the nature of science', *Proceedings of the Second International Conference on the History and Philosophy of Science in Science Education*, pp. 507–16. Ontario, Queen's University.
4 Milton, J., *Paradise Lost*, Book VIII, lines 76–84 (Raphael speaking to Adam).
5 *A priori* reasoning [from what comes before] is reasoning carried out without reference to experience, as distinct from *a posteriori* reasoning [from what comes after] carried out only by referring to how, as a matter of contingent fact, things are.
6 Koestler, op. cit., pp. 59f., 77.
7 Milton, op. cit., lines 126–31 (Raphael speaking to Adam).
8 Kuhn, T. (1976) *The Copernican Revolution*, pp. 179f. Cambridge, MA, Harvard University Press.
9 Hooykaas, R. (1974) 'The impact of the Copernican transformation', Unit 2, p. 63, Open University Course AMST 283, *Science and Belief: From Copernicus to Darwin*. Milton Keynes, Open University Press.
10 Quoted by F.R. Johnson (1937) *Astronomical Thought in Renaissance England*, p. 207. Baltimore, MD, Johns Hopkins University Press, cited in Kuhn (1976) pp. 189f.
11 Brooke, op. cit., p. 199.
12 Watson, J.D. (1970) *The Double Helix*. Harmondsworth, Penguin.
13 Santillana, G. de (1958) *The Crime of Galileo*, p. 290. London, Heinemann.
14 Seeger, R.J. (1966) *Galileo Galilei, His Life and Works*, pp. 270–74, *passim*. Oxford, Pergamon Press.
15 Cited in Hooykass, op. cit., p. 62.
16 Ibid., p. 61.
17 Langford, J.J. (1971) *Galileo, Science and the Church*, p. 89. Ann Arbor, MI, University of Michigan Press.

18 Ibid., p. 89.
19 Ibid., pp. 102f.
20 Koestler, op. cit., p. 479.
21 Santillana, op. cit., p. 138.
22 Koestler, op. cit., p. 490.
23 Goodman, D.C. (1974) 'Galileo and the Church', Unit 3, p. 110, Open University Course AMST 283, *Science and Belief: From Copernicus to Darwin*. Milton Keynes, Open University Press.
24 Ibid., p. 120.
25 Santillana, op. cit., p. 241.
26 Koestler, op. cit., p. 493.
27 Santillana, op. cit., p. 255.
28 Ibid., p. 312.
29 Hesse, M. (1975) 'On the alleged incompatability between Christianity and science'. In Montefiore, H. (ed.), *Man and Nature*, pp. 122f. London, Collins.
30 Whitehead, A.N. (1975) *Science and the Modern World*, p. 218. Glasgow, Collins.
31 Brooke, op. cit., p. 199.
32 Hummel, C.E. (1986) *The Galileo Connection*, p. 116. Downers Grove, IL., Inter-Varsity Press.
33 Santillana, op. cit., p. xiif.
34 Koestler, op. cit., p. 432.
35 Hummel, op. cit., p. 113.
36 Santillana, op. cit., p. 98.
37 Brooke, op. cit., p. 197f.
38 Cantor, G. (1991) *Michael Faraday, Sandemanian and Scientist*, p. 290. Basingstoke, Macmillan.

Chapter 7: 'God knows what the public will think'

1 For accounts of the voyage, see Stanbury, D. (ed.) (1977) *A Narrative of the Voyage of H.M.S. Beagle*. London, The Folio Society; Moorehead, A. (1969) *Darwin and the Beagle*. Harmondsworth, Penguin.
2 Sulloway, F.J. (1984) 'Darwin and the Galapagos', *Biological Journal of the Linnean Society*, **21**, 42.
3 Ibid., p. 50.
4 Darwin, F. (ed.) (1958) *The Autobiography of Charles and Selected Letters*, p. 184. New York, Dover.
5 Gould, S.J. (1980) 'Darwin's deceptive memories', *New Scientist*, **85** (1195), 577.
6 de Beer, G. (ed.) (1974) *Charles Darwin: Thomas Henry Huxley, Autobiographies*, p. 71. London, Oxford University Press.
7 Gould, op. cit., p. 578.

8 Ibid.

9 Huelin, G. (1978) *King's College London 1828–1978*, pp. 1f. London, University of London, King's College.

10 Ibid., pp. 3f.

11 Ibid., p. 3.

12 *Natural theology* is taken as knowledge about God which human reason can acquire without the aid of revelation.

13 Darwin, F., op. cit., p. 196.

14 Cited in Berry, R.J. (1988) *God and Evolution*, p. 35. London, Hodder and Stoughton.

15 Bowler, P. (1990) *Charles Darwin: The Man and His Influence*, pp. 214ff. Oxford, Blackwell.

16 Act IV, Scene 1.

17 Sprat, T. (1667) *History of the Royal Society, London*, Cope and Jones, 1959 edition, pp. 58, 154. London, Routledge and Kegan Paul.

18 Augustine (*c*.410) *The City of God*, Book XI, Ch. VI.

19 Blocher, H. (1984) *In the Beginning* (trans. D.G. Preston), p. 57. Leicester, Inter-Varsity Press.

20 Hooykaas, R. (1974) 'Genesis and geology', Unit 11, p. 68, Open University Course AMST 283, *Science and Belief: From Copernicus to Darwin*. Milton Keynes, Open University Press.

21 Russell, C.A. (1985) *Cross-currents, Interactions between Science and Faith*, pp. 13ff. Leicester, Inter-Varsity Press.

22 Ibid., pp. 127ff.

23 Ibid., pp. 139.

24 Ibid.

25 Mason, S.F. (1962) *A History of the Sciences*, pp. 497f. New York, Macmillan.

26 Darwin, F., op. cit., pp. 221f.

27 10 February 1860.

28 Moore, J.R. (1979) *The Post-Darwinian Controversies*, pp. 88f. Cambridge, Cambridge University Press.

29 Livingstone, D.N. (1987) *Darwin's Forgotten Defenders*. Edinburgh, Scottish Academic Press/Eerdmans.

30 de Beer, op. cit., p. xiii.

31 For example, the 1978 BBC television series on Darwin.

32 For example, Lucas, J.R. (1979) 'Wilberforce and Huxley, a legendary encounter', *The Historical Journal*, **22**(2), 313–30; Jensen, J.V. (1988) 'Return to the Huxley–Wilberforce debate', *British Journal for the History of Science*, **21**, 161–79.

33 Raven, C. E. (1968) *Science, Religion, and the Future*, p. 41. Cambridge, Cambridge University Press.

34 Wrangham, R. (1979) 'The Bishop of Oxford, not so soapy', *New Scientist*, **83**, 450–51.

35 Lucas, op. cit., p. 320.

36 Ibid., p. 318.

37 Jensen, op. cit., p. 164.

38 Ibid., p. 168.

39 Brooke, J.H. (1991) *Science and Religion: Some Historical Perspectives*, p. 41. Cambridge, Cambridge University Press.

40 Ibid., p. 172.

41 Ellegard, A. (1958) 'Public opinion and the press, reactions to Darwinism', *Journal of the History of Ideas*, **19**, 380.

42 Raven, op. cit., pp. 33–50.

43 Cantor, G. (1991) *Michael Faraday, Sandemanian and Scientist*, p. 290. Basingstoke, Macmillan.

44 Russell, C.A. (1989) 'The conflict metaphor and its social origins', *Science and Christian Belief*, **1**(1), 3.

45 Gauld, C. (1992) 'Wilberforce, Huxley & the use of history in teaching about evolution', *The American Biology Teacher*, **54**(7), 406–10.

46 de Beer, op. cit., p. 109.

47 MacLeod, R.M. (1970) 'The X-Club: A social network of science in late Victorian England', *Notes and Records of the Royal Society of London*, **24**, 308.

48 Jensen, J.V. (1970) 'The X Club: Fraternity of Victorian Scientists', *British Journal for the History of Science*, **5**, 63.

49 Russell (1989), op. cit., pp. 14–18.

50 Ibid., p. 26.

51 Moore, J.R. (1982) 'Charles Darwin lies in Westminster Abbey', *Biological Journal of the Linnean Society*, **17**, 111.

52 Barton, R. (1990) '"An influential set of chaps": The X-Club and Royal Society politics 1864–85', *British Journal for the History of Science*, **23**, 78 and 81.

53 See Templeton Foundation (1992) *Who's Who in Theology and Science*. Winthrop Publishing Co.

54 Announced in *The Independent*, p. 7, 18 March 1993, 'Writer donates £1m to strike blow for theology'.

55 Cited in Brooke, J.H. (1985) 'The relations between Darwin's science and his religion'. In Durant, J. (ed.) *Darwinism and Divinity*, p. 56,. Oxford, Blackwell.

56 Numbers, R.L. (1992) *The Creationists*. New York, Alfred Knopf.

57 Mabud, S.A. (1986) 'Theory of evolution: An

assessment from the Islamic point of view', *Muslim Education Quarterly*, **4**(1), 9–56.

58 A response is given in Van de Fliert, J.R. (1969) 'Fundamentalism and the fundamentals of geology', *Journal of the American Scientific Affiliation*, **21**(3), 69–81.

59 Morris, H.M. and Whitcomb, J.C. (1961) *The Genesis Flood*. Philadelphia, PA, Presbyterian and Reformed Publishing Co.

60 Poole, M.W. and Wenham, G.J. (1987) *Creation or Evolution – A False Antithesis?*, Oxford, Latimer House.

61 Kitcher, P. (1983) *Abusing Science*. Milton Keynes, Open University Press; Montagu, A. (ed.) (1984) *Science and Creationism*. New York, Oxford University Press.

62 Laws, C.L. (1920) *The Watchman-Examiner*, **8**(27), 834, cited in 'The future of science and belief: Theological views in the twentieth century', Unit 15, p. 32, Open University Third Level Arts Course A381, *Science and Belief: From Darwin to Einstein*. Milton Keynes, Open University Press.

63 Flew, A.G.N. (1970) *Evolutionary Ethics*, p. 30. London, Macmillan.

64 Durant, op. cit., p. 33.

65 *Nature*, **254** (5495), p. 4, 6 March 1975.

66 Midgley, M. (1985) *Evolution as a Religion: Strange Hopes and Stranger Fears*. London, Methuen.

67 Brooke (1985), op. cit., p. 42.

68 Darwin, F. (ed.), op. cit., p. 61.

69 'A' Level Studies, Biology – Mechanisms of Change, Parts 1 & 2, BBC schools, Francis Hitching (narrator).

70 Durant, op. cit., p. 34.

71 Brooke (1985), op. cit., p. 45.

72 Ibid., p. 47.

73 *The Blind Watchmaker*, BBC 2 *Horizon*, 19 January 1987; book published by Longman, Harlow, 1986.

74 For example, Bartholomew, D.J. (1984) *God of Chance*. London, SCM Press; Peacocke, A.R. (1979) *Creation and the World of Science*, pp. 86–108. Oxford, Clarendon Press; MacKay, D.M. (1977) *Science, Chance and Providence*. Oxford, Oxford University Press.

75 Carroll, L. (1962) *Through the Looking Glass*, pp. 83ff. London, The Folio Society.

Index

PRACTICAL SCIENCE
THE ROLE AND REALITY OF PRACTICAL WORK IN SCHOOL SCIENCE

Brian Woolnough (ed.)

Science teaching is essentially a practical activity, with a long tradition of pupil experimental work in schools. And yet, there are still large and fundamental questions about its most appropriate role and the reality of what is actually achieved. What is the purpose of doing practical work? – to increase theoretical understanding or to develop practical competencies? What does it mean to be good at doing science? Do we have a valid model for genuine scientific activity? – and if so do we develop it by teaching the component skills or by giving experience in doing whole investigations? What is the relationship between theoretical understanding and practical performance? How significant is the tacit knowledge of the student, and the scientist, in achieving success in tackling a scientific problem? How important are such factors as motivation and commitment? What do we mean by transferability and progression in respect to practical work? – do they exist? – can they be defined? How can we assess a student's practical ability in a way which is valid and reliable and at the same time encourages, rather than destroys, good scientific practice in schools? This book addresses such questions.

By bringing together the latest insights and research findings from many of the world's leading science educators, new perspectives and guidelines are developed. It provides a re-affirmation of the vital importance of practical activity in science, centred on problem-solving investigations. It advocates the need for students to engage in whole practical tasks, in which all aspects of knowledge (tacit as well as explicit), of practical ability, and of personal attributes of commitment and creativity, are interacting. While considering the particularly pertinent issues arising from the National Curriculum for Science in England, its discussion is equally germane to all concerned with developing good practical work in schools.

Contents
Setting the scene – Practical work in school science: an analysis of current practice – The centrality of practical work in the Science/Technology/Society movement – Practical science in low-income countries – a means to an end: the role of processes in science education – Practical work in science: a task-based approach? – Reconstructing theory from practical experience – Episodes, and the purpose and conduct of practical work – Factors affecting success in science investigations – School laboratory life – Gender differences in pupils' reactions to practical work – Simulation and laboratory practical activity – Tackling technological tasks – Principles of practical assessment – Assessment and evaluation in the science laboratory – Practical science as a holistic activity – References – Index.

Contributors
Terry Allsop, Bob Fairbrother, Geoffrey J. Giddings, Richard Gott, Richard F. Gunstone, Avi Hofstein, Richard Kimbell, Vincent Lunetta, Judith Mashiter, Robin Millar, Patricia Murphy, Joan Solomon, Pinchas Tamir, Kok-Aun Toh, Richard T. White, Brian E. Woolnough, Robert E. Yager.

224pp 0 335 09389 2 (Paperback) 0 335 09390 6 (Hardback)

LEARNING AND TEACHING IN SCHOOL SCIENCE
PRACTICAL ALTERNATIVES

Di Bentley and Mike Watts

This book provides a series of different approaches to teaching school science. These approaches will be of use not only to science teachers but also to teachers outside science and in different parts of the education system.

The book is organized as follows. The first chapter looks at pressures for change: the authors show that science teachers need to adopt new and different approaches to teaching and learning. In particular, the authors focus on the notion of active learning – a theme that runs through the remainder of the book. In the following chapters, case studies are clustered around a series of themes. The final chapter summarizes the approaches and their implications for teaching science for the National Curriculum.

In general, the book is a useful, practical guide to a variety of strategies and classroom activities: a collection of experience and ideas about different teaching methods which will benefit both trainee and practising teachers. It will appeal to those engaged in initial training and in-service work, as well as to teachers who are keen to innovate.

Contents

Preface – Acknowledgements – Learning to make it your own – Practicals and projects – Talking and writing for learning – Problem solving – Encouraging autonomous learning – Games and simulations: aids to understanding science – Using role play and drama in science – Media and resource-based learning – Summary and discussion – Index

The Contributors

Brigid Bubel, Bev A. Cussans, Margaret Davies, Rod Dicker, Mary Doherty, Hamish Fyfe, John Heaney, Martin Hollins, Joseph Hornsby, Andy Howlett, Pauline Hoyle, Harry Moore, Robin Moss, Phil Munson, Philip Naylor, Jon Nixon, Mick Nott, Anita Pride, Peter Richardson, Linda Scott, Brian Taylor, David Wallwork, Norma White, Steve Whitworth.

224pp   0 335 09513 5 (Paperback)   0 335 09514 3 (Hardback)

BIOTECHNOLOGY IN SCHOOLS
A HANDBOOK FOR TEACHERS

Jenny Henderson and Stephen Knutton

In recent years there has been spectacular growth in biotechnology and in its importance for the school curriculum. This handbook offers teachers:

- an overview of the significance and scope of biotechnology
- an introduction to the content of biotechnology and its relevance to the everyday world
- a guide to how biotechnology fits into the National Curriculum, within and across subject disciplines
- appropriate teaching strategies
- suggestions for practical work
- case studies and other material which can be used directly with sixth form students
- a glossary of terms
- a guide to resources
- coverage of safety issues.

This is an essential resource for practising and trainee teachers of science and technology.

Contents
What is biotechnology? – Biotechnology and the school curriculum – Biotechnology and the food industry – Biotechnology and medicine – Biotechnology in agriculture – Biotechnology and the environment – Biotechnology, fuels and chemicals – Biotechnology through problem solving – Biotechnology through discussion-based learning – Practical considerations – Resources – Glossary – Appendix – References – Index.

176pp   0 335 09368 X (Paperback)   0 335 09369 8 (Hardback)

SCIENCE EDUCATION FOR A PLURALIST SOCIETY

Michael J. Reiss

Science Education for a Pluralist Society is the first book to explore how a school science education should be provided that is appropriate for the entire school population. It argues that all too often the model of science held in school science education, the way science is taught, and the specific content matter learned, are too narrow in outlook. The consequences of a narrow male Western view of school science are far reaching and of two main sorts. Firstly, many pupils feel alienated from school science and drop it once they can. Secondly, the minority that continue (beyond the years in which it is compulsory) then learn an impoverished form of science.

A valid science education for a pluralist society will encourage and permit greater equality of standing between science as carried out and perceived by different cultural, ethnic, gender, class, ability and religious groups. *Science Education for a Pluralist Society* looks at how a science education could be taught across the 5 to 16 age range. There are chapters on the nature of science, the design of science curricula, organizing and running science departments, and teaching controversial issues in science. In addition, there is a wealth of bibliographic material on the contributions by women, black people and other minorities to biology, chemistry and physics. Throughout the book there are suggestions as to how specific topics might be taught to pupils and students of various ages.

Contents
What this book is about – What is science – Science curricula for a pluralist society – A science department for all – Teaching controversial issues in science – Life and living processes – Materials and their properties – Physical processes – The way forward – References – Bibliography – Resources – Index

128pp   0 335 15760 2 (Paperback)   0 335 15761 0 (Hardback)